AMERICA'S
CONDEMNED

AMERICA'S CONDEMNED

Death Row Inmates in Their Own Words

Dan Malone and Howard Swindle
The Dallas Morning News

**Andrews McMeel
Publishing**
Kansas City

America's Condemned copyright © 1999 by The Dallas Morning News, Inc. All rights reserved. Printed in the United States of America. No part of this book may be used or reproduced in any manner whatsoever without written permission except in the case of reprints in the context of reviews. For information, write Andrews McMeel Publishing, an Andrews McMeel Universal company, 4520 Main Street, Kansas City, Missouri 64111.

99 00 01 02 03 RDH 10 9 8 7 6 5 4 3 2 1

www.andrewsmcmeel.com

Library of Congress Cataloging-in-Publication Data

Malone, Dan.
    America's condemned : death row inmates in their own words / Dan Malone and Howard Swindle.
    p. cm.
    ISBN 0-8362-8198-5 (pbk.)
    1. Death row inmates—United States—Case studies. 2. Capital punishment—United States—Case studies. 3. Criminals—United States—Case studies. I. Swindle, Howard, 1945–   . II. Title.
HV8699.U5M34   1999   99-19522
364.66'0973—dc21   CIP

All photographs (except where noted) by David Leeson
Designed by John Reinhardt Book Design
Composed by Steve Brooker at Just Your Type

Dedication

For writers (also our wives)
Kathryn Jones and Kathy Swindle

Contents

• • •

Preface

• • •

SAMMY PETTIT'S TRIP to Florida's death row began with the pull of a trigger on the bank of a dark creek in Punta Gorda and ended with the clang of a cell door at the Union Correctional Institution in Raiford.

Those two moments, each occasioned by the snap of metal against metal, are now a decade old. And Pettit, as of this writing, doesn't know when, if ever, he might be fed his last meal and strapped into the electric chair.

Not long ago, we retraced Pettit's 250-mile journey from crime scene to death row, a short trip in what would become our four-year, coast-to-coast odyssey through America's death rows. We set out to look at violence through the eyes of the people who commit violence and see what we learned.

We had sent a detailed questionnaire to every man and woman on death row with no idea what response we might receive. No comprehensive national survey of condemned inmates had ever been undertaken as far as we could determine. But our mailboxes soon overflowed with long handwritten answers to our questions, personal photographs, court records and audiotapes from more than 700 men and women sentenced to die, roughly one-quarter of everyone then on death row throughout the country.

Our rather clinical attempt to examine the causes of crime inevitably turned personal as we sorted through their wrenching and wretched histories. Through no design of our own, we became curious pen pals with some of the country's most disturbing criminals.

Our journey led us to death rows and execution chambers in a dozen states: the egg-shaped gas chamber in Arizona, the mobile home that doubled as a death house in Montana, the collegial, dormitory-style cell block for women in Texas and a state-of-the-art prison in Kentucky. However they appeared, they were way stations and destinations for the condemned.

We interviewed about 50 death row inmates from California to Florida, and from Idaho to Louisiana. We talked with killers who admitted guilt, killers who didn't and a few, as it turned out, who weren't killers at all. In every case, we recorded lies and sad truths about their lives and crimes, their straight-faced denials and matter-of-fact accounts of butchery. In the process, we grew accustomed to eerie echoes of voices off concrete and steel, the smell of body odor and the pallid flesh and dead eyes of the condemned.

Sammy Pettit was among those we met. We wanted to talk to him because he broke the death row mold in at least one significant way. Unlike the overwhelming majority of condemned killers who fight for their lives, Pettit wanted the state of Florida to kill him.

We flew to Florida and drove up the lush coastline to Punta Gorda. We met the woman Pettit shot and tried desperately to kill. She told us about the crazed Manson-like figure who killed her friend and left her for dead. She took us past Pettit's home, to the bank of Alligator Creek where the shootings occurred and past the beach where police found Pettit collapsed in drug-induced sleep. We drove past the police station where he confessed, past the courthouse where he pleaded guilty.

The next day, knowing more about Pettit than we would about most death row inmates we encountered, we drove through the gates of the prison where Pettit hopes for death. Nothing we had seen or heard prepared us for what we were about to experience.

● ● ●

The bureaucracies that decide where prisons are built rarely select sites in big cities near airports. Prisons, particularly those that house society's most violent offenders, almost always are isolated and remote. In the desert. On an island. In a distant mountain range. In the "death belt" of the South, where most of the nation's executions take place, death row seems to always carry an address in the middle of flat, sparsely populated farmland.

For a crime-conscious public, it makes sense. No one wants an adrenaline-crazed escaped convict prowling through backyard suburbia. Besides, the struggling folks who eke out livings in rural America often welcome the business and jobs that come with a new prison—even if it is packed floor-to-ceiling with killers.

This peculiarity of prison geography meant it took us a while to get to any of the places we wanted to visit. We had plenty of time in rental cars to discuss what we saw or heard—or what we expected to see or hear—driving along the twisting, two-lane blacktops that dead-end at America's death rows.

Our odyssey coincided with a busy period for the nation's executioners. When we began, 2,850 prisoners had addresses on death rows in 36 states, and only 245 had been executed during the two decades since capital punishment was reinstated by the Supreme Court. When we finished our last trip four years later, the nation's death row population had burgeoned to more than 3,500, and the number of executions had doubled. Among those put to death were nine prisoners we met and another 43 who told us their stories in writing or during telephone conversations.

Despite the escalation of executions, some prisoners we interviewed had been on death row for mind-numbing spans, a handful for more than 20 years. One man we met, a former Texas police officer, had been convicted and sentenced to death three times for the same murder. When we interviewed him, he was awaiting yet another sentencing. His guilt in the 1975 crime has never been an issue—he confessed—but he was no closer to execution than he was when first sentenced to death in 1976.

There are many explanations for why death row appeals take so long, and none of them plays very well with politicians or a public more concerned with crime than criminals. And it is rare when a year goes by in which at least one execution isn't clouded by substantial doubt about whether justice is being served.

Certainly there is not a more chilling example of the effectiveness of the cumbersome appellate process than a recent conference in Chicago. At a convention of capital-punishment lawyers, they presented 74 people who once had been sentenced to death, but had since been freed. While some were released on so-called technicalities in the law, others used the appellate process to produce evidence that destroyed the prosecution's cases of guilt beyond a reasonable doubt.

For the most part, the people we interviewed were garden-variety murderers. Celebrity killers like Karla Faye Tucker, the first woman executed in Texas in more than 100 years, and Richard Ramirez, the so-called Los Angeles Night Stalker, shunned us. And other infamous killers like Charles Manson and Jeffrey Dahmer were serving long prison sentences, but were not on death row.

Many of the prisoners we met had undergone self-professed transformations while awaiting the executioner. Among a few, we suspected the change was genuine. Age sometimes mitigated whatever rage a killer might have had when he was younger. But more often, the changes were difficult to judge. About half, who admitted to drug and alcohol problems in their pasts, were now sober by circumstance. We could never tell whether the change these people underwent behind bars was tangible and lasting, or as ephemeral and fleeting as the rushes from alcohol and methamphetamines they knew so well on the outside.

Nor was it possible to come to a firm conclusion about the religious conversions prisoners claimed to have undergone during the monotony of solitary life. Many claimed rebirth in the name of Jesus, Allah, Buddha or some other higher power. Occasionally, the change and remorse appeared genuine. Tears and confession don't flow freely in a world of hard souls. And prison guards who have seen it all don't often volunteer testimonials about holy men with blood on their hands. But remorse from a man wanting out of a cage, like forced sobriety, was suspect when it intertwined bids for clemency with talk of spiritual rebirth.

The theological notion that one can hate the sin but love the sinner was one we sometimes encountered. Even when dealing with prisoners convicted of the most heinous crimes, we were surprised to feel tinges of compassion when they described the familial cesspool in which they were reared or the perverse abuse they endured as children. And no one deserves to be buried, as some executed killers have been, in unmarked desert graves we saw riddled with sandy burrows of foraging lizards.

The gulf between a man who kills and one who does not is not as great as many might suppose. Disturbingly, the lives of some—except, of course, for the single aberrational act of violence that landed them on death row—were so unremarkable, or the demons that motivated them so familiar, that we found ourselves thinking, more often than we might like to admit, "There but for the grace of God go I."

That is not to say that we didn't encounter a fair number of veteran sociopaths. Who else would respond to a survey by sending packages that contained what appeared to be body fluids and human waste? What else could you call a recidivist pedophile who dismembered his mother on a prison furlough, then tossed her bones to dogs? Or a drug dealer who fed a woman's body through a tree shredder?

• • •

It was with some of those experiences in mind that we headed off in a rental car on a Thursday morning down yet another highway to yet another death row. Florida State 16 is a snake of asphalt that runs flat and narrow from Starke to Raiford, the home of Florida's electric chair. Old Sparky, as it is called, is infamous for malfunctioning and on one occasion set fire to a prisoner before it dispensed the state's justice.

Together, we counted 45 years of journalism between us, much of those years shuttling in and out of prisons interviewing convicts. At face, we seemed the philosophical counterbalances of capital punishment, ostensibly the perfect pairing of opposites to achieve objectivity. We killed time on the drive to see Sammy Pettit, reurging the familiar points of view that we carried with us on our travels.

One of us expressed as little sympathy for the condemned as he supposed the killers had had for their victims. If 12 strangers sorted through the facts of a murder, summoned a hangman, and their verdict was repeatedly validated by a succession of courts, who, he argued, was he to second-guess such a decision? Once legitimate questions about guilt or innocence are resolved, even Gary Gilmore—the first prisoner executed after the death penalty was reinstated 20 years ago—had said, in his final words to a Utah firing squad, "Let's do it."

The other writer, even when confronted with the conclusiveness of guilt beyond a shadow of doubt, argued about the moral uncertainty of imposing death on a fellow human being. Mitigation could be found, he contended, in a killer's background, in alcohol and drugs, in mental instability and maybe even in his genes. Moreover, he was too cynical about the administration of jurisprudence to place another man's fate in the hands of laymen so easily manipulated by lawyers and rigid rules of evidence that sometimes had no room for facts.

Neither of us, however, would be the same after Raiford. If our thoughts on capital punishment had been as disparate as the ditches on either side of Florida 16, an hour alone with Sammy Pettit brought us to the center stripe.

There were no ubiquitous Plexiglas shields at the Union Correctional Institution that separated us from Pettit. After we were thoroughly searched, we were led down a hallway and locked inside a small room.

Pettit, we had been warned, suffered from Huntington's chorea, a hereditary deterioration of the nerves that leaves its victims twitching and jerking uncontrollably like a run-over snake. Guards rolled Pettit into the tiny room in a wheelchair, his hands cuffed in his lap and his head jerking violently from side to side. His mouth was contorted and revealed a gaping hole where his front four upper teeth once had been. He bore the stereotypical jailhouse tattoos on the knuckles of both his hands: L-O-V-E and H-A-T-E. The tattoo on the back of his right hand said LOONY, his alias on the outside.

Pettit slurred his words, forcing us to lean toward him in our chairs, his spittle peppering our shirts and skin like shotgun pellets.

Unintelligible growls gave way to snippets of perfectly clear speech, as if something inside him were switching his humanity on and off.

Slowly and agonizingly, Pettit told us, growling and spewing saliva, that he intended to kill his victims even before he randomly abducted the man and woman from the parking lot of a west Florida hotel and restaurant. He already had been diagnosed with Huntington's, but hadn't had the courage to commit suicide. He assumed that cops, when they finally found him, would kill him. They would do for him what he was too cowardly to do for himself.

Arrested without incident as he lay passed out on the beach, he pleaded guilty to capital murder. Florida, he thought, would help him commit suicide, just as his father had committed suicide when he no longer could handle the ravages of Huntington's. But Sammy Pettit, notwithstanding 29 previous arrests, misjudged the system; the state appointed two appeals lawyers who were keeping him from the electric chair against his will.

Pettit had left the woman for dead, slumped in the front seat beside her friend, who would die within hours. When we talked to her a day earlier, she had asked us to deliver a message to her assailant: "Ask him how it makes him feel to know that I take pleasure every day that he's in constant pain."

Pettit's eyes narrowed when he heard the question, and a contorted jack-o'-lantern grin appeared on his face.

"I should have killed her," he said, fighting to trap air in his lungs. "She was a fat woman, but she had a tiny little head."

He had aimed at her head in the darkness, but the best he could do was shoot her multiple times in her forearms as she shielded herself.

We noticed the tattoo of the devil on Pettit's own forearm and asked what would happen when he died. "I don't believe in God," Pettit said, gasping. "Gonna come back as an animal. . . . A bulldog . . . so I can kill that girl. . . ."

The 13 miles from Raiford to the next town were unremarkable, and we said little to each other as we watched the occasional cluster of tall pines fly past at 60 miles an hour. Finally, one of us broke the silence: "That's as close to evil as I ever hope to get."

At the first convenience store we found, one rushed to the restroom to wash the spit from his shirt and face. The other bought a bottle of mouthwash and went outside to gargle. Still we couldn't cleanse ourselves of Sammy Pettit.

The writer who had once argued privately for the death penalty wondered what role Pettit's disorder played in his makeup. How much of what the wheelchair-bound inmate intoned came from a forlorn genetic heritage and how much from a blood-black heart? He could not tell whether his own repulsion stemmed primarily from Pettit's physical condition and the froth he slung through the air, or from the remorseless clarity that occasionally pierced the animal sounds from the killer's mouth.

The reporter who originally couldn't imagine any facts compelling enough to condemn someone to death now wondered aloud if some people were simply too evil and too unsalvageable to live. How, he wondered, would he have felt about Pettit if, say, his wife had been the target of his dark fury that night? He knew the Huntington's diagnosis wouldn't have changed his mind.

Both of us, like society, had viewed capital punishment in broad brush strokes. Raiford and Sammy Pettit changed that. What we discovered is that the death penalty isn't about broad brushes at all, but rather the individual hairs in the brush.

—Dan Malone and Howard Swindle
October 31, 1998

Prologue

. . .

A View from Death Row

JERMARR ARNOLD, whom Texas prison officials call the meanest man on death row, knows the public's stereotype of condemned killers: "Someone without feelings, someone prone to violence, someone with no moral principles."

But sitting in the caged visitors' room at the Ellis I Unit near Huntsville, he is polite, soft-spoken and bright, more like the college scholarship candidate he once was than the man who wantonly shot a jewelry store clerk and later used his bare hands to drive a bolt through another inmate's skull.

Arnold is among the more than 700 inmates who responded to the most extensive survey ever of the approximately 3,000 men and women on death rows throughout the United States. He and most others condemned to die view themselves as normal people caught up in abnormal circumstances.

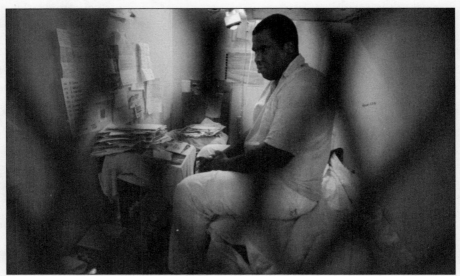

CONVICTED, SENTENCED AND WAITING: Jermarr Arnold, who killed a jewelry store clerk and another inmate, has been called the meanest man on death row by Texas prison officials.

A survey by *The Dallas Morning News* shows, however, that most death row inmates share certain characteristics in their backgrounds and beliefs. For example:

- Crime shaped their lives long before they were convicted of capital murder. Seven out of 10 began their criminal careers as juveniles and went on to commit serious crimes, often murder or other violent felonies, even before the killings that landed them on death row. Almost four of 10 said other members of their families, typically fathers and brothers, also have been convicted of serious crimes.

- The childhoods of almost nine of 10 were marred by poverty, abuse, drugs, alcohol, broken families or lack of any high school education. Specifically, four of 10 were experimenting with alcohol, three of 10 were having sex, and one-quarter were using drugs—all before age 13.

- Even while executions are soaring to historic highs, few inmates take the death penalty seriously, either as a deterrent to violent crime or as a threat to their lives. Nine of 10 condemned prisoners believe the death penalty deters violent crime not at all. And despite spending an average of seven years on death row, almost half have never been given an execution date. Still fewer—about one-third—believe that they will ever be executed.

- Eight of 10 black inmates and six of 10 Hispanic inmates believe that race discrimination played a role in their sentences. The American Bar Association, in its national conference in February, called for a moratorium on the imposition of the death penalty, citing, among other reasons, "the corrosive effects of racial prejudice in capital cases."

- Although the *Morning News* survey did not ask inmates about their guilt because many of their cases are on appeal, one in seven nonetheless volunteered that he or she was guilty as charged.

The *Morning News* received responses from all 36 jurisdictions that had inmates on death row at the time of the survey: 602 prisoners completed questionnaires, and more than 100 others sent letters, court records and photographs. The more than 700 responses represented about one-quarter of the 2,851 then on death row, a population that has since grown to more than 3,500. About two-thirds agreed to be named.

Additionally, more than three dozen death row inmates in 15 states were interviewed. Four of those—two in Missouri, one in Montana and one in Arkansas—have since been executed.

LEAVING VICTIMS IN THEIR WAKE: Violence was a common thread in the lives of many inmates long before they reached death row. Of those surveyed, 69 percent had a previous conviction, many for violent crimes including murder, attempted murder and assault. Here, Shawn Garrison lies wounded on a Baltimore street corner after assailants shot him repeatedly. Garrison survived; his assailants are still at large.

Death penalty no deterrent

Opinions on death row are as varied as the men and women who live there. On only a handful of topics in the survey was there anything approaching a consensus.

Slightly more than half of death row inmates said that except for their death sentences, they consider themselves average people, not much different, in fact, from the jurors who condemned them.

Before he was executed in South Carolina on July 19, 1996, triple murderer Fred H. Kornahrens described himself as a hardworking "decent citizen" and family man who snapped after his father died and his marriage fell apart. Everyone, Kornahrens said, has a breaking point.

"All it takes is enough pain, torment, or stress and pressure, and each one of us can go over the edge," he wrote.

Kornahrens, armed with a handgun and bayonet, ambushed his former wife, Patricia J. Avant; her father, Harry J. Wilkerson; and her stepson, 10-year-old Jason Avant.

Prisoners rejected by an overwhelming majority the notion, sometimes called the bad-seed theory, that anyone is born inherently

MEN IN BLUE: Charles Cleary, of Washington, D.C., holds a photograph of slain police officer Brian T. Gibson at the corner where Officer Gibson was shot February 4. Sen. Kay Bailey Hutchison of Texas responded to the killing by introducing a bill to impose the death penalty for murdering a District of Columbia police officer.

evil. Nine of 10 believe that upbringing and experience make people what they are.

"We are individuals, and must be considered as such," wrote a three-tour Vietnam veteran convicted of abducting and murdering a 10-year-old girl. "If you and I lived on the same street at the same time in the same town and were next-door neighbors, the pressures, the circumstances, life in general, would evoke a different response for each of us.

"Your life, my life, won't tell anybody anything about what we are capable of doing any time," said the inmate, who is awaiting execution in a southwestern state.

And in another area of broad agreement, prisoners challenged one of the most widely cited arguments in favor of the death penalty: Executions, according to almost nine of 10, do not deter violent crime.

"When someone is about to kill someone," wrote a double murderer in a southern state, "they don't think about the death penalty or premeditation or the consequences. Their rage is so great . . . [the] act of killing is so powerful over your whole mental state that you have no thought of right or wrong.

"Ninety percent of people on death row could be released today and live crime-free, productive lives because their crimes were heat of the moment or just being at the wrong place at the wrong time."

"On death row too long"

The "typical" inmate in the *Morning News* survey is a 37-year-old white male who has spent an average of seven years on death row. But death row has startling diversity.

Jeffrey Allen Farina was 16 when he and his 18-year-old brother, Anthony, killed an employee of a Daytona Beach fast-food restaurant and wounded three others in 1992. Jeffrey Farina was at the time the youngest person in recent U.S. history to be sentenced to death.

Others on death row are old enough to qualify for Social Security and Medicare. Viva LeRoy Nash, a twice-convicted murderer and escape artist on Arizona's death row, is 81, the nation's oldest condemned prisoner.

And although the average stay on death row is seven years, some have stretched their appeals for more than two decades. Jimmy Paul Vanderbilt Jr., a 44-year-old former Amarillo, Tex., police officer, was sentenced to die in 1976 for the murder of 16-year-old Katina Moyer, whom he abducted from a high school parking lot. His sentence has repeatedly been overturned, and his fate remains in limbo.

When Vanderbilt first arrived at the Ellis I Unit on December 1, 1976, death row was home to about 50 inmates. Today, it houses more than 400.

"There have been people on death row who weren't conceived when I first got here," Vanderbilt said in an interview at the Jefferson County Detention Center in Beaumont, where he is awaiting yet another resentencing. "That tells you you've been on death row too long."

Vanderbilt, like most on death row, is white. Nationally, about half of all people on death row are white males, and more than half of those responding to the survey were white.

Black prisoners, though a numerical minority on death row and in the survey, are disproportionally represented when compared with white and Hispanic prisoners. Just over one in 10 American adults is black, but on death row, black inmates account for four of 10 prisoners. One in three respondents to the *Morning News* survey is black.

The overrepresentation of blacks on death row has been at the heart of numerous challenges to the death penalty over the years.

The role of race in capital punishment is debated even among death row inmates.

Eight of 10 black death row inmates and six of 10 Hispanic inmates believe that race discrimination played a part in their convictions, while only one in 10 whites made the same claim.

"Quintessentially, I see the death penalty as merely another evil device . . . by the white man to do away with blacks under the pretext of crime and punishment," wrote one black death row inmate.

"In this country, there's two types of justice: one for whites and the rich, and another for blacks and the poor."

Others contend that the inequality is more about the color of money.

Executed in April 1997, Kenneth Gentry, 36, said most death row inmates, regardless of race, don't have the money to hire the Johnnie Cochrans and F. Lee Baileys of the legal world.

"I would say 90 percent of men and women on death row had court-appointed lawyers," said Gentry, who was convicted of murdering 23-year-old Jimmy Don Ham on September 10, 1983, at Lake Lewisville, Tex. "When a good lawyer would cost $100,000 to $1 million, a court-appointed lawyer gets only $15,000 or so. So just how hard do you think a lawyer will work?"

Death row historically has been a predominantly male domain. At the time of the survey, only 41 of the approximately 2,850 people on death row were women.

Though women—such as homemaker Darlie Routier of Rowlett, Tex., convicted in 1997 of killing her 5-year-old son, Damon—traditionally make their way to death row by killing family members, other women dramatically defy the stereotype.

In Nevada, Priscilla Ford, a 67-year-old widow, turned her car into a crowd of people on a packed Reno gambling row in 1980, killing seven and injuring 21 others. In Kentucky, LaFonda Fay Foster, 33, was sentenced to death after she and a female accomplice stabbed, shot, burned and ran over five people in Lexington one afternoon in 1986.

Dropouts and college graduates

Death row inmates in the survey are poorly educated. Although some have earned high school equivalency degrees, only one in seven graduated from a traditional high school, and a third got no farther than the ninth grade. One in five attended some college, but only one in 26 convicts said he or she graduated from college. Nationally, one in five Americans earns a college degree.

A LIFE IN SHACKLES: Timothy Allen, who is on death row in New Mexico, has his handcuffs removed after entering his cell.

One in four death row inmates said that a lack of education is an important cause of crime. But fewer—one in seven—expressed regret for not having stayed in school or going to college. Fewer still—one in 11—believe that additional education would have made a difference in their lives.

Illiteracy was apparent in the questionnaires that inmates returned.

One death row inmate asked his cellmate to complete his questionnaire because he couldn't read or write. Correspondence from other inmates frequently was laced with bad grammar and misspellings.

On the other hand, although he dropped out of high school, Ronald Keith Spivey, a Georgia inmate convicted of killing two men on December 28, 1976, has an IQ of 137 and is a member of Intertel, an exclusive society whose members rank in the top 1 percent of the world's most intelligent people.

Big families, broken homes

More than half the inmates in the survey were reared in broken, impoverished homes, and two of 10 were reared by single mothers. Their families average five children, about three times the national average. Statistically, death row inmates are far more likely to be a middle child than the youngest or the oldest. Six percent were only children.

More than half said their families were poor. And as adults, they were likely to continue the cycle of poverty, with half reporting that their last legitimate job paid less than $250 a week. They worked primarily in manual labor jobs, such as construction, maintenance and agriculture.

But a few also owned businesses or came from professional ranks. In recent years, for example, a lawyer and four police officers have been condemned to death row.

About half believe that the breakdown of the family is an important cause of crime. More than one in three inmates is divorced or separated. About a third believe that poverty is an important cause of crime.

"Crimes I have committed, I was in need of money," said Eugene Alvin Broxton, an orphan and veteran thief on Texas's death row for the 1991 robbery-murder of 20-year-old Sheila Dockens in a Channelview, Tex., motel.

"I lived on the streets," he said, "so I stole to eat and have someplace to live."

As splintered as their domestic lives may be, inmates profess strong family ties, even after they're sent to death row. About one-third said they were prouder of their children than of anything else in their lives. By the same margin, they list one or both parents as the people they most admire.

In a few cases, the inmates accused of committing society's most serious crime have been touched, too, by the same specter of violence. Freddie Lee Wright, 45, convicted of the 1979 murder of Warren and Lois Green during a robbery of a Western Auto Store in Mount Vernon, Ala., learned firsthand what it is like to lose a family member to violence. While awaiting execution at Holman Prison, Wright was informed that his daughter had been slain.

"I understand how it really feels to lose someone we really love to violence," said Wright, who was convicted of shooting the Greens in execution-style murders. "I sometimes feel that it's my fault my daughter was raped and murdered because if I was out there, my family and myself would have still been together and most likely we would have been living in a better area, where girls were not forced from the streets and raped.

"This is my way of handling my loss, but then I tell myself even if I was out there, this could still have happened no matter what area my family was living in, because our kids today have so little respect for each other and life in general."

BIDING THEIR TIME: Jerry McCracken (left) and Dion Smallwood wait in the visiting room of H-Unit at McAlester, Okla.

Almost two-thirds of the inmates, underscoring the importance of family ties, said they would rather spend a single day of freedom with family and friends than have sex, get high or flee the country, as a few mentioned. Other responses ran the gamut, from a midwestern inmate who wrote he would "nuke Washington, D.C., Israel, and Rome" to James P. Bonifay, a Muslim on Florida's death row, who would visit Mecca, then "visit the grave of the victim and pay my homage and shed my tears for my ignorance."

The environmental theory of crime—that it is bred by poverty and broken families—can't account for everyone on death row. More than four in 10, for example, were reared by their biological parents, and four of 10 described their families as middle class.

Michael Ross, 37, is white, a graduate of Cornell University and comes from a middle-class family in rural Connecticut.

"I am a serial killer," Ross said. "I raped and murdered eight women in three states—New York, Connecticut, Rhode Island. I confessed to everything."

Ross blamed his crime spree on a psychiatric disorder that created violent fantasies.

"If I had been able to face what was going on in my head—I was in denial—and sought help and received treatment . . . nobody would have died," he wrote from his death row cell in Connecticut.

Even with psychiatric treatment, many still turn violent. About one-third said they had been treated for mental problems—from playing with fire to attempting suicide.

Joseph Murphy, 32, convicted of killing Ruth Predmore, an elderly Marion, Ohio, woman during a 1987 robbery, said he was hospitalized for seven months as a child to recover from burns he suffered when a relative set him on fire in his bed. As a child, he said, he was in "17 nut houses in four states."

"I was a sick child who set fires," wrote Murphy. "The state sent me away for setting a fire at school. I was six years old. Because of fires, I was in a hospital for kids in four states from ages six to 12."

Addictive families, kids

Drugs and alcohol, according to more than half the death row inmates, are among the most important causes of crime in America. And the inmates speak from experience.

Almost half said at least one person in their family, most frequently a brother or sister, was a regular drug user. Two-thirds said a family member, usually a father, had problems with alcohol. And more than a third said their families were plagued by both alcohol and drug abuse.

An inmate on death row in the Southeast is grateful he wasn't free to repeat the mistakes his father made during his drunken rages. The inmate, convicted of a murder during a robbery, said that his sisters once had to stop his father from forcing him to commit bestiality, and that his father frequently subjected him to "brutal beatings."

"My father used to beat the . . . [expletive] out of me. Especially when he was drunk. That's every day," the inmate said. "He's alcoholic. He's a shell of a man now. But I still love him, because he is sick, and he is my father. . . . I thought it was legal to whip your children when they was bad. Thank God . . . I was in prison during my children growing up."

Death row inmates in the survey were far more likely to have had drug or alcohol problems than the average person. Four of five inmates said they had used drugs, some before age nine. Three of every five said their experimentation eventually led to regular use.

Michael Lacava, a 32-year-old Pennsylvania death row inmate, started smoking marijuana as a young teenager. He went on to become a twice-convicted drug dealer before killing Philadelphia police officer Joaquin Montijo with a shot between the eyes in 1990.

"There isn't much to say. I messed up my life dealing drugs, got caught up in something with an off-duty cop, he shot at me twice. I shot back in self-defense and hit him once," said Lacava, who spent

CAPITAL PUNISHMENT IN THE U.S.

☐ States with a death penalty*

WA
MT
ND
MN
VT NH ME
OR
ID
SD
WI
NY
MA RI
WY
IA
MI
PA
CT
NV
NE
IL
IN
OH
NJ DE MD
UT
CO
KS
MO
WV VA
CA
KY
NC
AZ
NM
OK
AR
TN
SC
MS AL GA
TX
LA
FL

Alaska and
Hawaii do
not have the
death penalty

*The federal
government
and U.S.
military also
have capital
punishment
statutes.

DEATH ROW INMATES BY STATE

% total inmates in U.S. Total inmates			% total inmates in U.S. Total inmates			% total inmates in U.S. Total inmates		
California	444	14%	Indiana	49	2%	Utah	10	1%
Texas	**394**	**12%**	Arkansas	42	1%	U.S. gov't	10	1%
Florida	349	11%	Kentucky	28	1%	U.S. military	9	1%
Penn.	201	6%	Oregon	22	1%	Nebraska	9	1%
Illinois	172	5%	Idaho	19	1%	Montana	6	1%
N. Carolina	154	5%	Maryland	17	1%	Connecticut	5	1%
Alabama	151	5%	New Jersey	16	1%	Colorado	4	1%
Ohio	150	5%	Washington	13	1%	New Mexico	3	1%
Oklahoma	124	4%	Delaware	11	1%	S. Dakota	2	1%
Arizona	122	4%				**Total**	**3,153**	
Georgia	108	3%						
Tennessee	102	3%						
Missouri	94	3%						
Nevada	81	3%						
S. Carolina	71	2%						
Louisiana	58	2%						
Mississippi	53	2%						
Virginia	53	2%						

Size of death row 1955-1995

3,000
2,000
1,000
0
'55 '60 '65 '70 '75 '80 '85 '90 '95

At the time of *The Dallas Morning News* survey, New York and Kansas had no death penalty.
SOURCE: Death Penalty Information Center, as of July 31, 1996.

LIVES, CRIMES AND TIMES OF DEATH ROW

Excerpts from a nationwide survey by **The Dallas Morning News** of inmates convicted of capital murder reveal early trouble with the law, broken homes, abuse and addiction. Their death sentences notwithstanding, most maintain hope. Results do not always total 100 percent because of multiple responses.

CASE RELATED

■ Even if you are innocent, what did officials say happened in your case?

Someone was killed during a robbery	48%
More than one person was killed	22%
Someone was killed during a kidnapping	13%
Someone was killed during a rape	11%
Someone was killed	10%
Someone was hired to kill someone else	6%
A child was killed	5%
A police officer was killed	5%

■ Even if you are innocent, please tell us which statement describes what you were convicted of.

Actually causing someone's death	71%
Being a party or accomplice to a death	18%
Both	3%
No answer	8%

■ How long have you been on death row?

Less than 2 years	11%
2 to 4 years	25%
5 to 7 years	20%
8 to 10 years	18%
More than 10 years	24%
No answer	2%
Average = 7 years	

■ Guilty or innocent?*

Guilty	15%
Innocent	23%
Not stated	62%

*These answers are based on inmates' verbatim comments in their questionnaires. To be counted as "guilty," the inmate must have outright admitted commiting the crime. To be counted as "innocent," the inmate must have claimed he/she did not commit the crime.

THE TRIAL

■ Believe race discrimination helped convict them

White	Black	Hispanic
11%	84%	59%

DEATH PENALTY & EXECUTIONS

Finish this sentence: The death penalty discourages people from commiting violent crime:

A lot	2%
A little	8%
Not at all	87%
No answer	3%

■ In your opinion, which manner of execution is the most humane?

Lethal injection	48%
Firing squad	13%
Electric chair	5%
Hanging	5%
Gas chamber	4%
None	27%

five years on death row before his sentence was commuted to life without parole. "I chose to involve myself in drugs and the fast lane. Nobody or nothing could change my lifestyle."

Additionally, nine of 10 inmates said they had used alcohol, two-thirds of them experimenting with it before age 16. Four of every 10 believe they eventually had a problem with alcohol.

Few of either group—alcohol drinkers or drug users—were ever treated for their addictions. One-quarter of the inmates said they had been treated for drug or alcohol use. Just one in four of those, however, believed the treatment was successful.

Before he was sent to Louisiana's death row at Angola for killing a police officer in 1984, Hakim El-Mumit was known as Tommy Sparks. He drank, he snorted cocaine and he can't remember actually killing the officer, Tangipahoa Parish Deputy Sheriff Edward Toefield.

"I believe I killed the officer," El-Mumit said in an interview. "I like to be a responsible person, but there are events in my life I cannot account for."

ATTITUDES TOWARD CRIME

■ **Which of these statements is closest to your view?**

People are neither born good nor bad; it's circumstances and experiences that make them what they are	89%
People are born good or born bad	6%
No answer	5%

■ **Under what circumstances do you think violence is OK?**

To defend yourself	73%
It's never okay to act violently	27%
To punish wrongdoing	10%
To protect your standing or reputation	5%
To get what you want	2%
Other: to protect, defend loved ones; to protect the country, in times of war	16%
No answer	3%

■ **What do you think are the most important causes of crime in America?**

Drugs or alcohol	56%
Breakdown of the family	47%
Poverty	37%
Lack of values or morals	33%
Lack of education	26%
Lack of parental supervision/discipline	22%
Racial prejudice	18%
Lack of religion in people's lives	17%
Failure of the justice system	16%
Violence on TV or in movies	11%
Children or teens joining gangs	10%
Availability of guns	9%
Pornography	2%

Though he knew he had a problem with alcohol and drugs, rehab didn't fit with his game plan. "I didn't like the idea of standing there and telling people I'm an alcoholic," El-Mumit said. "It wasn't what I was about."

Abuse scars childhoods

Virtually half of the surveyed inmates condemned to die in America said they were subjected to physical abuse as children, most frequently at the hands of a parent or other relative. And almost three of 10 said they were sexually assaulted or abused as a child, most frequently by a family member.

Whatever abuse they said they suffered as children, about one-quarter said the abuse was the worst thing that occurred during

MENTAL ILLNESS

■ **Have you ever been treated for a psychiatric problem?**

Yes	34%
Childhood-related	6%
Suicide attempt	6%
Depression, anti-social behavior	5%

Case-related evaluation	3%
Sex-related	2%
Drug or alcohol abuse	1%
Military-related	1%
Other	7%
No answer	4%
No	62%
No answer	4%

CRIMINAL HISTORY

■ **Have you ever been arrested for driving while under the influence of alcohol or drugs or for public intoxication?**

Yes	30%
No	69%
No answer	1%

■ **Have you ever been arrested for a sex crime?**

Yes	14%
No	83%
No answer	3%

■ **Besides your current capital crime conviction, what crimes, if any, have you been convicted of?**

Have been convicted before	69%
Burglary	24%
Robbery	20%
Assault	12%
Theft	11%
Murder	10%
Drugs	8%
Auto theft	7%
Sex crimes	6%
Weapons violations	4%
Escape	4%
DWI, DUI	3%
Forgery	3%

Kidnapping	3%
Arson	2%
Manslaughter	2%
Fencing	2%
Credit cards, checks	2%
Attempted murder	2%
Other	12%

NOTE: Results do not add to 69% due to multiple responses.

Have not been convicted before	21%
No answer	10%

their childhood. They also rated as traumatic the deaths of family members, accidental injuries and abandonment.

Seven of 10 said they were subjected to some form of physical punishment. Four percent reported bizarre or cruel punishment, and 1 percent said they were shot or threatened with death.

The abuse, in many cases, was horrific. A Texas death row inmate said his father punished him by forcing him to strike a book of matches, match by match, and then rub them out in his own flesh.

Another inmate from a southeastern state said he was "forced to hold a couple of wires on a hand-crank telephone while my father cranked it."

Others reported having been beaten with a Hot Wheels racetrack, an electrical cord, a skillet, a chain, a two-by-four, a telephone, a bullhorn, a water hose, a fire poker, a razor strap, a baseball bat, a pipe, an antenna and a golf club.

PREDICTIONS

■ In your opinion, how many inmates on death row in the United States are guilty?

Nearly all of them	32%
More than half of them	28%
About half of them	15%
Less than half of them	9%
Almost none of them	2%
No answer	14%

■ What do you think will happen to most of the inmates on death row today?

Their convictions will be overturned and they will be cleared of any wrongdoing	4%
Their convictions will be overturned and they will get a new trial	12%
Their death sentences will be changed to life in prison	38%
They will eventually be executed	57%
They will die on death row of other causes before they're executed	10%
No answer	8%

■ What do you think will happen to you, personally?

Your conviction will be overturned and you will be cleared of any wrongdoing	21%
Your conviction will be overturned and you will get a new trial	37%
Your death sentence will be changed to life in prison	20%
You will eventually be executed	30%
You will die on death row of other causes before you're executed	7%
No answer	8%

Crime runs in family

Overwhelmingly, the condemned inmates polled were no strangers to the criminal justice system even before the murders that put them on death row. And in many cases, rampant crime was a family affair.

Seven of 10 facing execution said they began their criminal careers as juveniles when they were arrested for mostly nonviolent property crimes.

Their run-ins with the law, however, made little impression on them as juveniles. Only one in 50, according to the survey, said such encounters were the worst things to happen to them as children.

Seven of 10 also said they later went on to be convicted of serious crimes as adults. One in seven, for example, said they had been previously arrested for a sex crime. One in 10 said they had been

PERSONAL PROFILES

Age	Survey respondents	U.S. adult population
18-24	7%	14%
25-34	37%	22%
35-44	37%	21%
45-54	15%	15%
55-64	3%	11%
65+	1%	17%
Married	13%	56%
Single	46%	27%
Divorced	31%	8%
Separated	5%	2%
Widowed	4%	7%
No answer	1%	

	Survey respondents	Total inmates	U.S. adult population
Men	99%	99%	51%
Women	1%	1%	49%

Survey respondents

White	57%
Black	34%
Hispanic	5%
Other	4%

Total inmates

White	49%
Black	40%
Hispanic	7%
Other	4%

	Survey respondents	U.S. adult population
Not a high school graduate	50%	24%
1st – 5th grade	2%	
6th – 7th grade	6%	
8th – 9th grade	24%	
10th – 11th grade	18%	
High school graduate	25%	30%
High school graduate	15%	
Vocational/technical	6%	
GED	4%	
Some college	20%	25%
College graduate	4%	21%
No answer	1%	

U.S. adult population

White	75%
Black	11%
Hispanic	10%
Other	4%

convicted of an earlier murder.

Four of 10 said other members of their family, usually a brother or father, also had been convicted of a serious crime.

In a few instances, brothers and fathers and sons went to death row together for murder. Brothers Lester and Vern Kills-on-Top, American Indians of Cheyenne descent, are awaiting execution in Montana for the drunken abduction, torture and murder in 1987 of Marty Etchemendy, a 23-year-old father of two boys.

In Arizona, William Diaz Herrera and three of his sons—William Jr., Mickel and Ruben—were arrested for the kidnapping and execution-style murder of Sheriff's Deputy Vernon Marconnet in 1988. William Sr. and William Jr. were sentenced to death. Mickel was sentenced to life and Ruben to 10 years.

Although serial killers such as John Wayne Gacy or child killers such as Routier dominate headlines about death row, the typical

FAMILY PROFILES

■ Raised by:

Birth mother and birth father	45%
Natural mother/father only	40%
Natural mother/father, plus others	5%
Birth mother only	20%
Birth father only	2%
Birth mother and a stepfather	18%
Birth father and a stepmother	5%
Another relative	13%
An adoptive parent or parents	7%
In an orphanage	2%

■ Family income

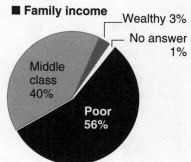

Wealthy 3%
No answer 1%
Middle class 40%
Poor 56%

■ Number of siblings

None	6%
1 to 2	26%
3 to 4	33%
5 to 6	16%
Seven or more	17%
No answer	2%
Average = 4	

■ Have any members of your immediate family ever been convicted of a felony?

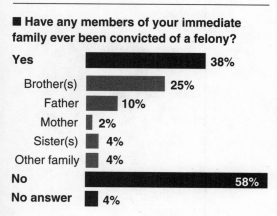

Yes	38%
Brother(s)	25%
Father	10%
Mother	2%
Sister(s)	4%
Other family	4%
No	58%
No answer	4%

■ Position in the family

Only child	6%
The oldest	29%
The youngest	18%
In between	46%
No answer	1%

death row inmate awaits execution for murder that generally created little notice outside the local area.

Indeed, almost half were convicted of capital murder for killing people during robberies. Although most on death row were convicted of actually killing someone, nearly one in five said they were assessed the death penalty although they did not kill anyone. Their capital convictions stemmed from being an accomplice to murder.

Sometimes, even in robberies gone haywire, inmates admitted killing a person but distanced themselves from their actions by claiming the murders were unintentional.

"I robbed a woman, tied her up, she was old and she ended up suf-

CHILDHOOD PROBLEMS

■ As a child or teenager, were you ever in trouble with the law?

Yes 71%
No 28%
No answer 1%

■ During your childhood, what was the harshest punishment you received from your family?

Beaten, whipped, spanked	69%
Restricted, grounded	10%
Bizarre, cruel punishment	4%
Privileges taken away	3%
Rejected, abandoned, ostracized	3%
Verbally or mentally abused	2%
Kicked out of house, sent to reform school	2%
Threatened my life, shot	1%
Sexually abused	1%
Humiliated	1%

■ What was the worst thing that happened to you as a child?

Physical abuse by family member	15%
Death of family member or friend	12%
Accidental injury	10%
Sexual abuse	10%
Abandoned, separated from parent	8%
Witnessed something bad	6%
Lack of love, rejected, neglected	5%
Beaten, stabbed, shot	3%
Verbal, mental abuse; humiliation	3%
Incarceration: jail, reform school	2%
Parents divorced, separated	2%
Illness, disease	2%
Pet-related	2%
Growing up poor	1%
Nothing	6%

■ Were you ever sexually assaulted or abused as a child?

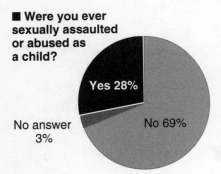

Yes 28%
No 69%
No answer 3%

■ Were you ever physically abused as a child?

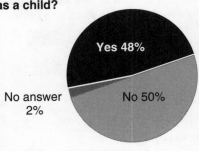

Yes 48%
No 50%
No answer 2%

focating," wrote an inmate from a western state, neglecting to say that he also sodomized the elderly woman. "But the DA lied and speculated to the jury that it was intentional."

Although half of the death sentences stemmed from armed robberies, only 2 percent of the inmates said they believe that it is okay

DRUGS/ALCOHOL

■ **Did you ever become a regular drug user? If so, what drug did you use most?**

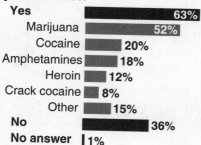

Yes	**63%**
Marijuana	52%
Cocaine	20%
Amphetamines	18%
Heroin	12%
Crack cocaine	8%
Other	15%
No	**36%**
No answer	1%

■ **If you have ever used drugs or alcohol, how old were you when you first tried each?**

	Drugs	Alcohol
Under 9	6%	17%
9 to 12	22%	25%
13 to 15	28%	25%
15 or older	29%	26%
Never tried drugs	13%	
Never tried alcohol		5%
No answer	2%	2%

■ **Do you believe that you ever had a problem with alcohol?**

Yes	41%
No	58%
No answer	1%

■ **Have you ever been treated for drug or alcohol abuse?**

Yes	24%
Drug abuse	8%
Alcohol abuse	6%
Treated for both	10%
No	75%
No answer	1%

■ **Did you consider the treatment successful?**

Yes	6%
No	18%

■ **Have any members of your family been regular drug users?**

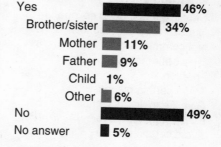

Yes	46%
Brother/sister	34%
Mother	11%
Father	9%
Child	1%
Other	6%
No	49%
No answer	5%

■ **Have any members of your family ever had a problem with alcohol?**

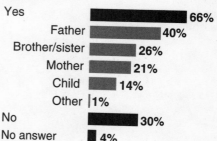

Yes	66%
Father	40%
Brother/sister	26%
Mother	21%
Child	14%
Other	1%
No	30%
No answer	4%

to act violently to get what they want. Supporting claims by some that they killed in self-defense, seven of 10 think violence is permissible to defend oneself.

David Brown, awaiting execution in Oklahoma for the murder of his father-in-law, Eldon Lee McGuire, doesn't deny responsibility for the killing, but he said he was only protecting himself.

RELIGION

■ Since you've been on death row, how important would you say that religion is in your own life?

Very important	50%
Fairly important	21%
Not very important	26%
No answer	3%

■ Is that more than, less than or about the same as it was before you were sent to death row?

More	42%
Less	9%
About the same	45%
No answer	4%

REGRETS

■ If there were one thing that you could do differently in your life, what would it be?

Stay in school, go to college	14%
Not use drugs or alcohol	13%
Not commit crime	8%
Be a better father/husband/ person	7%
Avoid certain places	6%
Give life to Jesus Christ	5%
Everything, start over	4%
Avoid certain people	4%

■ What events or circumstances would have changed the direction in your life so that you would not be on death row today?

Stayed off drugs or alcohol	14%
Case-related	14%
Had more love, discipline, more stable home	13%
Stayed in school, gone to college	9%
Avoided certain places	7%
Changed an incident or action	7%
Had more faith in Jesus Christ	6%
Hung around with better people	6%
Gotten professional help	5%
Gotten a job, stayed with my job	4%
Stayed married	2%
Done what I was taught or told	2%
Nothing	2%
Joined or stayed in the military	2%
Made better choices	1%
Been born white	1%

Brown, a fugitive on a charge of kidnapping his wife at the time of the murder, said he returned to Oklahoma with the intent of surrendering. When he appeared at his father-in-law's home, the two men got into an argument and his wife's father, he said, announced, "I'm gonna kill you, you little son of a bitch."

"He shot and fired and missed," said Brown during an interview at the underground H-Unit at McAlester. "I started shooting. What made it look so bad was I hit him two times in the head.

"I had no intention of harming anyone. . . . I feel sorry for him, but he left me no choice. . . . I should have just turned myself in that night and not gone out there."

Because virtually every death row case is in some stage of appeal, and to avoid questions that could jeopardize those proceedings, the *Morning News* survey did not specifically ask whether the inmate was innocent or guilty of the capital case for which he or she was convicted.

Most made no specific claim either way. However, about one-quarter of the inmates made spontaneous statements that they were innocent. And contrary to the stereotype that virtually all death row inmates profess their innocence, 15 percent voluntarily admitted their guilt.

"I am totally guilty of my particular offense," wrote a condemned inmate from a southeastern state who killed during a robbery. "I can't see sitting in this six-by-nine cell for endless years. In my opinion, the entire appeals process needs to be speeded up. One trial and one appeal unless the individual claims innocence, which isn't the case in my particular case.

"They ought to make a distinction between those claiming innocence and those such as myself, who are definitely guilty as charged. Then allow the ones who claim to be innocent to challenge the legality of their sentences. By letting everyone linger and pursue needlessly, it becomes quite frivolous. That's what is bogging down an already burdened judicial system and at an outrageous cost to tax-paying citizens."

For many, death row is a place of introspection. Deprived of drugs and alcohol and forcibly removed from the streets, some sober up to disturbing realizations and scathing self-evaluations.

"I have failed life," said a robber, convicted thief and drug user in a northwestern state. "I am proud of nothing."

Almost six of 10 prisoners said they believe that most of their fellow inmates eventually will be executed. But when that same question is applied to their own circumstances, only a third said they believe they will be put to death. More than half believe that their convictions will be overturned and that they will win a new trial or be cleared of wrongdoing.

Nearly three-quarters of the prisoners said religion plays an important role in their daily lives. Second only to family photographs, holy books are the most prized possessions on death row—more so than the ever-present televisions and radios.

Two-thirds said those inmates who turn to religion after confinement to death row do so primarily to achieve peace of mind. Four in 10 profess to be Christian; one in 10 follows the Muslim faith.

Jusan William Frank Parker, one of a handful of Buddhists on death row, said his conversion to faith after killing his in-laws and wounding two others gave him peace he had never known.

"I . . . could actually look at myself in the mirror and like what I saw," said Parker, a former air-conditioning repairman who was on death row in Arkansas. "What you can do is face everything with a smile. That's all I try to do. I'll try to face death with a smile."

Three weeks after he was interviewed, he was executed by injection at the Cummins Unit near Little Rock.

PART ONE

Faces of Death Row

CHAPTER 1

. . .

A Life of Crime

Oldest death row inmate's lawlessness spans 60 years

FLORENCE, ARIZ., APRIL 1997—Viva LeRoy Nash, at 81, spends his days feeding birds outside his window, getting what little exercise he can and typing long letters adorned with colorful stickers of stuffed animals and angels. He reads. He watches TV. He talks about his hiatal hernia and his heart condition, his great-grandchildren and his strict Mormon upbringing.

A decade-old photograph shows him as a thin old man with sagging skin and gray, wispy hair parted down the middle.

Outwardly, little about this man—the oldest person on death row in America—hints at his past: a criminal history spanning thefts, cons, multiple escapes, robberies and murders over six decades, about 10 states and two countries.

I have never been convicted of anything," Nash said, "unless the prosecutor used both false evidence and perjury."

Law enforcement officials, however, describe Nash—an accomplished jailhouse lawyer and self-educated seventh-grade dropout—as a cunning and violent predator unable to function in the free world, a poster boy for the death penalty.

Even a lawyer who once tried to keep him out of prison said the elderly career criminal has the "coldest eyes and coldest heart" of any man he's defended.

At times, Nash's tumultuous criminal career has perplexed even him. As he once told a prison official: "I'm the black sheep and no one seems to know why."

SCENE OF THE CRIME: In 1977, 63-year-old Viva LeRoy Nash targeted this site, which used to be a jewelry store, for a robbery. Nash fatally shot a postman while loading jewelry into bags.

Nash more recently blamed his sociopathic nature on his child-hood, which, he said in his response to the *Morning News* survey of death row inmates, was marred by beatings at the hands of both parents and reformatory guards.

An acquaintance believes that, given a different childhood, Nash could have been a "risk-taking, admired entrepreneur." Had he been born a century earlier in the American West, said another of his attorneys, the same bare-boned individualism that has kept Nash in trouble with the law would have made him a "tremendous hero."

Instead, Nash left home in Utah as a teenager, only to be arrested almost immediately for car theft. During the next 60 years—a period that spanned the Great Depression and the Cold War—Nash was in and out of prisons across the country.

His misdemeanors turned to felonies and his property crimes became violent, just as they did in the cases of seven of 10 death row inmates who responded to the *Morning News* survey.

In 1982, while serving a life sentence for killing a letter carrier, Nash escaped from the Utah State Prison. Nineteen days later, he killed a jeweler in Phoenix in another botched stickup.

When he could have been living off Social Security or playing with his grandchildren, the 67-year-old Nash came to rest at Cell Block 6, Arizona's death row, in the desert outside Florence.

A lifelong enigma

Viva LeRoy Nash is a man of contradictions: A bumbling thief able to successfully represent himself in court. A defendant who acknowledges his guilt but stretches for ways to blame his victims. A man who, in his own words, "abhor[s] violence, and yet my criminal record seems to be filled with crimes of violence."

A throwback to a different era, Nash boasts in tough-guy chatter of being a "quick-change artist," of having "waylaid" a bond courier, of being "bush-whacked" and of outsmarting the "stupid bastards" in authority.

He is not, however, so old-fashioned as to reject a modern, almost routine rationalization for criminal conduct. His lifelong war with society stems, he says, from child abuse.

"I hesitate telling anyone the real truth regarding my personal history and criminal record because it sounds like a damned string of lies," he said. "Nobody ever wants to hear anything good about a man . . . called a career criminal. But in many ways that was my category most of my life."

He blames his actions on his parents, who, he said, "had beaten me repeatedly and humiliated me to an unendurable extent as a little boy. . . . They turned me into a criminal psychopath. . . .

"That battered-child syndrome caused me to become antisocial and distrustful of almost all authority. That turned into a disrespect of society's laws and rules."

Arizona prison officials do not allow face-to-face interviews with death row inmates. This story is based on a telephone interview with Nash, about a dozen letters, news accounts, a tour of the death row where he lives, and court and police records.

Except for his contentions of childhood beatings, Nash is unwilling to share much information about his family.

"I have been doing my best to shield them from adverse publicity for 60 years," he said. "The old folks are all dead now, but the many grandchildren are alive and happy. Not a single one of them ever has been in prison, and they are all respectable people. I wouldn't even tell prison officials their names or addresses. I want them left alone."

Fleeing the country

Nash says he left home as a teenager in the early 1930s. His arrest in Utah in 1931 on auto theft charges resulted in probation, according to FBI records. In 1932, he was arrested on a charge of interstate vehicle theft and sentenced to a year and a day in an Ohio prison.

After an escape in 1933, he was sentenced to 30 months in the U.S. Penitentiary at Leavenworth in Kansas. He was released in May 1934 and apparently remained free until January 1936, when he was arrested in connection with a robbery in Salt Lake City.

It was during that 18 months of freedom, when Nash was 19, that he married Myrtle Beth Curtis, 17, according to Utah records. Their union, Nash said, produced one child, a son. Nash said that he and his wife divorced after he returned to prison, that she remarried and that his son was adopted by her new husband and took his name.

Nash told Arizona authorities that he was divorced after eight years of marriage. His son, who Nash said died several years ago, had four children, and they in turn have had children of their own.

During the next 10 years, Nash worked his way across the country, committing a series of robberies, burglaries and larcenies in Utah, Georgia and Alabama.

He was arrested November 5, 1946, in Mobile, Ala., and charged with burglary, grand larceny and receiving stolen property. Records show he was carrying $29.75, a knife, a screwdriver and a flashlight when arrested. Police confiscated a typewriter and some silverware and jewelry that had been reported stolen. Nash escaped from the jail before he was tried, and fled to Mexico.

He also says he "waylaid" a Wall Street bond courier and stole $400,000 in bonds, which he sold for the $25,000 he used to finance the trip.

Nash said his status as an American fugitive became known to members of the Mexican Mafia, who nicknamed him *"El Tigre Grandote"* or the Big Tiger. When his money ran out, he returned to the United States and began a check-writing scheme that eventually would lead to his first documented crime of bloodshed.

"In Detroit, I got a bunch of business checks printed on several big companies and got some credentials and began cruising from city to city across the country cashing those 'beautiful' checks. That was in 1946," he said.

While the country was retooling to a peacetime economy, Nash's scam, he said, was netting him about $10,000 a week.

"But I got caught after a couple of months and was put on trial in Connecticut for grazing a tough police captain with a bullet when he tried to make an illegal arrest and threatened to kill me if I did not submit to it."

Career turns violent

According to court records and contemporary news accounts of the incident, Nash strolled into Mack's Men's Store in Danbury in May 1947 wearing a cocoa brown suit and toting a black satchel. He took a straw hat and two pairs of shorts to a clerk and offered to pay for them with a $57.50 check made out to Wesly Hanninen, one of the numerous aliases Nash used.

The clerk accepted the check for the purchases, which totaled less than $5, and gave Nash the difference in cash. Nash left the store $50 ahead but forgot his black satchel.

By the time he returned to retrieve the bag, store employees had found a gun in the satchel and phoned police. The responding officer, Capt. Eugene F. Melvin, a 25-year veteran of the Danbury Police Department, had also discovered ammunition, road maps of various states, automobile registration plates from Florida and Vermont and 96 blank checks.

Capt. Melvin escorted Nash to his police car. As the detective replaced the radio microphone on the dash, Nash, who had not been searched, pulled a .25-caliber revolver and shot Capt. Melvin point-blank in his right side. When the officer reached for his own gun, Nash fired a second shot, striking him in the right arm. Nash escaped and headed south.

He was arrested two days later in Dallas for speeding. He was driving a car stolen in Detroit, and police found a .25-caliber handgun like the one used in the Danbury shooting and a suitcase containing 10,000 checks, assorted inks and a blackjack. Additionally, officers confiscated a two-shot, .41-caliber derringer, which they found Nash clutching as he was being booked into Dallas County Jail, and two hacksaw blades that he had sewn into his belt.

While in custody in Texas, Nash confessed to the Melvin shooting, two forgeries totaling about $6,000, an escape from a Georgia jail, and the theft of the car he had been driving.

Police in Connecticut matched the .25-caliber pistol confiscated in Dallas to the bullets that struck Capt. Melvin, who identified Nash as his assailant. On July 9, less than six weeks after the shooting, Nash was convicted of attempted murder and sentenced to 25 to 30 years in the Connecticut State Prison at Wethersfield. He was 31.

"His defense was he was such a good shot that if he intended to kill the guy he would have shot him right between the eyes," said attorney Igor Sikorsky, who assisted Nash on his appeal. "He was insulted by the charge because it attacked his competency as a gunman."

Nash ended up serving 25 years in prison for the Melvin shooting. He probably would have served less time had he not, starting in the mid-1960s, attempted a series of escapes. Records show he was sentenced to two to five years for an escape attempt in 1965, three to 10 years for another in 1969 and one to five years for a final try in 1972.

Finally released in 1972, Nash was in his mid-50s and had spent about half of his life behind bars.

Fighting for rights

When he wasn't trying to escape, Nash was transforming himself from gun-toting hoodlum to what defense attorney Sikorsky described as a precedent-setting jailhouse lawyer.

Court records show that he attempted to mail a required notice of his intent to appeal to court officials, but prison employees failed to send his mail. Years later, a federal judge ordered Connecticut officials to hear his appeal promptly or release him.

Although Nash ultimately lost, he nevertheless "won procedural safeguards for inmates," including their right to appeal, Sikorsky said. "He actually made law. Lots of cases actually cite *Nash v. warden.*"

Nash was in and out of trouble during the next five years, according to FBI records. He was arrested in Michigan for car theft and in Nevada for fraud and served time in federal prisons in Atlanta and Leavenworth. He was paroled at some point in the mid-1970s.

In an interview, Nash said childhood beatings "made me hate authority, and it took me 20 years to get over it. By the time I got over it, I had such a criminal record that every time I ever got looked at by a cop, I got stuck in jail. That creates more hostility and then pretty soon it builds up and it takes another 10 years to get over that and by that time I'm 40 years old."

In the mid-1970s, Nash returned to Utah, where he met his granddaughters for the first time. "They know practically nothing about me or my activities," he said. "All they knew was that I had spent about half my life in prison, but that I was also a gentleman."

Murder in Salt Lake

The execution of Gary Gilmore before a Utah firing squad in January 1977 made news throughout the country, marking the resumption of executions in the United States after five years. But the execution was no deterrent to Nash, who would soon be faced with the threat of capital punishment himself.

By May, the 63-year-old Nash and an accomplice targeted a jewelry store for a robbery. They tied up the clerk and were loading jewelry into bags when a postman, David J. Woodhurst, walked in with the mail. The postal employee was shot to death, and the pair of robbers fled with more than 150 pieces of jewelry.

The accomplice pleaded guilty and identified Nash as the mastermind and the gunman. Faced with the possibility of a death sentence, Nash agreed in February 1978 to a plea bargain that sentenced him to two terms of five years to life for robbery and murder.

Nash was quarreling with his court-appointed attorneys in the month before he was sentenced and had failed in an attempt to persuade his judge to dismiss them. In an indignant letter to the judge, Nash complained as if he were one of Utah's finest citizens:

"My people have helped populate the area since 1947, and frankly, your Honor, I strongly protest being treated as a skid row character . . . especially because I've never hung around skid row in my life and haven't been in any trouble in Utah for about 35 years."

At Utah State Prison, corrections officials sized up Nash as an unlikely candidate for rehabilitation.

"At age 63, Nash has spent a goodly portion of his life in prisons," an official noted in his file. "His arrest record is extensive and varied. He should be considered extremely dangerous. According to Nash, he is a disabled, retired senior citizen. Retired from a life of crime. However, he came out of retirement long enough to murder a law-abiding citizen. It is felt that he is not amenable to change."

Five years later, on October 15, 1982, Nash escaped while working on a prison forestry crew. He said he simply walked away and his absence was not noticed for several hours. His escape and eventual arrival in Phoenix are another aspect of his life for which there is no available documentation.

Trip to death row

What is known is that, upon arriving in Phoenix, he acquired a gun. Records show that Nash went to the apartment of a man who had placed a classified ad in a newspaper to sell a .357-caliber revolver.

Nash looked the gun over, loaded it with six cartridges he was carrying, then told the man he was taking the gun and left.

On November 3, 1982, Nash went to the Moon Valley Coin and Stamp Shop. Gregory West and Susan McCollough were working at the store, located in a strip shopping center in suburban Phoenix.

The ensuing robbery, like the one in Salt Lake City, went awry. Nash killed West and, as he bolted from the store, was wrestled to the ground by two men who held him until police arrived. Near the coin shop, police found a van, reported stolen earlier in the day, with its engine running.

Nash's story: "Coin shop clerk tried to bushwhack me during an attempted robbery. I am not sure what happened after he shot at me, but unfortunately, and to my surprise, he was killed. The whole thing was idiotic and should not have happened; the actual shooting was not even intentional."

A pretrial assessment of Nash by officials describes a man who had been locked up so long that his understanding of the free world was tangential at best:

"The defendant is obviously institutionalized and has learned over his forty-eight years in prison to think like a convict rather than to think like a 'normal person.' . . . His lifestyle in the free world is that of a predator.

"This officer feels that the defendant was, as much as he is able, genuinely sorry that Gregory West was killed. While the defendant was accepting of this responsibility for West's death, he did not seem to understand that it was also his responsibility for setting up a situation, i.e. a robbery with a gun, wherein it would be possible for someone else to die. That is, the defendant looked at the robbery as a justifiable need for survival."

Nash told a court official, "I do not seem to be able to function in a normal society."

Deputy Maricopa County Attorney Gregg Thurston agreed: "If ever there was a case where a person should receive the death penalty, this was it."

An Arizona court agreed and sentenced Nash to death.

News of Nash's involvement in the Phoenix murder eventually filtered back to Utah. Keller, the Salt Lake City attorney who had represented Nash in the Utah murder case, said he was once an ardent opponent of the death penalty. Today, the lawyer said, he sees a need for such an ultimate sanction when it comes to people like his former client.

"I have told people for 20 years that this man was responsible for me changing my firm opinion against the death penalty," Keller said. "Of all the people I ever represented, he had the coldest eyes and the coldest heart."

Keller came to realize that his client would kill for the "lightest of reasons" and that if freed, he would kill again.

AWAITING EXECUTION: This is the cell in the Arizona death house where prisoners await their execution.

Friends on the outside

After decades behind bars, Nash, who claims an above-normal IQ of 125, has become what he calls a "glutton for knowledge." He reads just about anything but fiction and has become a student of parapsychology and positive thinking.

"Negative thinking ruins character, and positive thinking can bring about the needed corrections," he said. "Over the intervening years, I have learned that the ordinary common cold, no matter which of the many kinds of germs involved, can be whipped by the proper application of the subconscious mind to the problem . . . therefore, I simply don't think negative. . . . The result, or one of them, is that in the 14 years I've been here, I have never been punished for any rule infraction."

According to prison records, Nash has been cited three times for rules violations, once for using obscene language and twice for disobeying orders. All three are considered minor infractions, and Nash, despite his murder convictions and history of escape, is no longer considered much of a threat inside the prison.

Officials say the old man is quiet and has the respect of younger inmates, some of whom look after him.

"He feels like he should be in a retirement home" instead of a maximum-security prison, said a prison official.

Estranged from his family, Nash corresponds regularly with a small group of female pen pals.

Virginia C. Trader, a civilian supervisor at the Yakota Air Force Base in Japan, has exchanged letters with Nash since 1984, when she read an article he wrote for a prison newspaper.

"Given a different childhood," Trader wrote in a letter to the *Morning News,* "he could have been a risk-taking, admired entrepreneur."

In his letters to her, Nash calls her "Dearest Vicky" and "darling," and quotes old song lyrics ("The g-r-e-a-t-e-s-t thing you'll e-v-e-r learn is just to l-o-v-e and be loved in return.") and tells her the "most peaceful times" of his life were spent taking time out "to just settle back for a few moments and contemplate the natural beauties around me, the magnificence of it all. But I always submitted to that crazy urge to go-go-go."

Another pen pal, Barbara Krepps of Auburn, Pa., said Nash was a great comfort after the deaths of her parents and husband.

"He was very concerned about the effect it would have on me," Krepps said. "Believe me, if not for his concerns, I don't know what I would have done."

This student of the world's natural beauty and consoler of grieving widows expects to die of old age or other causes before Arizona, which has executed only four men in the last 20 years, gets around to carrying out his death sentence.

Barring an escape, it is unlikely that he will ever again be free, though he said he could still make it in the outside world. To a survey question about how he might spend a day of freedom, Nash printed: "Killing judges and lawyers. Christ was right! So was Shakespeare!"

CHAPTER 2

• • •

Purging His Murderous Past

Faith provided peace, but no mercy

A Sentence Executed

TUCKER, ARK., APRIL 1997—Three weeks before the state of Arkansas announced it was calling its debt on Jusan William Frank Parker, the affable, soft-spoken prisoner ran his hand over his shaved head and contemplated the uncertainty of his fate.

Jusan, as he preferred to be called, was an incongruous sight for Arkansas's death row, a squatty fire hydrant of a man with a black prayer vestment draped over his stenciled prison whites. He bowed graciously and smiled, a condemned killer with an execution date and a Buddhist name that means "mountain of eternal life."

"It's hard to walk around two bodies," he said of the murders he committed in 1984.

Jusan's chances at last-minute clemency, a rarity in the annals of Arkansas penology under normal conditions, had become even more of a dice roll earlier in the day: The state's brand-new governor, untested on the issue of capital punishment, was also an ordained Southern Baptist minister.

Gov. Mike Huckabee, who ascended to the governor's mansion when incumbent Jim Guy Tucker was convicted in the Whitewater scandal, had spoken openly against abortion. But Jusan wasn't sure how the new chief of state would come down on the death penalty. How would the onetime Pine Bluff preacher equate the two forms of death, each sanctioned by the laws of the land?

"I'm not a carnate god, so I don't know," Jusan said finally. "You're born here and you die here, and what moves you from

Point A to Point B is your karma. Everything you've done is there. . . .

"If it's for me to die, then I die," the Buddhist monk said, "and if it's not, I won't."

The siege

On August 8, 1996, the day that Arkansas designated for Jusan's execution, and 250 miles to the northwest in the foothills of the Ozarks, M. Raymond Feyen was a busy man. He walked into his claustrophobic office on the third floor of the Rogers Police Department at 7 A.M. The office, not much larger than a big closet, is the nerve center for the department's computer system, a labor of love that Feyen built from scratch.

By early afternoon that day, Feyen, 53, was off for his moonlighting job, supervising his landscaping crew. It was mowing season, Feyen's busiest time of the year.

William Frank Parker, Feyen acknowledged, was at the back of his mind, but he wouldn't allow the thought to alter his schedule. Both the former district attorney of Benton County and Feyen's boss, the police chief, had assumed Feyen would want to be at the death house that night, watching through the plate-glass window as an IV dripped the lethal mixture of sodium Pentothal, Pavulon and potassium chloride into Jusan's arm.

"I was told if I wanted to go, they'd get me in," said Feyen.

Feyen and Jusan go back more than 12 years, to a raw minute sometime around 8 P.M. November 5, 1984, in the basement of Rogers's decrepit police headquarters.

Jusan, an air-conditioning technician then known as Frank Parker, was dressed to kill. He already had, twice in fact, before he showed up at the red brick police station. Feyen was the only uniformed officer in the building, sorting warrants in a tiny cubicle next to the radio dispatcher. The handful of other on-duty officers had run out minutes earlier, answering a rare call that multiple gunshots had been fired at a residence.

Feyen heard the swoosh of air entering from an opened door and heard the loose skid plates creak on the three steps that led into a tiny reception area. As he walked through the doorway from his warrant office, he caught a fleeting profile of Parker, dressed in camouflaged fatigues and combat boots. Parker also had his former wife, Pam Warren, as a hostage.

Feyen still doesn't remember seeing Warren, nor does he remember hearing anything.

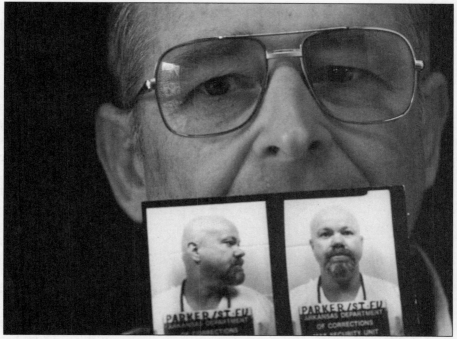

VICTIM AND CRIMINAL: Ray Feyen of the Rogers, Ark., Police Department was wounded by William Frank Parker, shown in the mug shots, during a shootout and hostage ordeal at the police station. Parker became a Buddhist while he was on death row.

"Things happened too quick."

But he remembers vividly the black Interdynamics KG99 9mm automatic in Parker's hand and seeing the muzzle blast. Nearly simultaneously, the officer felt a jackhammer blow over his heart. The Kevlar vest deflected the slug, but the impact knocked Feyen backward four feet, onto the floor.

The scene, on an otherwise placid Monday night in a small town known as the chicken capital of Arkansas, was surreal. Feyen thought: "What the hell? This is the *police* station."

Monty Balk, the unarmed dispatcher, watched the scenario unreel in a convex security mirror in the corner of the basement, and he dived beneath his desk. He fell inadvertently onto the foot pedal that keyed the microphone for all Rogers police units.

Officers had just discovered the bodies of Parker's former in-laws, Sandra and James Warren, at their white-frame home when they heard at least seven gunshots crackle through the portable radios on their belts.

"I missed him on all four shots," Feyen recalled. "But another officer told me that I blasted hell out of the door facing. As much as a .357 weighs, I guess I would have done more damage just throwing it at him."

The man in camouflage fired at least three more times at Feyen's prone body: one hit the officer's soft body armor again, traveling straight down, deflecting and slamming into his lower stomach, piercing his intestines; one hit him in the left leg beneath the knee; another struck a chair.

As mysteriously as he had appeared, Parker was gone, apparently moving deeper into the police station. Balk dragged Feyen into a tiny cubicle. The officer gave the dispatcher his pistol; the dispatcher bolted through a rear exit to get help from the fire department next door.

The ensuing siege of the Rogers Police Department would last three hours. Feyen, a retired army sergeant who had survived two tours in Vietnam and barely three years as a police officer in Arkansas, was pulled, critically injured, from a ground-level window by a state trooper. He had lost so much blood he was barely conscious.

Pam Warren was sitting on the tile floor outside the booking room. Parker would say later that if he couldn't have her, no one would. He turned the automatic on her; she was wounded, also critically, by a slug that went through her liver.

In periodic phone calls during the standoff, all of them monitored and recorded by police, Parker cursed his former sister-in-law, Cindy Warren, who narrowly escaped the gunfire that killed her parents at their home. He also consoled his mother, admitted killing his in-laws, and frequently screamed and cursed into the phone before hanging it up.

Officers began firing into the building. Ricocheting slugs struck Parker in his upper left leg and just beneath his left armpit, alongside a rib. Another slug severed the middle finger from his right hand.

No one, not even Parker, according to Feyen, can say why he ended up at the police station. "I've always wondered," said Feyen, who retired as a commissioned officer in 1995 and came to work the next day as a civilian for the same department.

Over the next few months, Feyen and Pam Warren would recover, but not without permanent physical effects. Periodically, Feyen would see Parker at the Benton County Jail when he transported prisoners.

"We would nod, acknowledge each other," Feyen recalled recently, "but I wasn't comfortable talking to him. Plus, I didn't want to say anything that would jeopardize the case."

The former officer saw him later, seated at the defense table at his trial.

"He was very unemotional, somewhere between cocky and arrogant. He had this smirk."

Even today, Feyen, quiet and dispassionate by nature, still refers to the man who nearly killed him as "Mr. Parker." There are no adjectives, no apparent venom, and he's been told repeatedly his reaction is curious.

"Maybe it's how I survive," he said. "When I look back at Vietnam, for example, when killing was commonplace, well, I've just never been emotional. I cry at the national anthem, that's about as close as I come to crying."

On the day last summer when his assailant was scheduled to be executed, Feyen and his landscaping crew worked until nightfall.

"I would have gone, but that was my mowing season," he said. "I had too many things to do to watch someone die."

Becoming Buddhist

The sergeant of the guard for death row, a tall, quiet man in blue, watched guards unshackle Jusan for the interview.

"Is Parker for real?" he was asked. "Does he really believe the Buddhist beliefs he talks about?"

It's a cliché among prison guards: If anyone's looking for God, or Buddha, or Allah, or Jehovah, they'll find him in prison. Born-again belief is a trait that prisoners believe impresses parole and clemency boards.

(The *Morning News* survey showed that 50 percent of death row inmates, including Jusan, regard religion as "very important in their lives"; 42 percent said religion is more important since they've been sentenced to death. One in three condemned inmates said other prisoners turn to religion "to help their case.")

"He's for real," the sergeant said, not hesitating. "He helps people. He helped me. He gave me a book that helped my marriage. And he talked to me about it."

Inmates and guards alike called him Jusan, the name bestowed on him since his death row conversion to Buddhism. Likewise, by all accounts, Jusan managed to maintain his credibility with both groups in the distinctly distrusting world of death row.

SYMBOL OF FAITH: Jusan William Frank Parker says other inmates harassed him when he first started wearing his Buddhist vestment.

A month earlier, condemned inmate Kirt Wainright learned he had just been denied relief by the U.S. Supreme Court, leaving only clemency standing between him and execution.

"This guy came out of the cuffs, almost killed two guards," Jusan said. "He knew that a clemency hearing, particularly in this state, is a joke, you're wasting your time."

The courts, when they take all hope from inmates, Jusan said, "invent a society so . . . violent they'll never have a guard that'll want to work here.

"These guards, I've known them for years," he said, "then this guy Wainright tries to kill them. I was mad at him for hurting those two guys, and then here come the guards, and they rush him and stomp him, and then I was mad at the guards for hurting him."

The apparent transformation of Frank Parker—the enraged gunman who wantonly tried to kill Officer Feyen to the Buddhist monk who professes compassion for two prison guards stabbed in the line of duty—was, by his own account, as unlikely as it was unplanned.

Jusan recounted transfer officers pulling beside the highway as they neared the Arkansas State Penitentiary, allegedly beating and kicking him in a ditch until he was almost unconscious, then dumping him on death row.

He tells the story now as if there were some justification for the purported beating, which is not substantiated in any court record: "I was a crazy, mean . . . when they brought me down here."

His first capital murder conviction was thrown out by the Arkansas Supreme Court on an interpretive issue of law. He was tried again a year later and again sentenced to death.

After both convictions, Parker asked that his court-appointed attorneys withdraw his appeals so that he could be executed. In June 1988, following his last conviction, he stood before the judge and pointed to the prosecutor:

"No matter how many trials I get, I'm fighting this man, his money and you. . . . It's like me going against the Dallas Cowboys. Eventually, I'm going to get a soft head banging against the crowd. I'm giving up. Take me down there . . . and kill me. But leave me alone."

The judge agreed; the Arkansas Supreme Court didn't. It stayed his execution, and the appeals continued.

Ultimately, Parker ended up in The Hole. He knew his rights and demanded writing material, a No. 2 pencil, and a religious book, assuming it would be a Bible. Instead, a guard pitched him a copy of the Sutra, a book of Buddhist scriptures. He read the first page, Jusan said, and he was enthralled. The teachings, which hold that right thinking and self-denial enable people to achieve Nirvana, or a divine state, changed his life, he said.

"When you're doing all that stuff," Jusan said of his former life on the streets, "you think you're a genius, and you're just a . . . idiot."

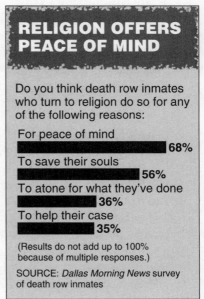

RELIGION OFFERS PEACE OF MIND

Do you think death row inmates who turn to religion do so for any of the following reasons:

For peace of mind

68%

To save their souls

56%

To atone for what they've done

36%

To help their case

35%

(Results do not add up to 100% because of multiple responses.)

SOURCE: *Dallas Morning News* survey of death row inmates

When he first began wearing the rakusu, the Buddhist vestment, he said, other death row inmates harassed him.

"This is a fundamentalist Christian state," Jusan said, "and when you start worshiping the Buddha, you're just a devil-worshiping heathen. . . .

"I actually threatened to throw a preacher off the top tier if he kept refusing my books to come into this prison. I know I meant it . . . but I wasn't as spiritually grown then. But it was the truth."

His faith, Jusan said, was challenged by staff and inmate alike.

"Pot is offered to me," he said. "Cocaine is offered to me. Homemade hooch. I refuse it. I know they're testing me.

"It's amazing, isn't it, this war on drugs? They're going to keep drugs out of this country, and they can't keep them out of this prison, every prison. . . . For money, there's anything you can get. Anything. A few years back, they had a prostitute out here in a horse barn."

Ultimately, Jusan's conversation with visitors turns back to his execution date and his chances of dodging the lethal needle.

"I know that there are a large amount of people that don't want to see me die, and they are fighting daily," Jusan said, referring to the Buddhist monks who have mentored him, particularly the Rev. Kobutsu Kevin Malone in New Jersey, who was already trying to arrange a meeting with Huckabee in Little Rock.

Jusan had been within hours of death before, having taken the short van ride from death row at Tucker across the flat cotton fields to the death house at Cummins. He got a reprieve; 11 of his fellow prisoners on death row hadn't.

"I seen where Clinton executed Ricky Ray Rector," Jusan said of the days when Bill Clinton's highest post was still governor of Arkansas. "The guy was brain-damaged. He had been shot in the head. He was a nut. I medicated him. I gave him 100 milligrams of antitripolene. I made sure he bathed. This guy was a big black man, but he was a kid. He was afraid of the dark.

"When I saw Clinton executed . . . Rector, I knew that none of the rest of us had a chance."

Realistically, his own chances of clemency were slim and none, Jusan said. Warren, his former wife, had testified before the pardons and paroles board earlier in Little Rock, where she unequivocally urged the death penalty for the man who killed her parents.

Nor was the public record an ally. For four months before the shootings, according to police reports and affidavits, Jusan, who admits having been a heavy cocaine user, had terrorized his estranged wife and her family, blaming his former in-laws for encouraging his wife to divorce him.

And he had blamed his former sister-in-law, Cindy Warren, for flushing $2,000 in cocaine down a toilet. That triggered threatening phone calls to the Warren family, tire slashings on her car, and a burglary of his former wife's apartment, during which he stole her clothes.

When he was jailed for the burglary and looking at the possibility of serving five years in prison, Parker wrote a letter to Pam Warren, begging her to drop the charges.

The undated letter was chilling when it was introduced months later during his trial for capital murder. Addressed to "Pam, honey," Parker swore he would "never bother you again."

"They have done nothing but good for me and are loving parents . . ." he wrote of his former wife's parents. "But please explain to them that I was crazy mad at the time and have since cooled down and I would never do anything to them or anything of theirs."

After 11 years on death row, Jusan said he knew the Warren family still hates him for what he did.

"I have great sympathy for them, but there is nothing I can do or say to alleviate their hate, their pain, so I try to avoid thinking about it," Jusan said. "They have been very adamant about their viewpoint. I'm terrible's all I can be.

"I'm not a killer. I killed, but I'm not a murderer," he said. "There are people who murder who enjoy it."

Just a few weeks earlier, Jusan had seen a piece on *PrimeTime Live* that had chronicled the last few hours of a Louisiana inmate before he was executed.

"What I hate about the whole thing is, when you're walking to the chamber, they hold you," he said. "They hold you. I want to walk by myself. I don't want to look like some guy is carrying me.

"A good death," he said, "does honor to a whole life."

Lingering pain

Hollis Warren, brother of the late James Warren, and Nola, his wife, joined Ray Feyen, Cindy and Pam Warren and a handful of others in Little Rock early last year to argue against clemency for Jusan.

"I didn't realize how painful it still was until I sat down and started writing out what I was going to say," said Nola Warren.

Her late brother- and sister-in-law were "just good, decent people," Warren said. "They were a strong church family. Sandra was a perfectionist in her housework and with the family. And James—we called him Julian, his middle name—had worked for the same can company in Springdale for 30 years."

She and her husband, Nola Warren said, had been dubious of Parker from the beginning, when he and Pam Warren showed up for their daughter's wedding.

"He wasn't the type person I'd normally associate with," she said. "His language was vulgar. . . . He was very fidgety, very nervous. He couldn't sit still."

He also had an ego, she recalled. "At a family reunion later, he had to be the center of attention."

Nola Warren sat through each trial, every minute. "Parker never showed any remorse, he never said he was sorry," she said. "He just tried to stare a hole through us."

Warren, like Feyen, suspects that the tragedy from one night in Rogers affected survivors and family members for years in ways they can't document.

THE FINAL DAYS OF D

The following process preceded the execution of Jusan William Frank Parker on Aug. 8 at the Cum confidential execution protocol, the 18-page death watch log and the certificate of death. Some exa

The Director will select two executioners. . . . The identity of the executioner(s) will be kept secret.

The execution shall not be witnessed by more than 25 persons. . . . No inmate's family member nor family member of the victim will be present at the execution. Seven calendar days prior to the scheduled execution date, the warden . . . will explain to the condemned inmate his option of electrocution or lethal injection . . . and document his choice.

A security officer will be stationed as determined by the warden to observe the condemned inmate and record activities. The Arkansas State Police will provide two cars to escort the body off the premises. If the method of execution is electrocution, the Deputy Director . . . will ensure that a good conductor will be available for the condemned inmate's head and leg and will ensure that elephant ear sponges will be in the leg and cap covers. . . . [If the choice is lethal injection] have the lethal injection, the gurney, straps, etc., available for use on the scheduled date of execution.

8-6-96

5:08 a.m.: Inmate arrived at Death House, Cummins Unit.
5:15 a.m.: Inmate shook down/changed clothing/signed for personal property. . . .
6:36 a.m.: Inmate removed from cell to check vital signs. . . .

SOURCE: Arkansas Department of Corrections

7:10 a.m.: Mr. Long in death house to talk to inmate about diet. . . .
9:10 a.m.: Inmate visiting with spiritual adviser. . . .
11:54 a.m.: Inmate interviewed by Mr. Moore from Mental Health. . . .
12:08 p.m.: Inmate strip searched. . . .
12:19 p.m.: Inmate given noon meal. . . .
12:36 p.m.: Inmate requested and received two Pepto-Bismol tablets. . . .
1:34 p.m.: Inmate visits with Lucy Sauer, Frank Parker, Janie Parker, and Sharon Bottorff. . . .
3:03 p.m.: Inmate receives second visits. They are Rev. (Kobutsu) Malone, Elizabeth Potter, Ann Cox & Sandra Formica. . . .
6:02 p.m.: Inmate Parker's dinner tray in by Ofc. Bills. Meal consists of five slices of bread, ravioli, beans, carrots and two cups of ice. Inmate Parker also given one Coke out of property. . . .
6:07 p.m.: Inmate Parker asked what time it was and if the TV could be turned on. TV was turned on to Ch. 4 at inmate's request. . . .
10:13 p.m.: Inmate Parker using restroom. Asked that the toilet be flushed. Sgt. McDaniel flushed toilet. . . .
10:45 p.m.: Inmate Parker asked that water be turned on so he could brush his teeth. . . .
10:47 p.m.: Inmate Parker asked that light and TV be turned off. . . .
11:15 p.m.: Inmate lying on bunk, appears to be sleeping.

3:30 a.m.: Inmate bunk.
3:50 a.m.: Ofc. L with Inmate Park hotcakes, two sa grits and two cup Inmate Parker gi Sgt. McDaniel. .
6:48 a.m.: Inma Officer Berry. . . .
7:35 a.m.: Inmat to Jeff Rosenzw
8:08 a.m.: Capt. take picture of Ir
8:35 a.m.: Inma
12:15 p.m.: Inm
12:25 p.m.: Inm Kobutsu Shindo Jeff Rosenzweig
3:27 p.m.: Inma friends. . . .
4:06 p.m.: Inma Bldg. to remove
6 p.m.: Inmate talking to Warde
9:45 p.m.: Inma cell. . . .
11:30 p.m.: Inn appears to be a

Feyen, who still suffers the effects of irreversible intestinal damage, points to his graying, thinning hair: "Before that night, I had beautiful hair. Stress does unusual things. Plus, there's the effect of all the medicine."

In the immediate aftermath of the murders, Nola Warren said, her elderly mother-in-law questioned reasons to continue living. Her own husband, Hollis, suffered a stroke, and she, too, became incapacitated. Two of the late Sandra Warren's brothers died: "One quit eating, and the other had a heart attack.

"For whatever reason, we lost contact with the girls Pam and Cindy and don't see them anymore. It changed everything."

TH ROW INMATE SK899

Jnit of the Arkansas Department of Corrections. The entries are excerpted from Arkansas'
es and times are not known.

	8-8-96	given socks and undershorts by Capt.

r meditating on

Quiet Cell area
akfast (three
three syrups,
pefruit juice.)
lactate pill by

•day's paper from

'egal phone call
er. . . .

Death House to
rker out of cell....

visitation. . . .

ved lunch tray....

ues visit with
and his lawyer,

with family and

enters East
s. . . .

ng on bunk
.

around inside

g on bunk,

8-8-96

3:17 a.m.: Inmate Parker asked and was told what time it was. . . .
3:45 a.m.: Sgt. McDaniel in with inmate's breakfast (6 pancakes, 2 slices bologna, oatmeal, 4 syrups and 2 cups of apple juice. . . .)
4:48 a.m.: Inmate requested the television to be turned on and turned to channel seven. This was done. . . .
7:25 a.m.: Inmate asked for razor and shaving cream. It was given to him & placed in shower.
8:35 a.m.: Mr. Reed, Capt. Harris and Kobutsu Shindo [Malone] enter death house into Quiet Cell to see Inmate Parker. . . .
9:57 a.m.: Inmate receives lunch meal containing barbecue beef, corn, rice, stewed tomatoes, cornbread and peach cobbler. . . .
12:20 p.m.: Inmate still visiting with spiritual adviser Kobutsu Shindo [Malone]. . . .
5:08 p.m.: Inmate received telephone call from son, William Parker. . . .
5:09 p.m.: Mr. Long in death watch area with 12 beef tacos, Spanish rice, refried beans, cheese enchiladas 6, sliced avocado 2, tostado chips, onions, and 8 jalapeno peppers, 2 yellow onions, 12 oz. cheese and 2 tomatoes and 1 2-liter Coke.
5:45 p.m.: Jeff Rosenzweig (attorney) in Quiet Cell to talk to Inmate. . . .
6:41 p.m.: Inmate finished with shower,

given socks and undershorts by Capt. Harris. . . .
6:46 p.m.: Spiritual advisor Kobutsu Shindo [Malone] in Quiet Cell area, escorted by Ofc. Ladd. . . .
7:33 p.m.: Jeff Rosenzweig (attorney) in Quiet Cell area.
8:03 p.m.: Inmate asked and was told what time it was. . . .
8:49 p.m.: Inmate Parker and Kobutsu Shindo [Malone] praying.
8:50 p.m.: Tiedown Team enters Quiet Cell. Inmate Parker removed from Quiet Cell 22.
8:51 p.m.: Inmate Parker and Kobutsu Shindo [Malone] praying together in front of Buddha. They hug each other. . . . Turned log over to Mr. Gibson (Internal Affairs).
8:52 p.m.: Catheters placed in arms; witnesses enter viewing room.
9:01 p.m.: Curtains of viewing room opened; Inmate Parker's last words: I seek refuge in the Buddha. I seek refuge in the Dharma. I seek refuge in the Sangha.
Lethal injection administered/switch activated.
9:04 p.m.: Coroner pronounces death.
9:09 p.m.: Witnesses exit the viewing room.
9:23 p.m.: Body departs Death Chamber.

(Certificate of death dated Aug. 9, 1996, lists cause of death as "mixed drug intoxication." Duration of illness: "3 minutes." Manner of death: "homicide.")

Final pleas

Jusan was well aware of the vagaries of execution dates. He had seen them come and go, delayed generally by state and federal appeals. Now his appeals were exhausted.

Most recently, his execution had been set for May 29, 1996. In preparation, Jusan's spiritual adviser, Kobutsu, had flown from New Jersey to Arkansas to spend the final few hours with him. But on May 28, Tucker was convicted.

"He leaves office the 15th of July and didn't think it would look right if he killed me before he left office a convicted felon," Jusan wrote in a letter to the *Morning News*.

"He didn't hesitate murdering six of my friends while he was in office knowing in his heart he was a criminal just like those he was killing."

Kobutsu, part of the Engaged Zen Foundation, a prison ministry in Ramsey, N.J., said he was told the new date would be September 17. But on July 22, he said, Huckabee moved Jusan's execution date to August 8.

"In effect, with his signature, he cut six weeks off Jusan's life," Kobutsu said. "We were stunned."

The Buddhist priest launched an extensive letter-writing campaign throughout the country, aimed at swaying Arkansas's governor. Mario Cuomo, the former governor of New York, wrote, "If the death penalty fails . . . as a deterrent to others—which history requires us to concede—then how does the death penalty ever succeed?"

The Dalai Lama, the exiled Tibetan spiritual leader, appealed, too, on Jusan's behalf: "I believe that as long as one is alive there is the possibility to change and redress whatever wrong one has done."

Perhaps no one was more vocal in Jusan's behalf than his sister, Sharon Bottorff. Bottorff and her brother, according to court records, are from a family that has been plagued by depression. Their brother, sister and a grandfather each committed suicide.

"My parents are little old people who have never been religious," Bottorff wrote in her letter to Huckabee. "I have tried for years to get them to accept Christ as their Lord and Savior, and I'm afraid they never will if a man of God (you) kills a child of God. They will never understand, and frankly Brother Huckabee, neither will God."

Kobutsu, meanwhile, tried—and failed—to get a personal meeting with the governor to plead Jusan's case.

On August 8, Huckabee's office released a terse, three-graph statement.

"After careful consideration and review of the files, documents and clemency application," the statement said, "Parker's request has been denied."

The governor's signature on the execution warrant, his spokesman said, was not a philosophical departure from his staunch anti-abortion views.

"The governor makes a distinction between the death of an innocent, unborn child," press aide Jim Harris said, "and a man who has committed capital murder."

On the day that Jusan was to be executed, Kobutsu arrived at the prison at 8:40 A.M. Virtually all of Jusan's actions—talking to

Buddhist mentors on the phone and writing letters—were observed and recorded by guards minute by minute in the "death watch" log.

At 5:20 P.M., Jusan shared his last meal with Kobutsu. Jusan, according to his mentor, went through his belongings, all of which fit in a small cardboard box, and told Kobutsu to whom they were to be forwarded.

At 8:50 P.M., according to Kobutsu, the "tie-down team," a group of prison officers in black body armor and shielded helmets, arrived in the "quiet cell," manacling Jusan's ankles and cuffing his hands in front of him, attaching them to a belly chain.

Jusan, Kobutsu said, walked on his own the 15 feet to the death chamber. He wore his Buddhist robes, to which he had paper-clipped a photo of the Dalai Lama. He was strapped to the gurney, and the injection was begun.

At 9:03 P.M., he was dead.

Minutes later, Ray Feyen's phone rang. Officials from Rogers, who had witnessed Jusan's execution, phoned from a car phone.

"From my standpoint, as a law enforcement officer," Feyen said, "justice was done."

Postscript

Three weeks before his execution, Jusan had been prophetic about his fate.

"There is no way to mitigate a murder," he had said. "There is no way to mitigate your behavior anyway, once you are a condemned man. You know the old cliché, 'How do you rehabilitate a murderer?'"

He recalled a conversation he had had with a friend, who maintained that capital punishment would be abolished if the murder rate dropped.

"And I said, 'Sweetheart, the murder rate's been steadily rising since Cain killed Abel.'"

CHAPTER 3

. . .

When the System Fails

Cuban immigrant freed 14 years after death sentence

A shattered dream

*L*AS VEGAS, NEV., APRIL 1997—Roberto Hernandez Miranda, like many immigrants, had the most American of dreams: He wanted a decent job, a house to call home, and freedom.

What he got was a 7-by-14-foot cell at Ely State Prison in the desolate copper and gold mining country of central Nevada.

While Miranda languished on death row, justices on Nevada's Supreme Court occasionally questioned whether the state was about to execute an innocent man. But the full court consistently voted to uphold his conviction.

"When they put me in prison," Miranda, now 53, said, "they killed everything I dreamed of. Those dreams are dead."

Finally, a judge new to the case reviewed newly discovered evidence and ruled that Miranda's conviction was unconstitutional. In September 1996, Miranda emerged—after 14 years—from prison with his freedom, but little else.

His release came with neither an official exoneration for the murder he steadfastly has denied nor an apology from the state of Nevada for the years he spent awaiting death.

"I have faith," Miranda wrote to *The Dallas Morning News*, "that God will clear my name."

Miranda left Cuba in the freedom flotilla of 1980. He had been in Las Vegas only a few months when he was implicated in the August

FRESH AIR AND FREEDOM: Former inmate Roberto Miranda celebrates his newfound liberty after being released from death row in Nevada. The charges against him were dismissed.

1981 murder of Manuel Rodriguez Torres, a 30-year-old Mexican, who, like Miranda, had entered the United States illegally.

The Cuban defendant and the Mexican victim had both been part of the large, often faceless pool of cheap workers on whom Las Vegas relies to cook the meals and clean the rooms that draw gamblers the world over to the Strip.

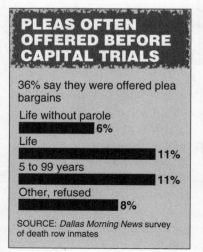

PLEAS OFTEN OFFERED BEFORE CAPITAL TRIALS

36% say they were offered plea bargains

Life without parole
6%

Life
11%

5 to 99 years
11%

Other, refused
8%

SOURCE: *Dallas Morning News* survey of death row inmates

Neither man's passing—Torres from living to dead, or Miranda from free world to death row—would have aroused much interest except for the heightened fears that Las Vegans had at that time of crimes committed by illegal immigrants.

Prosecutors, in fact, initially offered Miranda a plea bargain so lenient, according to records, that he might have spent as few as 10 years behind bars. Miranda's attorney, a public defender with only a year's experience who inherited the case when a colleague died, urged his client to accept the deal.

The plea bargain offered Miranda was the sort of offer prosecutors routinely make, an incentive for a defendant to admit guilt without putting his life in jeopardy, and one that provides a shortcut for an overburdened court system. In fact, a third of the prisoners who responded to the *Morning News* death row survey reported that they were offered deals prior to the trials that condemned them to death.

A guilty man might have accepted the deal with a thank-you. But Miranda insisted that he was innocent.

"Believe me," he said in a letter from death row, "if I were guilty I would take the 10 years and not the death sentence, but no matter what, when you are innocent, you go all the way because of your convictions."

Miranda refused the offer. Prosecutors later tried him for capital murder and persuaded a jury to send him to death row.

His decision almost got him killed before a judge determined something was catastrophically wrong with *State of Nevada v. Roberto Hernandez Miranda.*

Lumped with the dregs

The Cuban exodus of 1980 landed more than 100,000 illegal immigrants in the United States. Known as "Marielitos," taken from their port of departure in Mariel, most were simply fleeing oppression and seeking a fresh life in a new land. But Fidel Castro, seizing on an opportunity to purge his country of undesirables, salted the Marielitos with inmates from his jails and asylums. In the United States, "Marielito" quickly became synonymous with "outlaw."

"The prosecutor was saying, 'Look at him. He comes from Cuba, he's a criminal.' American people say everybody was criminals and crazy and did bad things," Miranda said. "That's lying. You have to live with that."

Miranda was drawn to the United States, he said, to make "a home I can call my home, to be able to help my family, my children, especially my mother, to be able to sleep without fear of being wakened by police, to stay away from Communists and earn the money I deserved to be paid—not the 49 cents a hour Castro pays in Cuba."

Miranda, according to a biographical account given to his appellate lawyer, had experienced his share of trouble even before fleeing his home country.

Born in Havana in 1943, he was the second of four children. His father, Marcelino, cleaned and polished tile floors for a living. Mother

Maria Teresa worked as a maid. Young Roberto quit school in the third grade to take care of a younger brother while his parents worked.

His relationship with his father, who died while Miranda was on death row in Nevada, eventually would drive the young boy from his home and into the streets. The senior Miranda, whose abuse of family members appeared to be proportionate to the amount of alcohol he consumed, once served nine months in prison "for slicing Roberto's mother with a machete," according to the account.

Roberto Miranda told an investigator that his fights with his father stemmed from his attempts to protect the women in his family. His father responded by chaining him by his ankles to a door or by forcing him to strip and sit naked in a chair with his legs propped so that circulation was restricted.

Miranda said he left home at 13. He lived on the streets, in homeless shelters, or hiding out in movie houses. He worked when he could, pushing a fruit cart, helping an uncle in construction and assisting a mailman. He took a wife and fathered two children, but the marriage faltered in the mid-1970s.

Once, police arrested him for no reason, he said, and placed him in a prison work crew for about a year before freeing him. Another time, he said, he was sentenced to "three to four" years in prison for stealing a dozen eggs and two pairs of socks. Additionally, there were troubles stemming from an accident in which a bus he was driving collided with another vehicle, killing at least one passenger. The accident also sent Miranda to the hospital and put him back on the streets just before the boat lift began, according to his defense team.

U.S. Immigration and Naturalization officials said federal privacy laws prevent them from discussing Miranda's case without his written permission. But a spokesman said the legal problems he described are typical of those experienced by many Marielitos.

"Such stories are certainly not impossible," said INS spokesman Russell "Pete" Ahr. Being detained by police or locked up in a Cuban prison is not, he said, "in and of itself a guarantee you were a criminal."

One print nets arrest

The best anyone could tell, Manuel Torres had been dead about 24 hours when his body was discovered by a hotel coworker who stopped by his modest, furnished one-bedroom apartment near downtown Las Vegas. Police determined that his apartment had been burglarized and his pickup truck stolen.

The next day, records show, police got a tip that Torres's abandoned truck was in an alley just off the Strip, the city's neon-lit main drag and home to back-to-back casinos. The truck led police to another Marielito, Fernando Gonzalez Cabrera, now 39, who was spotted near the stolen truck when police arrived.

Arrested a short time later, Cabrera was carrying the dead man's Longines watch and peace-symbol ring in his pocket. Police also found one of Cabrera's fingerprints on the victim's truck. And the stains on his pants, police thought, looked suspiciously like blood.

Cabrera initially denied knowing anything about the victim or the crime. Confronted with the incriminating fingerprint, Cabrera changed his story, settling on a version that would be used against Miranda at trial.

Yes, he told police, he had been to Torres's apartment. And yes, he said, he had driven the victim's truck. But it was Miranda, he said, who killed the Mexican after being tricked during an alleged drug deal. The killer, Cabrera said, had given him the watch for his help moving the truck.

The search of Torres's apartment turned up a piece of broken glass in the sink which had one of Miranda's fingerprints on it. Before the murder, Miranda and Cabrera often ran in the same circle of friends and acquaintances. The weekend of the murder, both had attended the same barbecue.

Miranda said he believes that Cabrera planted the incriminating glass shard in Torres's sink after the murder.

However it got there, that fingerprint, coupled with Cabrera's most recent account, persuaded police to issue a warrant for Miranda's arrest.

Defense lawyer pushes plea

The workings of the American justice system were as difficult for Miranda to understand as the language. He often had to communicate with his attorney through a translator. As a Marielito, he sometimes was suspected of being a criminal, or a lunatic, or both. And as a black Cuban, he was further ostracized within his own community because some of the light-skinned Cubans looked down upon their black kindred.

Compounding the problem, Miranda didn't get along with his attorney, a young Clark County public defender named Thomas Rigsby. Miranda, according to records, had failed a defense polygraph. Although lie detector results are not admissible in court, Rigsby nonetheless tried to persuade him to accept the plea bargain.

Rigsby said later in an interview that he does not believe Miranda was responsible for the murder. But in a memo to a defense investigator, Rigsby mentioned "strong indicia of guilt and deception" by his client. In another, the attorney said he believed that Miranda, on trial for his life, and Cabrera, the state's chief witness, committed the murder together.

Miranda was undeterred and asked the judge to appoint another lawyer. His request was denied, but not before Miranda vented his frustration during a pretrial hearing.

"From the very beginning, I have told my attorney that I am innocent in this case," Miranda told the judge. "They have tried to tell me if I don't plead guilty, they are going to give me the gas chamber . . . and the attorney tells me no matter what happens, I will be convicted, just because of the fact that I am black and I am Cuban."

Miranda began to recite to the court the names of six witnesses whose testimony he said would prove his innocence. But he was interrupted by Rigsby, who expressed concern that Miranda was giving away his defense to prosecutors who were in the courtroom.

Testimony began August 4, 1982. Cabrera, the state's key witness, told the jury that Miranda admitted the murder. The fingerprint on the shard of glass was introduced. Miranda had wanted to testify, but his attorney, concerned about how the prosecutor might discredit him, persuaded him to sit still until a verdict was returned.

Of the six witnesses Miranda wanted to testify on his behalf, none appeared in the courtroom.

Rigsby, according to records, said he had difficulty locating some of the witnesses.

The jury began deliberations August 18, and the next day, Miranda was found guilty of murder, robbery and grand larceny. Two weeks later, Miranda was sentenced to death.

In Cuba, people sentenced to death are quickly executed. Miranda expected to be put to death as soon as he arrived at death row. Waiting in a Las Vegas jail to be transferred to state prison, records show, Miranda attempted suicide three times, first slashing his wrist, then fashioning a noose from his bandage, and finally ripping the sutures from his arm in an attempt to bleed to death.

Doubts, but no relief

The balding bear of a man spent much of the next decade lost in the numbing routines by which condemned inmates pass time. He worked as a porter. He wrote his family in Cuba. He gazed out the slit of a cell window at the no-man's-land outside. And he waited for good news on his appeal.

He was steadfast in claiming his innocence, writing letters to an assortment of Nevada officials. His case made its way to the Nevada Supreme Court three times. On several occasions, individual judges expressed concern about whether the state had convicted the right man.

In one such instance, according to court documents, Nevada Supreme Court Justice John Code Mowbray said he had a "very uncomfortable feeling that this man did not receive the most zealous representation."

That view was echoed by a second justice, Thomas L. Steffen, the jurist who wrote the opinion that upheld Nevada's death sentence.

"I have no hesitancy to impose death in this case if we have the right man," Justice Steffens said. "But . . . the fact that Cabrera had a fight with the decedent, the victim; the fact that Miranda had an affair with Cabrera's girlfriend; the fact that there was apparently another witness who . . . would have stated that Cabrera had indicated to him about the time of the murder in this case that he had killed someone . . .

"Now if all of these facts are true . . . if there's any truth to them, I'm sure that no one on the part of the state would want to participate in executing someone who's innocent of murder."

Despite such reservations, the court upheld Miranda's conviction on three occasions.

Rigsby, who also represented Miranda during the early phase of his appeal, eventually was replaced by another lawyer, Laura Fitzsimmons, a former public defender then in private practice. Fitzsimmons remembered the Miranda case from the early 1980s because Las Vegas, she said, had been whipped into a frenzy about the Marielitos. The atmosphere at the time, she recalled, was: "Lock up your women and children. The mongrel horde is coming."

That fear had largely passed when she took over the case in 1991. She interviewed Miranda, took down the names of the witnesses he had wanted to testify and began to investigate the case. Fitzsimmons placed the total cost of appealing Miranda's case at more than $250,000, a bill paid by taxpayers.

Aided by such resources, Fitzsimmons said the defense was able to find all six elusive witnesses, though one had returned to Cuba and would not be available for a possible retrial.

Perhaps the most important was Belkys Ibarra, a young woman who had at one time shared an apartment with Cabrera. Miranda said he and Cabrera had vied for Ibarra's affection.

According to Ibarra, Cabrera encountered her and Miranda sitting on a bed in his apartment. Cabrera, she said, had told Miranda: "I'm going to make you pay."

Ibarra corroborated Miranda's earlier accounts and, Fitzsimmons would argue, provided a motive for Cabrera to falsely incriminate Miranda.

Fitzsimmons developed additional evidence that questioned Cabrera's truthfulness. Cabrera testified at trial that he did not know Torres. But the man who discovered Torres's body, Roberto Escobedo, a coworker at the Stardust Hotel, told the defense that the two men knew each other. Fitzsimmons said that Escobedo's statement, had it been used in trial, would have created doubt in the jury's mind about Cabrera's testimony.

Escobedo, in a statement he gave the appellate team, also complained about the lax investigation into his friend's death.

"It was like they didn't even care Manuel got killed," Escobedo said. "The police never did any investigation, nothing at all. . . . At one time, I wanted to shoot Fernando. I knew he was involved."

In one of her motions, Fitzsimmons argued the jury surely would have returned a different verdict with the new evidence.

"The simple and inescapable fact is that Roberto Miranda was convicted and sentenced to die by a jury that was denied important information," she said.

The new evidence was gathered up in a 200-page petition for habeas corpus, the legal process routinely used in the final stages of death case appeals. Miranda had been "represented by counsel who conducted no meaningful investigation into the state's allegations, and who failed to locate, interview and call known witnesses whose testimony would have materially altered the outcome of the trial," Fitzsimmons wrote.

The appeal was heard by Clark County Senior District Court Judge Norman C. Robinson. In his January 1996 ruling, the judge said Rigsby's failure to "pursue and discover witnesses who would have provided exculpatory evidence and testimony, thereby casting doubt on the veracity of the state's primary witness, is sufficient to rise to the level of ineffective assistance of counsel.

"Subsequent evidence presented indicates that the state's primary witness had threatened the defendant prior to this murder. This coupled with other new facts presented demonstrate that there is a strong likelihood that the outcome of this trial would have been different had the evidence been submitted to the jury."

Judge Robinson also noted that both the original trial judge and the Nevada Supreme Court "had repeatedly expressed that the penalty of death in this case was harsh and not warranted."

Bottleneck to freedom

Things changed dramatically in Las Vegas during the 14 years since Miranda's original conviction. The neighborhood where Manuel Torres was killed was torn down to make room for the Stratosphere, the towering hotel and casino with a roller coaster on top. Bob Miller, the district attorney at the time Miranda was convicted, was elected governor of Nevada. And the prosecutor who actually tried the case, Thomas Ferraro, became an assistant U.S. attorney in San Diego.

The task of deciding what to do with the case fell to Eric Jorgenson, a chief deputy to district attorney Stuart Bell, a prominent Las Vegas defense attorney before his election to the prosecutor's office.

By May 1996, Jorgenson had reviewed the case and concluded that even if it were retried, he wouldn't ask a jury to sentence Miranda to death. Agreeing with judges who had thought the death penalty too harsh for this case, he said, "I just don't think it warrants the death penalty."

The decision on whether to retry the case on a lesser charge than capital murder, or to let Miranda go free, was more difficult to make. A new trial date was set for mid-September, and a few weeks before, Jorgenson still had not decided how to proceed. At a September 3 hearing, Jorgenson announced that his office would no longer challenge Fitzsimmons's attempts to obtain Miranda's release. The case against Miranda was dismissed.

Jorgenson said he usually decides first whether he thinks a defendant is guilty, then looks at the facts and determines whether they are strong enough to win a conviction.

Although he said he believed Miranda was "involved" in the murder, the prosecutor never had to "get to that issue of whether he was guilty."

"I just looked at whether or not I could prove it, and I decided I could not prove it," Jorgenson said. "I went backwards on this particular case."

Too, Jorgenson said, he was having trouble finding the state's witnesses. Foremost among the missing: Fernando Gonzalez Cabrera.

In the movies, men released from prison are given a suit of clothes, a little spending money and a bus ticket. In real life in

WORLDLY POSSESSIONS: Miranda carries his belongings after he was released from the Clark County Detention Center on September 3, 1996. He had been accused of killing a Mexican immigrant.

Nevada, Miranda was returned to the Clark County Detention Center within moments of the dismissal of the case against him.

Miranda, still wearing a jail uniform, had time to embrace his attorney before he was led from the courtroom. Fitzsimmons, unable to find anyone who could tell her when Miranda would be released, returned to her office.

When officials finally released Miranda about four hours later, he stumbled onto the streets of Las Vegas with little more than the clothes on his back and a bag filled with his belongings. He walked across the street to a casino, found a phone and called Fitzsimmons.

"I know I'm supposed to feel happy, but I'm so afraid, like a bird out of a cage," Miranda told Fitzsimmons. "We have an expression in Cuba that happiness in a family doesn't last long."

In Miranda's case, happiness lasted less than a day. The day after his release, the Immigration and Naturalization Service telephoned Fitzsimmons. Miranda's release from prison, immigration officials said, had been a mistake. The detention center overlooked a "hold" that the INS had placed on Miranda.

As a Marielito, Miranda had been arrested on the Torres murder before the INS held a hearing to determine if he could remain in the

GRATITUDE OF A FREED MAN: Roberto Miranda (right) celebrates with his private investigator, Tom Casler, after his release from death row in September. At right is Miranda's attorney, Laura Fitzsimmons.

United States. The federal detainer placed on Miranda was meant to assure that he wasn't released without the knowledge of the INS.

Fitzsimmons escorted Miranda to INS headquarters, where he was again taken into custody for what turned out to be an overnight stay. The next day he was released again, and he has remained free since.

Minds don't change

The simplest things in life, things most people take for granted, have proved difficult for Miranda. Fitzsimmons said she tried several hotels before she could find one that would allow her to pay for a room for Miranda. Clerks were reluctant to rent a room to a man with no identification, much less a man just released from death row.

Upon his release, Miranda eventually got a job and an apartment. At the time of this writing, however, he had lost one and was on the brink of losing the other.

"When I got out from death row, I said this is the beginning. So I can make my dream come true," Miranda said. "But now I don't know. . . ."

RELISHING MORE THAN FREEDOM: Roberto Miranda, a Cuban, anticipates a steak dinner at a Cuban restaurant as he celebrates his freedom with his lawyer, Laura Fitzsimmons. As he rubbed his hands together, he noted that in Cuba "only Castro can eat like this."

"I don't know if I'll be in this apartment, be able to pay rent, to get a job. I don't know if people will change their minds about me."

Miranda said he has been unable to get a job despite two dozen applications. That week, he said, he had gone three days without food. He said he was days away from living on the streets, just as he had in Havana.

Thomas Ferraro, now assigned to an organized crime and drug enforcement task force in San Diego, said it is possible that Miranda did not receive an adequate defense, but he said he remains convinced he committed the murder.

"No single court found that this defendant did not commit the murder," Ferraro said. Having the case overturned because of inadequate counsel, he said, is "not even close to being a statement of innocence on the part of the defendant."

It is foolish, he said, to seek "perfect justice" and give appellate courts a "bottomless pit" of money when the defense lawyers whose competency they attack are denied even a fraction of those funds at trial.

"Even if Hitler could not be sentenced to death under the kind of system we've set up," the career prosecutor said. "There is no such thing as perfect justice here on earth. We may get perfect justice, but not here."

Fifteen years after defending Miranda, Thomas Rigsby is still a Clark County public defender. And even though it was his work as an attorney that was put on trial to win Miranda's freedom, Rigsby said, "No one was happier than I was when his death penalty was overturned."

Miranda's capital murder trial, it turned out, not only was Rigsby's first, it was also his last. Today, his office has a team of capital murder specialists who handle such cases. He wishes such a team had existed in the early 1980s.

"I don't think at that point in my career I should have been assigned a capital murder case," Rigsby said. "Did I do the best job I could? I think I did."

But he, too, acknowledges that it was very possible adequate investigation was not done.

"The returning of the death penalty was one of the most emotionally shocking experiences I've ever had," Rigsby said. "I went home and cried. It wasn't because I loved Roberto Miranda. It was an evil decision. I pledged that I would never be a part of that again."

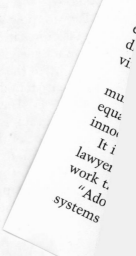

CHAPTER 4

• • •

Lives Gone Awry

Backgrounds, crimes show variety of those awaiting execution

Profiles

THEIR personalities had cracks, to be sure, but sometimes the flaws weren't obvious to anyone who wasn't watching closely. And unfortunately, no one noticed until it was too late.

From outward appearances, the life insurance salesman was engaging and intelligent. The uniformed police officer could have been the friendly cop who gave motorists directions. The couple with the 9-year-old son would be faceless in a packed Wal-Mart. Then there is the handsome young athlete with a confident smile; the guy on the bar stool with an encyclopedic knowledge of pro football; the teenage brothers loitering in a fast-food taco place; and the boyish foreigner with a student visa.

Most of them say they're no different from you. Except that they've been condemned to die. Among them, they have been convicted of killing 14 people.

Theirs are the diverse faces of death row:

Syed M. Rabbani
DATE OF BIRTH: June 12, 1965
DEATH ROW: Ellis I Unit, Huntsville, Tex.

Victim
Mohammed Jakir Hasan, 21
DATE OF HOMICIDE: November 1, 1987

His impish appearance, according to witnesses, was disarmingly deceptive. Put a pistol in his hands, they said, and Syed M. Rabbani becomes a laughing, arrogant killer.

During an animated interview at Texas's maximum-security Ellis I Unit, Rabbani, 5 feet 3 inches and barely 100 pounds, rambled incoherently about "evil talking machines," the CIA, Satan and God. At some point, he said he was "incompetent," a characterization that prison officials and other inmates on death row don't question.

He, like many on death row, has been plagued by some sort of psychiatric problem. One in three condemned inmates in the *Morning News* survey said they had been treated for a variety of mental impairments, ranging from depression and suicide to aberrant sexual behavior.

Rabbani, a native of Bangladesh, was barely 20 when he arrived in the United States on a student visa in 1984. In a questionnaire he completed for the *Morning News*, he said he was reared in a wealthy Muslim family that included four brothers and two sisters. He settled in Houston but never enrolled in college.

CAUGHT IN DELUSIONS: Texas death row inmate Syed Rabbani, a native of Bangladesh, says he was operating as a CIA agent and diplomat when he killed his former roommate, a convenience store clerk.

On November 1, 1987, three years after his arrival in the United States, Rabbani and another man robbed a Houston convenience store clerk, Mohammed Jakir Hasan —Rabbani's former roommate —of $300. They handcuffed the clerk, dragged him into a restroom and shot him twice in the head and once in the chest with a .38-caliber pistol. Officers said the clerk appeared to be kneeling at the time he was shot.

About two weeks later, in Brooklyn, N.Y., another clerk, Mohmed Salam, also a Bangladeshi immigrant, was robbed and dragged into the restroom of his store. Salam told Houston officials that Rabbani terrorized him for hours, laughing and bragging about killing Hasan. Rabbani would have killed him, too, Salam said, had it not been for Rabbani's companion, Shibli Khan, who intervened.

The monthlong crime spree ended November 30 when Rabbani and Khan killed a second Houston storekeeper, Khairul Kabir, 24.

Khan was sentenced to 45 years for robbing Hasan, but Rabbani was convicted of killing the clerk. He was sentenced to death in a trial that he called a "mockery."

Once on death row, Rabbani contended that he became a "victim of circumstance" while operating as a "CIA agent and diplomat."

"I've immunities," he wrote in his questionnaire. "I didn't kill anybody and didn't commit any crime."

In person, in the caged cell in the visitors' room, Rabbani acknowledged fleetingly in his singsong voice that he may not have all his mental capabilities.

"I lost all my brainpower," he said. "That's why I don't make sense. I was not always like this. . . . I don't pretend I am going through a crisis. I might even go to hellfire, I'm so afraid."

Before the guards returned him to his cell block, Rabbani's opinion again turned grandiose: "If I can be protected, I can protect the whole world because I am the eternal president."

How does he know that? "Because," he said, "my palm reading says that."

Jimmy Paul Vanderbilt

DATE OF BIRTH: November 25, 1952
DEATH ROW: Temporarily housed at the Jefferson County Detention Center, Beaumont, Tex., awaiting resentencing

Victim

Katina Moyer, 17
DATE OF HOMICIDE: April 1, 1975

Jimmy Paul Vanderbilt, a killer with an unlikely past and an uncertain future, has managed for two decades to elude not only the state's attempts to kill him but also the constant threat from the inmates around him.

Before he was sentenced to death for killing a teenage girl, Vanderbilt was an Amarillo patrolman. He became one of only four police officers in the nation to be sentenced to death in recent years.

"Being a cop in prison isn't a good thing," Vanderbilt said. "There's no such thing as an ex-cop."

While the average stay on death row among inmates surveyed by the *Morning News* is seven years, Vanderbilt has kept the executioner at bay more than 21 years.

"When I got here, there weren't any VCRs, no personal computers and gasoline was 50 cents a gallon," Vanderbilt said. "Now I probably wouldn't know how to make a collect call."

His protracted legal battle—and continued existence—is not rooted in the issue of whether he killed Katina Moyer, a straight-A senior at Amarillo High School and daughter of a well-known former Texas legislator. Vanderbilt admitted abducting Moyer. And, as he held a gun to her head, he said, it discharged accidentally.

Moreover, Vanderbilt, who had just been fired for using excessive force, also confessed to kidnapping and sexually molesting a 21-year-old woman just a few days before killing Moyer.

The reason he is alive today in a state that has achieved the most proficient record in America at execution is that Vanderbilt also has a tape recording that casts grave doubts about the legality and morality of the circumstances under which he signed the confessions.

Those doubts, which have been argued at virtually every level of court in Texas, have led to two trials and four sentencings.

In the tape, made April 12, 1975, in the presence of Vanderbilt, his defense attorney, three Amarillo police officers and a justice of the peace, Potter County District Attorney Tom Curtis outlined the plea bargain that he offered and signed during the same meeting.

"Upon the conviction of Vanderbilt for capital murder of Katina Moyer," the prosecutor said, "the state will not seek as punishment the death penalty. That will leave as the alternative punishment which he will receive, life in the penitentiary."

The plea bargain, Curtis said, also included the earlier abduction-molestation, for which he agreed to recommend "five years in the penitentiary and further recommend . . . that such sentence be made to run concurrent with any life sentence that Vanderbilt may receive as a result of conviction of capital murder for Katina Moyer."

The plea bargain, by local accounts, was widely rebuked in Amarillo, particularly by Moyer's father, Hudson Moyer, a former prosecutor.

Vanderbilt has contended in his appeals for two decades that Curtis reneged on the plea bargain "to save his own political career." In a motion in April 1994 to force the state to adhere to the plea agreement, Vanderbilt's attorneys wrote: "Curtis was practically tarred and feathered and carried out of town on a rail. The grand jury reindicted Vanderbilt and Curtis turned the case over to a special prosecutor. Curtis's political career was ruined by the episode."

Vanderbilt's attorneys ended their motion by saying: "Reasonable men may disagree about whether that unlawful ordeal was unjust for a confessed killer, but 'the temptation to prosecute' does not give the state a license to break its word."

Curtis, now in private practice in Austin, said the preliminary plea bargain neither damaged his political career nor jeopardized the state's ability to pursue the death penalty against Vanderbilt.

The last 21 years have been a netherworld for the erstwhile cop.

"I don't fit in the world," he said. "Maybe I didn't fit in the world before. . . . The real reason is, I didn't think right.

"I needed to be alone where I could think or in some kind of therapy. That didn't happen. It's hard to talk to people about mitigation without it sounding like justification."

Vanderbilt is awaiting his fourth sentencing for the murder of Katina Moyer.

Ronald Keith Spivey
DATE OF BIRTH: November 8, 1939
DEATH ROW: Georgia Diagnostic and Classification Center, Jackson, Ga.

Victims
Officer Billy Watson, Charles McCook
DATE OF HOMICIDES: December 28, 1976

Ron Spivey has a history of mental problems, including severe depression and a documented inability to deal with disappointment. In 1965, state psychiatrists diagnosed him as psychotic, a man who, when gripped in uncontrollable, violent rages, couldn't distinguish right from wrong.

He also is a member of Mensa and Intertel, an elite society whose membership is limited to the top 1 percent of the most intelligent people in the world.

Although his IQ establishes him as one of the brightest men on death row, Spivey, like half of the inmates surveyed by the *Morning News*, did not graduate from high school. He dropped out after the ninth grade.

In 1976, in a span of 4½ hours in cities 100 miles apart, he killed two men. His first victim was Charles McCook, who died in a

Macon, Ga., pool hall. Spivey, an avid sports fan with an uncanny recall for statistics, had been arguing with McCook over a gambling debt. A short time later in Columbus, Ga., Spivey killed Billy Watson, a moonlighting police officer, a devout Christian and a devoted husband and father.

The violent spree, during which three others were wounded, came after Spivey's wife and only child, a daughter, left him shortly before Christmas 1976.

"All five of these people were absolute, total, complete strangers to me," said Spivey, who said he had been taking tranquilizers and drinking before the shootings. "It later came out that I had freely identified myself and even handed out my own personal business cards."

The shootings and his self-described "subconscious desire" to be arrested and punished were part of a pattern that had been played out on at least three previous occasions, each after women had disappointed him.

In the '50s, he discovered two weeks before he was to be married that his fiancée had been sleeping with her stepfather since she was 12, including during the time she had been dating Spivey. He stole blank checks from his employer and cashed them, using his own name. He was arrested on the same day.

In 1965, when another woman declined his marriage proposal, Spivey used a toy gun and, without benefit of a mask, held up a liquor store. He was arrested within hours. Spivey, without psychotherapy or control, according to a psychiatrist who examined him at the time, would progressively become "more contemptuous of the rules and the laws of society."

The prognosis was prophetic. After a prison term and only two months of psychotherapy, Spivey married a teacher with three children. While he was hospitalized for hepatitis, a friend saw her with another man. She admitted having an affair and told Spivey she was filing for divorce.

He robbed a bar and took a taxi to a bank across the street. Wearing no mask, Spivey robbed a teller and left in the awaiting taxi. He was caught within hours.

"It seems that in each of these episodes, I have subconsciously . . . done everything within my power to see to it that I must be caught," wrote Spivey in an autobiographical account provided to the *Morning News*.

The murderous rage that landed him on death row began, once again, when he believed that a woman had betrayed him. He had married again, and the marriage had produced a daughter. He had begun a business in Tampa, but despite what he termed 14- and 16-hour days, the business failed.

He returned to Macon, found a house, and when he phoned for his family to join him, they had vanished. Through an intermediary, Spivey said, he learned that his wife planned to divorce him, prevent him from seeing his child and "use my past against me in court."

Using a handgun he had been given by a man on a bar stool, Spivey shot McCook to death, then drove to Columbus. Officer Watson, working as a security guard at the Final Approach Lounge, was killed trying to stop Spivey from robbing the mall establishment.

"There is no doubt about my guilt in relation to what I am charged with," Spivey wrote. "I never denied my guilt. . . .

"It has been hard for me to believe that even God could forgive someone like me whose sins have been so terrible," he wrote. "I can't blame anyone who does not forgive me. I am certainly unable to forgive myself."

Deeply introspective, quietly religious and painfully remorseful, Spivey has adopted causes during his two decades on death row that have made him an enigma to prison officials and a pariah among his condemned colleagues.

Spivey has fought continually for his legal right—and that of other death row inmates—to donate organs. His campaign, he says, is a means of repaying society for the crimes he committed against it, and it has attracted the support of actor Ed Asner and Dr. Jack Kevorkian, the controversial Michigan doctor who has assisted terminally ill patients in committing suicide. Although Spivey hasn't been successful in the courtroom, he made organ donation the first item in his will "so that my organs . . . may be used to continue human lives who would have otherwise perished without their use."

Thirteen years after he used a handgun to kill two people and wound three others, he attempted to sue the National Rifle Association for negligence, and he embarrassed the gun lobby by becoming a member from his death row cell. He became NRA member No. BRB 3001 C, he said, "to call attention to the NRA's selfish actions and complete lack of concern for thousands of people who die annually from gunshots."

Several times over his 20 years on death row, Spivey has notified prison officials about crimes by both inmates and guards that he has witnessed and about confessions he has overheard.

Branded by fellow inmates as a snitch, he has been beaten, stabbed and, on one occasion, firebombed in his cell. In April 1994, after he had asked prison officials for protective custody, three inmates attacked the 6-foot-4-inch, 280-pound Spivey. He suffered a broken jaw that had to be surgically corrected.

Spivey is 57 now and has spent more than half his life behind bars, from mental hospitals, state prisons and Leavenworth to, finally, death row in Jackson. The last stop, he said, is by far the worst.

"Some of the people on death row would gag a maggot," he wrote in a June 1995 letter. "But in killing them, we demean our society and ourselves. . . . Some here I loathe, and they make my skin crawl, and some would gladly kill me in an instant.

"But I would not vote to see them die," Spivey wrote. "Not even the ones who tried to beat me to death."

Harry Lee Gosier
DATE OF BIRTH: May 23, 1961
DEATH ROW: Menard Corrections Center, Menard, Ill.

Victims
Soynda Halcrombe, 24; Mae Francis Halcrombe, 44
DATE OF HOMICIDES: February 22, 1988

Harry Gosier was in the fourth grade when authorities caught him shoplifting a box of cereal and a carton of milk. Reluctantly, the 9-year-old led officers to a dilapidated West Palm Beach apartment, where they found his younger brother and sister. The children appeared to have been abandoned for weeks.

"All they had to eat," recalled Bill Waddell, who would become one of Gosier's several benefactors through the years, "was what Harry brought home. He was the oldest, and he was looking out for them as best he could."

Child welfare workers took custody of the younger children, but a couple who were teachers took in young Harry and, along with Waddell and others in the community, they raised him as a sort of community project.

"Everyone loved Harry and everyone helped take care of him," said Waddell, who taught young Gosier math and coached the football team at North Shore High. "If you were buying a pair of jeans for your kid, you'd buy a pair for Harry, too. People took sacks of groceries to help the family that gave him a place to live."

As a teenager, Gosier "had the respect of all the kids at school and teachers, too," Waddell said. "I had never heard Harry even cuss, not a filthy word ever."

Harry Gosier, in fact, became a local success story. He was president of his senior class, and according to Waddell, an above-average student. Equally important, young Gosier was a four-year starter on the basketball team and a prep school All-American in football, virtually assuring himself of a college education.

Widely recruited by some of the top football colleges in the nation in 1981, Gosier chose the University of Michigan. The Wolverines, with Gosier in their defensive secondary, would win the Rose Bowl that year. But not without skirmishes between legendary coach Bo Schembechler and the freshman defensive back over the color of his shoes and the right to become the school's first freshman defensive starter. Gosier lost both battles.

The former high school math and science standout also lost his eligibility to bad grades. Transferring to a smaller California college for a year, during which he married his childhood sweetheart, he boosted his grade point average and reappeared at the University of Illinois.

In 1984, when the Fighting Illini won the Big 10, Gosier became the only player in history to play in the Rose Bowl for two different teams.

But off the field, in Champaign, Ill., his life was falling deeper into chaos. He negotiated with the Canadian Football League, but his pro career ended before it began, apparently due to a contract dispute. He also had met Lesia Halcrombe, with whom he had a daughter, India, while he was married to his first wife. After divorcing his first wife, he married Halcrombe.

And, like 63 percent of death row inmates who responded to the *Morning News* survey, Gosier found himself coping with drug abuse, particularly cocaine, which he sometimes abused with alcohol.

Except for a few phone calls in which he said God had forgiven him, and a brief letter to the *Morning News* that gave no details, Gosier has declined to comment on the specifics of the case that sent him to death row.

"I pleaded guilty," he wrote, "so that's that."

In the span of five hours on an icy afternoon in February 1988, Harry Gosier, his second marriage almost as spent as his football career, exploded in a boozy, violent rage.

Sued for divorce two months earlier and barred by court order from "striking, threatening or harassing" his estranged wife and child, Gosier broke into the home of his in-laws, whom he had blamed for the breakup.

When his 24-year-old sister-in-law, Soynda Halcrombe, came home for lunch, he shot her to death, then raped her, according to court records. About 30 minutes later, Gosier confronted his wife and 3-year-old daughter at gunpoint as they came through the door. After raping her, Lesia Gosier said, he told her, "One down, four to go."

"Meaning he'd killed my sister, and he was going to kill me, my father, my mother and my youngest sister," Gosier told investigators.

Gagged and bound by her ankles and hands in a bedroom, Gosier said, she heard her mother at the front door shortly after 4 P.M. Mae Francis Halcrombe tried to reason with Gosier and, as the woman's granddaughter ran to her, three gunshots rang out.

"India . . . was right there in the same room when Harry killed my mother," Lesia Gosier said.

When word reached south Florida, Waddell was shocked.

"It was almost like when my dad died," the retired teacher said.

Unknown to his supporters but documented in extensive police records, Gosier had been traveling a downhill path in the three years before the shootings.

Barely two months after his second marriage, according to an FBI rap sheet, Gosier had been arrested in Lake Park, Fla., on charges of possession of cocaine and resisting arrest. He was arrested again in Florida a year later on similar charges. Authorities in Illinois had arrested him five times in three years on charges ranging from car theft to aggravated assault and home invasion.

Gosier later admitted to officials that he was spending $500 a week, some of which he borrowed from friends and former coaches, on cocaine. In the interim, he worked at pizza parlors and convenience stores. He also sold his Rose Bowl ring for $200.

Dr. Lawrence J. Jeckel, a psychiatrist who examined Gosier after the murders, said: "A sense of abandonment has dominated his entire life. High school sports was an island of tranquillity."

Gosier was found competent to stand trial and represented himself. The jury, impaneled only to determine punishment, sentenced him to death.

In the end, Harry Gosier's twisted childhood roots ran deeper than community support, athletic success, education or change in geography. He was, as Dr. Emanuel Tanay, another psychiatrist, wrote in his analysis, "a star as an adolescent, a complete failure as a young man, and a tragic figure before the age of 30."

Michael Bruce Ross

DATE OF BIRTH: July 26, 1959

DEATH ROW: Somers State Prison, Somers, Conn.

Victims

Wendy Baribeault, 17; Tammy Williams, 17; Debra Smith Taylor, 23; Robin Dawn Stavinsky, 19; April Brunais, 15; Leslie Shelley, 14

DATES OF HOMICIDES: May 12, 1981; January 4, 1982; March 1982; June 15, 1982; November 16, 1983; March 1984; June 13, 1984

The people who knew Michael Bruce Ross socially described him as handsome and charming. In the classroom or at work, he was known to be intelligent and industrious. He had grown up in rural eastern Connecticut on a poultry farm, where he hoped to return one day to help in the family's burgeoning egg business. He was a high school honor student and a graduate of Cornell University.

What wasn't apparent was that Michael Ross also was a sexual sadist and serial killer who quietly was turning longtime childhood fantasies into brutal rapes and murders in Connecticut, New York and Rhode Island.

In December 1985, he was sentenced to 120 years in prison—two consecutive life sentences—for the sex murders of Tammy Williams and Debra Taylor. On July 6, 1987, he was sentenced to death for the murders of teenagers Wendy Baribeault, Robin Dawn Stavinsky, April Brunais and Leslie Shelley. His victims, all of whom were strangers and some of whom he encountered as they walked along the street, were strangled or beaten to death.

Among more than 600 condemned inmates who responded to a survey by the *Morning News,* Ross was one of only a handful to have graduated from college. One in five adult Americans have college degrees, but only one in 25 inmates in the survey do.

He also was among 34 percent who were treated for psychological problems.

"If I had been able to face what was going on in my head . . . and had sought and received treatment for my paraphilia, a compulsive sexual disorder," Ross wrote, "nobody would have died."

Acquaintances and witnesses said Ross and his brother and two sisters, all younger, had a volatile relationship with their mother. Their mother, they said, blamed her pregnancy with Michael for forcing her into marriage. The marriage was stormy and, while the children were young, she left the family. Her husband and a minister found her and committed her to a mental hospital for treatment before returning her to the family.

During young Michael's childhood, according to family acquaintances, his mother burned his mattress on the front lawn after she caught him masturbating.

In recounting the worst event of his childhood, Ross wrote in the survey: "Mother used to give me enemas on a regular basis to 'clean out my system.'"

As a child, Ross said, he fantasized about taking women to an underground place, where he would keep them to love him. As a hyperactive adolescent, Michael was prescribed Ritalin, a psychostimulant, which he took three times daily for six years. By the time he was a teenager, he had molested girls in the neighborhood.

His condition at Cornell, where he was away from his parents' continually stormy marriage and no longer taking Ritalin, deteriorated. His girlfriend described him as sexually hyperactive. One day, he stalked a young woman student, pulled her into a secluded area and acted out his fantasies, dominating her, raping her and, ultimately, strangling her with his hands.

In and out of a series of relationships and jobs after graduating from college, Ross, from 1981 through 1984, sexually assaulted at least 11 women, strangling six of them. His victims ranged from 14 to 23.

Today, he receives monthly injections of Depo-Lupron, a chemical castration drug that reduces his testosterone and alleviates the symptoms of his sexual disorder.

Ross spends his time on death row writing articles and editorials against the death penalty: "We may be aware of the criminal acts that put an individual on death row," he wrote in *The Providence Journal*, ". . . but very few of us know of the human being whom society has condemned to death."

Ross's father visits him twice a year; he has had no contact with his mother since she assisted prosecutors in the cases against him.

Lynda Lyon and George Sibley Jr.

Lynda Lyon
DATE OF BIRTH: February 8, 1948
DEATH ROW: Julia Tuttwiler Prison for Women, Wetumpka, Ala.

George Sibley Jr.
DATE OF BIRTH: September 8, 1942
DEATH ROW: Holman Prison, Atmore, Ala.

Victim

Sgt. Roger Motley, 38, Opelika, Ala., Police
Department
DATE OF HOMICIDE: October 4, 1993

In cell blocks separated by 125 miles of Interstate 65 in Alabama, Lynda Lyon and George Sibley Jr. may be the only married couple on death row in America. The murder for which the couple was convicted, that of a 38-year-old police officer and father of four, was committed in front of Lyon's 9-year-old son.

The fatal shooting occurred at midday on October 4, 1993, in the parking lot of a Wal-Mart in Opelika, in eastern Alabama. But its bizarre stage apparently was set in Lyon's previous, acrimonious marriage in Orlando, Fla.

Lyon, now 49, and Sibley, her 54-year-old common-law husband, were publishers of what law enforcement officials termed "anti-establishment" magazines that offered, among other things, tips on avoiding federal taxes.

In late 1991, Lyon and her husband at the time, 78-year-old Karl Block, separated. During the summer of 1992, Block, who had been living in an apartment, filed a court action to win back the couple's house in Orlando.

According to Orlando police, Lyon and Sibley confronted Block in his apartment. Lyon warned him to drop the court action, then stabbed him in the chest.

Prosecutors filed charges of aggravated battery on a person older than 65 even though Block declined to press charges. Lyon and Sibley, neither of whom had criminal records, originally pleaded no contest after prosecutors offered to recommend probation.

But shortly before sentencing, the pair began sending facsimile messages to the court and to *The Orlando Sentinel* saying that the judge was an illegal alien and they were withdrawing their guilty pleas.

"We will not live as slaves, but would rather die as free Americans," they said in one of the faxes. They also said they were barricading themselves in their house, awaiting a siege from police.

There was no siege, and when a bail bondsman showed up a few days later to return Lyon to jail, the house was vacant.

The couple surfaced days later in Opelika, just a few miles from the Alabama-Georgia state line. Police said that Sgt. Roger Motley was driving through the Wal-Mart parking lot when he saw Sibley, Lyon and her son. For reasons that apparently were unclear, the officer approached Sibley. A struggle ensued, and the two men fired at each other.

According to witnesses, Lyon, who had been using a nearby pay phone, ran up and shot Sgt. Motley in the back. As the officer ran to his car and radioed for help, Lyon shot him several more times, killing him.

Lyon, in her response to the *Morning News* questionnaire, said she and her husband are appealing their convictions because the officer had attempted to make an illegal arrest.

"We were given the conviction of capital murder solely upon the fact that the 'victim' was a police officer," she wrote, "without allowing for the possibility that the officer was abusing his position as a law enforcement officer, and that he himself was breaking two laws by performing an unlawful arrest and then using threat of deadly force to make the arrest."

Sgt. Motley was married and the father of a daughter, 10, and a son, 14. He also had two stepchildren, 19 and 21. Lyon's 9-year-old was turned over to state child protective workers.

Jeffrey Allen Farina and Anthony Joseph Farina

Jeffrey Allen Farina
DATE OF BIRTH: July 27, 1975

Anthony Joseph Farina
DATE OF BIRTH: November 29, 1973

DEATH ROW: Union Correctional Institution, Raiford, Fla.

Victims

Michelle Van Ness, 17.
WOUNDED: Gary Robinson, 19; Derek Mason, 17; and Kimberly Gordon, 18.
DATE OF HOMICIDE: May 9, 1992

When Jeffrey and Anthony Farina were sentenced to die nearly four years ago, they made dubious history in Florida's legendary Union Correctional Institution.

They were the first pair of brothers condemned to die in Florida, and, at 16, Jeffrey Farina was among the youngest ever to be sent to death row.

Their trip to Raiford began on May 9, 1992, at a Taco Bell in Daytona Beach. The Farinas jumped two employees, Michelle Van Ness, 17, and Derrick Mason, 16, as they carried trash to a bin behind the restaurant.

Binding their hands and those of two other employees, Gary Robinson, 19, and 18-year-old night manager Kimberly Gordon, the Farinas herded all four teenagers into a walk-in freezer.

What happened inside the freezer, according to the prosecutor who argued for death sentences for the Farinas, was an "absolutely pitiless slaughter."

Jeffrey, 60 days short of his 17th birthday, shot Van Ness, Mason and Robinson. His gun jammed when he tried to shoot Gordon, and, witnesses said, he gave his 18-year-old brother a knife, which he used to stab her. Three of the victims survived, but Van Ness, who was shot in the face, died on Mother's Day.

The Farinas and an accomplice, who sat outside in the getaway car, netted more than $2,000 from the restaurant's safe.

The Farinas' mother, Susan Brant, testified that the boys were physically abused by their stepfather, a manic-depressive Vietnam veteran. The family was transient, she said, once living on the beach in their car, using an ice cooler to take baths.

If there was any empathy among the jurors for the Farinas' age, it was more than erased by a tape recording of a conversation between the two brothers in the backseat of a patrol car.

Jeffrey is heard laughing, then telling Anthony: "A guy asked me, 'Why did you shoot 'em?' I said I had a boring day."

Once transferred to Union, the brothers were assigned to adjoining cells.

The "typical" inmate in the *Morning News* survey was in his late 20s to early 40s. The Farinas were among only 7 percent who were in their teens or early 20s.

Over the last decade, according to law professor Victor L. Streib of the Cleveland-Marshall College of Law, homicide arrests among adults have risen by 25 percent. During that same period, he discovered, the number of juveniles arrested on murder charges has risen by 170 percent.

Texas had 30 inmates and Florida had 18 sentenced to death for offenses they committed as juveniles during the period from January 1973 through June 30, 1996, according to Dr. Streib's study.

"Texas and Florida are clear leaders in this practice, each having imposed at least twice as many juvenile death sentences as any of the other jurisdictions," Dr. Streib wrote.

During the 23½-year period covered by the survey, nine of those teen killers were executed, five of them in Texas: Charles Rumbaugh, Jay Pinkerton, Johnny Garrett, Curtis Harris and Ruben Cantu, all 17 at the time they committed murder.

Jeffrey Farina did not respond to the *Morning News* survey. His brother, Anthony, had been on Union's death row two years at the time he completed the questionnaire.

Responding to the question about events that could have changed the direction of his life, Anthony Farina wrote: "Usually, I do not think about this because the past is the past. However, if I would of had Jesus in my life, my life would be somewhere else. But I am glad I came here because it opened my eyes and showed me I needed Jesus."

Nationally, according to Dr. Streib's study, there were 47 inmates on death row on June 30, 1996, for murders they committed as teenagers.

Anthony Farina was not among them. While his guilt in the Taco Bell robbery-murder was upheld, the Florida Supreme Court remanded his case to another jury on the issue of whether he will spend the rest of his life in prison or die in the electric chair. The original trial court made a mistake, the Florida high court ruled, when it excluded a potential juror who was qualified to serve.

Jeffrey Farina, now 21, remains on death row.

CHAPTER 5

• • •

Different Paths, Same End

By injection, electrocution or firing squad, dozens of the survey's participants have since died

CONSEQUENCES: The cross at Charles Clifton Russell's grave at a prison cemetery in Huntsville shows the date of execution and his three-digit death row number, but not his name. The X before the number indicates that he was executed.

Epitaphs

*D*ALLAS—In the free world, a realm with which he had only a passing acquaintance, Kenneth Edward Gentry was a jack of all crimes: car thief, burglar, arsonist, escape artist and, ultimately, killer. He did them all with little concern for the consequences.

"When a person does a crime," Gentry said, "he or she doesn't think about what may or may not happen if they are caught."

Moreover, said the junior high school dropout, one of many prisoners in the *Morning News* survey who have been executed, some people enjoy crime for the "excitement of being on the edge."

Gentry, on the run from a Georgia prison, was on the edge himself when he killed Jimmy Don Ham and dumped his body at Lake Lewisville in 1983. Testimony revealed that Gentry killed Ham in a failed effort to assume his identity.

Nine days before the state of Texas planned to take his life, the lanky killer was moved from his cell at the Ellis I Unit in rural Walker County to the death house in The Walls in Huntsville. Inside the red brick compound built by convicts long dead, the 36-year-old inmate ate a final meal of butter beans and mashed potatoes.

A few minutes after 6 P.M., Gentry, wearing state-issued blues, was strapped to a gurney and injected with lethal drugs. In less time than it took a television newscaster to move from the day's top story to the weather, Gentry, a recidivist criminal, was dead.

Despite macabre aberrations—flames leaping from the mask of a man electrocuted in Florida, a botched and uncommonly long execution in Missouri, and an ominous threat made from a gurney in Arkansas—Gentry's execution, like most others, went off quietly, without incident.

Many of the condemned, having chosen to remain silent about their crimes, arrived on death row as riddles to the public. Gentry and many others volunteered information—sometimes a glimpse, sometimes a life story—to the *Morning News* before they were executed.

Pedro Medina, 39
ELECTRIC CHAIR, March 25, 1997
Florida State Penitentiary, Starke
14 years on death row

Medina, a Cuban of African descent, came to the United States in 1980 during the so-called freedom flotilla. He was convicted of the fatal stabbing in 1982 of Dorothy James, a 52-year-old schoolteacher who had befriended him.

In a letter to the *Morning News*, he complained that, early in his case, lawyers had failed to raise issues in court that "could have had my sentence overturned."

"I am innocent . . . and I'm tired of this," he wrote. "I'll keep it short. Take it easy. That's what I do."

Shortly after Medina was strapped into the electric chair, the jolt of electricity that killed him also ignited the mask that condemned men wear for execution. The flame renewed the debate over whether electrocution is humane.

Michael Carl George, 39
LETHAL INJECTION, February 6, 1997
Greensville Correctional Center, Jarratt, Va.
Six years on death row

George, a former computer operator, was convicted of the sexual torture and murder of 15-year-old Alexander Eugene Sztanko, who was abducted while riding his dirt bike in his neighborhood.

George, who had previous convictions for involuntary manslaughter, abduction and shoplifting, handcuffed the teenager to a tree, shocked his genitals with a stun gun, stole his billfold and shoes, then shot him in the head.

George was reared by his mother. He told the *Morning News:* "Children grow up with only one parent (or with no parents) to nurture and guide them. . . . No one shows them that their lives are valuable. . . . They feel unloved and unwanted, as if no one could care less whether they live or die. . . . As a result, life has little or no value to them—neither their own lives nor the lives of others."

Eric "Cockeye" Schneider, 35
LETHAL INJECTION, January 29, 1997
Potosi Correctional Center, Mineral Point, Mo.
11 years on death row

Schneider, who owed his nickname to having been clubbed in the eye with a police baton, called the *Morning News* frequently during the weeks before his execution. A longtime drug abuser and an amateur musician who formed a prison band of death row inmates, Schneider was optimistic until the last that he would be spared execution.

"The governor's going to give it [a stay of execution] to me," he said in his last phone call, two days before the execution. "I got too many people behind this."

His attorneys fought fruitlessly to obtain a stay, arguing that prosecutors misled jurors and that Schneider was mentally incapable of masterminding a robbery. As his appointment with the executioner drew near, the defendant worked on a diary about his life for his 2-year-old son, who was, Schneider said, conceived on death row during a loosely supervised contact visit.

Schneider said he lacked the ability to control his anger but said he was innocent of the double murder in January 1985 that sent him to death row. He was convicted of killing two St. Louis teachers, Ronald E. Thompson, 55, and Richard R. Schwendeman, 53, during a robbery at their antique-filled home in House Springs, Mo.

Schwendeman, a bullet wound in his forehead, was found in the basement. Thompson, stabbed 10 times, was found in the backyard swimming pool.

Randy Greenawalt, 47
LETHAL INJECTION, January 23, 1997
Arizona State Prison Complex at Florence
18 years on death row

After escaping from prison in 1978 while serving a life sentence for a 1974 murder, Greenawalt and a gang of four others kidnapped and killed a Good Samaritan and his family who had stopped to help them when their stolen getaway car broke down in the desert. John Lyons, 24; his wife, Donnelda, 23; their toddler, Christopher; and the Lyonses' niece, 15-year-old Theresa Tyson, were shotgunned to death.

During his almost two decades on death row, Greenawalt, once a hard-drinking truck driver, said he became a devout Christian who lamented not turning to his faith earlier.

"If a person learns to follow the Lord Jesus and the Holy Spirit and is willing," he wrote, "there is great blessing in life."

Billy Wayne Waldrop, 44
ELECTROCUTION, January 10, 1997
Holman Prison, Atmore, Ala.
14 years on death row

Waldrop was convicted of killing three men during his drug-addled life. He fatally stabbed two in 1973, carving his initials into both of their bodies. Released from prison, the erstwhile construction worker killed 72-year-old Thurman Macon Donahoo during a robbery of his home in Alpine, Ala., in 1982.

Waldrop first began using drugs as a grade school student and went on to abuse whatever was handy: marijuana, speed, heroin and cocaine. A few months before his arrest, he was shot in the head in an unrelated incident, and he contended that prosecutors framed him for Donahoo's murder.

Like many others on death row, Waldrop professed to have had a religious conversion. "Whatever the eventual outcome, the state of Alabama will never kill me," he wrote, citing a New Testament verse about everlasting life. "In light of that, I consider my death row experience to be a blessing."

Gregory Warren Beaver, 32

LETHAL INJECTION, December 3, 1996
Greensville Correctional Institution, Jarratt, Va.
11 years on death row

Beaver pleaded guilty and was sentenced to die for the 1985 shooting of a Virginia State Police trooper, Leo Whitt. The 21-year veteran was shot after he stopped Beaver, who had escaped from a drug treatment center. Beaver was high on drugs and driving a vehicle with only one license plate.

Before turning violent, the former construction worker had a long string of burglary convictions. He told the *Morning News* that crime for some is an emotional rush: "Depending on what the crime is, there is a certain high or adrenaline rush that accompanies the actions."

He also said he had matured while on death row. "I was 19 years old when my crime occurred," he wrote. "I am not the same person I was then."

Larry Lonchar, 45

ELECTROCUTION, November 14, 1996
Georgia Diagnostic and Classification Prison in Jackson
Nine years on death row

Lonchar came close to death twice before he was executed. Once in 1993, and again in 1995, he waived his appeals and expressed a desire to be executed, only to change his mind and file last-minute appeals that delayed his execution.

He was convicted of killing Charles Wayne Smith, 54; Smith's girlfriend, Margaret Louise Sweat, 45; and Smith's son, Steven Wayne Smith, 24, over a $10,000 gambling debt. Lonchar, who had previous convictions for burglary and robbery, also said he had a history of psychiatric problems stemming from his parents' divorce.

Describing one of his close encounters with the electric chair, he wrote of being taken to the death house and being "all prepared" up until the final half hour, when he was talked into starting a last-minute, and temporarily successful, appeal.

"Won't happen this time!" he wrote. "Just have too many reasons why it's best for me to die!"

Jusan William Frank Parker, 44

LETHAL INJECTION, August 8, 1996
Cummins Unit, Varner, Ark.
11 years on death row

Parker, consumed by the idea that his in-laws had undermined his marriage, stalked and killed them November 5, 1984, at their home in Rogers, Ark. After fatally shooting James and Sandra Warren, Parker, a heavy cocaine abuser, abducted his estranged wife, Pam, and took her at gunpoint to the police station. He wounded officer Ray Feyen, and before the siege ended, he had also shot his wife in the abdomen. Both victims recovered.

On death row for more than a decade, Parker became a Buddhist and spoke frequently of his remorse. "I was 30 years old and was going through my third divorce," Parker said in his questionnaire. "It became too much psychologically, and I lost it.

"The death penalty was never a concern to me, until now. Call it my karma."

He was an advocate of televising executions. "I wish they would . . . put them in people's living rooms, make them watch what they're paying taxes for," he said. "If you're going to execute me, so be it. But don't do it in secret."

Thomas Battle, 34

LETHAL INJECTION, August 7, 1996
Potosi Correctional Center, Mineral Point, Mo.
15 years on death row

As a young man, Battle trolled the streets of St. Louis learning lessons and picking up habits that would haunt him throughout life. He was convicted in 1980 of raping and killing Birdie Lee Johnson, an 80-year-old neighbor who called him by the nickname "Sweet Boy." Johnson, according to press reports, was discovered in her home with a butcher knife protruding from her head and numerous stab wounds.

Battle, a juvenile delinquent who gave his life over to the drugs he easily obtained on the streets, told the *Morning News* that he felt trapped by his environment. He said he needed "a larger view of the world" to learn that "the convictions and practices of the ghetto are not acceptable all over."

Emmet Nave, 55

LETHAL INJECTION, July 31, 1996
Potosi Correctional Center, Mineral Point, Mo.
12 years on death row

Nave was convicted in the shooting death of his landlord, Geneva Roling, in Jefferson City, Mo. The shooting took place less than a year after his parole from prison for robbery and rape. After shooting Roling, Nave took four women hostage at a nearby hospital and sexually assaulted them before he was arrested.

Nave, who said his father also served time for murder, said his criminal conduct was the result of a lifetime of drug and alcohol abuse. He started drinking in grade school and using drugs in high school, eventually coming to prefer cocaine, speed and heroin.

"My social problems have been caused by the use of drugs and alcohol," Nave told the *Morning News*. "I'm sure the victims of alcohol- and drug-induced death row inmates wished society would have recognized a disease that can so control a person's actions that they can murder at will while under the influence. I've known killers who have woke up after a drunk and have no idea they had killed someone."

Fred H. Kornahrens, 47

Lethal injection, July 19, 1996
Broad River Correctional Institution, Columbia, S.C.
10 years on death row

Kornahrens, a civilian employee in the military, was sentenced to death for killing his former wife, Patricia J. Avant; her father, Harry Lee Wilkerson; and her stepson, Jason. Domestic pressures and a lack of faith, he said, pushed him past his "breaking point." His victims were killed with a bayonet and a handgun.

"For years, I suffered one setback, problem and loss after another," Kornahrens wrote. "Among other things, my . . . [father] was killed by drug dealers" and his marriage broke up. "It's a long story, and the pain and stress of it all made me sick.

"I was not aware how sick I had become until I lost control of my actions."

Joseph J. Savino Jr., 37
LETHAL INJECTION, July 17, 1996
Greensville Correctional Institution, Jarratt, Va.
Eight years on death row

A bisexual bartender who had abused a pharmacopeia of drugs since he was in grade school, Savino was sentenced to die for killing Thom McWaters, his 64-year-old lover. McWaters was beaten with a hammer and stabbed with butcher knives. Savino, according to reports, said he killed his lover over his frequent demands for sex. He told the *Morning News* that he killed McWaters during a robbery.

His life, he wrote, was warped by sexual abuse and drugs, and he said a priest molested him. "Never," he wrote, "use any drugs!"

Daren Lee Bolton, 29
LETHAL INJECTION, June 19, 1996
Arizona State Prison Complex at Florence
Two years on death row

Unlike many who draw out their time on death row with repetitive appeals, Bolton "volunteered" to be executed. Sentenced to death February 22, 1993, for the kidnapping and stabbing death of Zosha Lee Pickett, 2, who was abducted from her bedroom in Tucson in 1986, he was executed just a little more than two years later. He also had been charged with the death of another Tucson girl, seven-year-old Cathy Fritz, in 1982, but that case was never tried.

An alcohol abuser and dope smoker, Bolton told the *Morning News* that he suffered from psychiatric problems stemming from his parents' divorce and that he once had his head "put through a plaster wall" for bringing home average grades on a report card. He said he wished he could spend time counseling troubled teens "to try to keep them from ending up here."

Jeffrey Sloan, 29

LETHAL INJECTION, February 21, 1996
Potosi Correctional Center, Mineral Point, Mo.
10 years on death row

Sloan was convicted of killing his 9-year-old brother, Jason, in 1985, and was suspected of also killing his parents, Judith and Paul, and another brother, Timothy, 18.

In his questionnaire, Sloan complained of physical abuse by his father, and said he might have turned out differently if he had "moved away from home."

"I am not a criminal. I know I was convicted of murders, but I was never into crime or would be into crime. It was something in my family that made me do the murders."

John Albert Taylor, 36

FIRING SQUAD, January 26, 1996
Southpoint Facilities, Utah State Prison at Draper
Five years on death row

When Taylor was executed, his death was national news, appearing in *The New York Times* and *The Los Angeles Times*, because he insisted on being executed by firing squad. He told the *Morning News* that he considered a firing squad most humane. He joined Gary Gilmore, the first person executed after the death penalty was reinstated in 1976, as the only condemned men to die before a firing squad.

Utah is the only state that still uses riflemen to carry out executions. As political pressure mounts to do away with the firing squad, the chance increases that Taylor will go down in history as the last person to be executed in the United States by gunfire.

Taylor was convicted in the 1989 rape and strangulation of Charla Nicole King one day before her 12th birthday. As a juvenile, Taylor was in trouble for burglary, mail fraud and shoplifting. As an adult, he was convicted of weapons and burglary charges but apparently received probation.

During his childhood, Taylor related, he was gang-raped by strangers and physically abused by a parent. "I was stripped naked and placed in an aluminum shed in the middle of winter in Colorado for seven days," he said.

Richard Townes Jr., 45

LETHAL INJECTION, January 23, 1996
Greensville Correctional Institution, Jarratt, Va.
Nine years on death row

Townes, a black man convicted of killing a 32-year-old white woman, believed the death penalty is immoral because it is not applied equally to all people accused of capital crimes.

"As long as there exists underlying factors such as race, sex, economical status or political influence in determining who shall or shall not be prosecuted for capital murder," he wrote a year before his execution, "the death penalty can never be considered morally or socially acceptable as a direct consequence of the arbitrary, capricious and discriminatory manner in which it is misapplied upon the people of color and the poor in America."

Townes, previously convicted of three robberies and a maiming, was sentenced to death for the 1985 murder of Virginia Goebel, a mother of two, during a convenience store robbery.

Lethal injections usually are administered in a prisoner's arm. But officials could not find a suitable vein in the arm of Townes, a onetime heroin user, and inserted the needle in his right foot.

Robert Sidebottom, 33

LETHAL INJECTION, November 15, 1995
Potosi Correctional Center, Mineral Point, Mo.
Eight years on death row

Stoned on drugs, Sidebottom, the courts found, killed his 74-year-old grandmother, May Sidebottom, in 1985 after an argument over $5. In an interview before his death, Sidebottom said he really wasn't sure exactly what happened that day. He and a friend were at his grandmother's house, but his memory, he said, was fogged by "drinking and doing drugs."

"I was there," he said. "I'm not real sure about . . . [who killed his grandmother]. I'm pretty sure it was him [the friend]. I don't think I did."

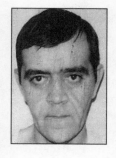

Dennis Wayne Stockton, 54

LETHAL INJECTION, September 27, 1995
Greensville Correctional Institution, Jarratt, Va.
12 years on death row

Stockton—sentenced to die for a 1978 contract murder of a Virginia teenager, Kenneth Ardner—became the 300th person to be executed since the practice resumed in the United States in 1977.

He published a prison newsletter, *Passin' Thoughts,* and the issue he sent the *Morning News* included a long fantasy piece about how he had escaped from death row, lived in the woods, married a young homeless woman and adopted her young son.

He consistently maintained his innocence and blamed his conviction on "crooked lawmen." "I am on death row, sentenced to die for a crime I'm not guilty of. I've been saying this long before it became fashionable to do so. I'm the victim of crimes by members of law enforcement. I want to be free."

Vernon Lamar Sattiewhite, 39

LETHAL INJECTION, August 15, 1995
The Walls Unit, Huntsville, Tex.
Nine years on death row

Sattiewhite was convicted in San Antonio for the 1986 slaying of his former girlfriend, Sandra Sorrell.

Sattiewhite accosted Sorrell as she was walking to nursing school, grabbed her by the head, dragged her several hundred feet, then shot her twice in the head. Turning his gun on himself, he repeatedly pulled the trigger, only to have the weapon misfire.

In his questionnaire, Sattiewhite spoke of the loss he felt from his own mother's death when he was four. Ironically, Sattiewhite's actions had the obvious effect of visiting upon his former girlfriend's two children the loss he endured as a child.

"I would have been better if my mother hadn't died when I was four," he wrote. If he could be freed for one day, he said, he would spend it with his own son.

Sorrell was the second person Sattiewhite had killed. The former forklift operator and 10th-grade dropout had previously been convicted of murder in 1977 and received a five-year sentence.

John Fearance Jr., 40
LETHAL INJECTION, June 20, 1995
The Walls Unit, Huntsville, Tex.
16 years on death row

Fearance was convicted for the December 23, 1977, slaying of a neighbor, Larry Faircloth, 32, a printing company executive, during a burglary in Dallas.

In his questionnaire, Fearance, a marginally literate ninth-grade dropout who wrote that he suffered from "brain danger [sic]," claimed to have suffered a "psychotic break" following an argument with his wife over a casserole. She had put meat in the dish; he wanted it on the side. After arguing with his wife, he broke into Faircloth's home and stabbed him 19 times.

Fearance, a car wash worker, previously had been convicted of theft and attempted rape. His last words: "I made a mistake 18 years ago. I lost control of my mind, but I didn't mean to hurt anyone. I have no hatred toward humanity. I hope He will forgive me for what I done. I didn't mean to."

Ronald Keith Allridge, 34
LETHAL INJECTION, June 8, 1995
The Walls Unit, Huntsville, Tex.
Nine years on death row

Allridge was convicted of murder for the 1985 shotgun slaying of Carla McMillen, 19, during a late-night holdup at a Whataburger in Fort Worth.

Allridge and his brother, James Vernon Allridge III, were members of a gang responsible for a series of robberies in 1985. James Allridge drove the getaway vehicle during the robbery in which McMillen was killed. Ronald Allridge was at the wheel when James killed a clerk in a convenience store robbery that netted $300. Ronald Allridge had been released from prison in 1983 after serving six years of a 10-year sentence for an unrelated 1976 murder he committed when he was 16.

"I feel some people commit crimes because they feel it is a necessity," Ronald Allridge wrote. "I feel others just enjoy the feeling of power or enjoy the material gain."

Allridge, an accomplished robber who grew up in a large middle-class family, said he might have been a better person had he stuck with the last regular job he had—at Domino's Pizza.

Varnall Weeks, 43

ELECTROCUTION, May 12, 1995
Holman Prison, Atmore, Ala.
13 years on death row

Weeks was sentenced to death after stealing a car and killing its driver, 24-year-old veterinary student Mark Anthony Batts of Murfreesboro, Tenn.

Weeks, a former bricklayer, had a long history of psychiatric problems and maintained that he shared his cell with an angel. "I sacrificed one life in order to save and reconcile them both," he wrote. "This is psychotic."

Duncan Peder McKenzie Jr., 43

LETHAL INJECTION, May 10, 1995
Montana State Prison at Deer Lodge
20 years on death row

Interviewed the week of his execution, McKenzie was eager to talk and had encouraged a reporter to "hurry" to the prison at Deer Lodge before his death. Sitting in a small room with his hands chained to his waist, McKenzie, with no expression of emotion, denied involvement, as he had for 20 years, in the murder that sent him to death row. Convicted of kidnapping, torturing and murdering 23-year-old teacher Lana Harding in 1974, the loner became the first man to be executed in Montana in more than 40 years.

Once a relatively fit man standing almost six feet tall and weighing 190 pounds, he bloated on death row to 265 pounds of sallow flesh. For his last meal, he ordered an entire beef tenderloin, french fries and a half gallon each of whole milk and orange sherbet.

Strapped to a gurney in the makeshift mobile home that Montana officials use for a death house, McKenzie died listening to a Marty Robbins recording through a pair of stereo headphones. He told the *Morning News* that he imagined death to be a void with endless sleep.

Emmitt Foster, 42

LETHAL INJECTION, May 3, 1995
Potosi Correctional Center, Mineral Point, Mo.
11 years on death row

Foster was convicted for the 1983 robbery and slaying of Travis Walker, 26. The two men were members of the same softball team.

As a child, Foster's science fair project had been featured in a local newspaper, but he dropped out in the 11th grade, opting for a life of drugs, alcohol and crime. The former maintenance man racked up four prison sentences before killing his friend during a robbery.

People enjoy crime, he said, because it allows a person to pit "your mind against someone else."

In his questionnaire, Foster said he believed that lethal injection was the most humane form of execution. When it came time to execute Foster, however, prison officials first had trouble finding a good vein on the onetime drug abuser, then had to loosen an overly tight restraining strap that had slowed the flow of lethal chemicals to his body. Death from lethal injection usually occurs in minutes. In Foster's case, it took almost half an hour.

Keith Zettlemoyer, 39

LETHAL INJECTION, May 2, 1995
State Correctional Institution, Rockview, Pa.
14 years on death row

Zettlemoyer was convicted of the 1980 murder of Charles DeVetsco, 29, of Sunbury, a onetime friend who had agreed to testify against him in a robbery trial. DeVetsco was kidnapped, taken to a wooded area and slain. According to the victim's mother, Zettlemoyer told officials that he had been "killing rats."

Zettlemoyer, previously convicted of robbery, was the first person to be executed in Pennsylvania since 1962.

While in prison, the former janitor said that he became a devout Christian and that his Bible was his most cherished possession. He said he would have been a better person had he "become a Christian much earlier in my life."

Richard Wayne Snell, 64

LETHAL INJECTION, April 19, 1995
Cummins Unit, Varner, Ark.
Nine years on death row

The morning of the day he was executed, Snell, an avowed white supremacist, was smiling and chuckling as death house television carried breaking news of the worst act of terrorism in U.S. history: the bombing of the Alfred P. Murrah Federal Building in Oklahoma City.

For a final meal, he consumed six pieces of fried crappie, part of a white onion, salad and five hush puppies. In his last words, the convicted double murderer issued an ominous warning to then-governor Jim Guy Tucker, who had rejected his bid for clemency.

"Look over your shoulder," Snell said, according to a death house prison log that recorded his last words. "Justice is on the way. I wouldn't trade places with you or any of your political cronies. . . . Hail his victories. I am at peace."

Snell had been linked to assorted ultra-right-wing and racist organizations. Twice sentenced to death, he was convicted of killing a black Arkansas state trooper, Louis Bryant, and a Jewish pawnbroker, William Stumpp. Snell described himself to the *Morning News* as a family man, married for 47 years, who believed "in law and order and the death penalty."

Noble D. Mays Jr., 41

LETHAL INJECTION, April 6, 1995
The Walls Unit, Huntsville, Tex.
16 years on death row

Mays was convicted for the 1979 robbery and murder of Jerry Lamb, a 34-year-old food service worker in Wichita Falls.

Mays, an oilfield roughneck and convicted robber, was tried four times for Lamb's death. One was declared a mistrial. Two were overturned on appeal. The fourth led to his execution.

He grew up in a world of drugs, violence and crime. In comments written four months before he was executed, he expressed hope that one day he would obtain his freedom "so I'll have a future to accomplish something good."

"People think life here is too easy," he wrote, "but I wouldn't wish this life on my worst enemy."

Clifton Charles Russell Jr., 33

LETHAL INJECTION, January 31, 1995
The Walls Unit, Huntsville, Tex.
15 years on death row

Russell was convicted of the 1979 robbery and murder of Hubert Tobey, a 41-year-old air traffic controller from Abilene. Tobey was stabbed and his head crushed with a heavy object.

Six weeks before his execution, Russell expressed remorse for having "taken a life" and said he longed for the stable family life he never had as a child. He said he spent four years at the Abilene Boys Ranch while his "mother was on the run" and was, at other times, left alone "for days at a time without knowing when or if my mother was ever coming back."

"I believe that if I had of been given a home where there were strong (lawful) morals and less or no drugs, parties and the like, I would have grown up into a productive person."

Kermit Smith Jr., 37

Lethal injection, January 24, 1995
Central Prison, Raleigh, N.C.
14 years on death row

Condemned for the death of a 20-year-old Wesleyan College cheerleader, Whelette Collins, Smith became only the second white person since 1976 to be executed for the murder of a black person.

Smith described himself as a suicidal, bisexual restaurant worker who was teased and assaulted by other children growing up. Reared in a middle-class family by his natural parents, he had a history of criminal conduct. Before committing murder, he had been convicted of assault, forgery, burglary and larceny.

He was convicted of kidnapping three cheerleaders and raping and killing one—Collins—while her friends were locked in the trunk of his car. In his questionnaire, Smith regretted that he had not developed a "better understanding of people." Free for a day, he said, he would be "leaving the country."

PART TWO

Causes of Crimes

CHAPTER 6

• • •

Playmates Turned Inmates

Four men share same wretched roots of poverty, gangs

COMPTON, CALIF., OCTOBER 1997—For four longtime friends now condemned to death, life began here 30 years ago in the aftermath of the Watts riots, in an urban miasma of despair, hatred and blood.

As young boys they played in the same parks, attended the same schools and roamed the same streets. They were raised in matriarchal homes, their fathers long gone or dead.

As teenagers, they saw mutual friends arrested, shot and killed. They partied together, joined the same gangs, committed similar crimes—sliding toward an end even more hopeless than their beginning.

Finally, as young men, these four childhood friends—Paul Brown, Tracey Carter, Alphonso Howard and Paul Watson—were convicted of unrelated capital murders in Los Angeles County and sentenced to die.

The four youths, who became members of two groups of Crips, were convicted of killing a total of seven people: four in robberies, two in a drive-by shooting and an 11-year-old girl during a rape.

Today, 400 miles up the coast, the four men are locked down on California's death row at San Quentin, a virtual Valhalla for gangsters. Their broken lives document yet another generation crippled by what some experts call the environmental theory of crime.

In the *Morning News* survey of death row inmates, nearly nine of 10 inmates cited family and community environment as one of the most important factors in shaping a person's life.

Many of those responding to the survey contend they, like the four from Compton and south-central Los Angeles, were products of a world scarred by poverty, broken homes, drugs and gangs—four important environmental influences—long before they were convicted of victimizing others.

Brown, Carter, Howard and Watson, like 56 percent of the death row respondents, came from poor households. Like 55 percent, they were reared in broken homes. They were among seven in 10 who reported having been in trouble with the law as juveniles.

Paul Madison Brown, now 30, grew up in what he calls a "concrete jungle" not far from the site of the 1965 riots that killed 34 people. Like many of his friends, he said he never envisioned what most Americans take for granted: a long life, a family of his own or a career.

"I didn't see no future," Brown said. "There was no sense of community. Don't even know what that means where I come from. It was every man and woman for themselves."

From playmates to inmates, the four lives seemed to tick to the same eerie clock. Born within two years of each other in the mid-1960s, they would commit capital crimes within a two-year period in the late 1980s and end up on death row during the first two years of the 1990s.

Watson's mother, Mary Cooper, said the boys not only grew up together, but often as not, the women in their families were friends as well.

"Tracey Carter used to live on our street," Cooper said, and often played with Paul. Cooper also was friends with Tracey's mother and the grandmother who raised him.

Paul Watson and Paul Brown got to be friends "from the streets," and their sisters grew up together, Cooper said.

Alphonso Howard, while visiting his grandmother who lived nearby, played basketball with Watson at nearby Oaks Park, she said.

School records obtained by the *Morning News* show that Howard attended some of the same schools as Carter and Watson.

Male role models were few and far between.

"I don't know of any stable or successful fathers where I grew up," Brown said. "Many were absentee fathers. Most males I saw beat up on their wives and were not good examples."

Brown won't talk about it publicly today, but the violent world which he and his three young friends routinely negotiated became profoundly personal in January 1977. He and his friends, still in grade school, were attending a party in a south-central Los Angeles apartment complex for one of his older brothers.

ROUGH STREETS, ROUGHER LIFE: Winnie McCloud (left), a Los Angeles County probation officer, talks with a woman about her gang member son, who is behind bars, charged with capital murder.

Eunice, another of his brothers, was gunned down in a gang war shooting. He died in Paul's arms as his young friends watched.

"It just so happened that the shooters got Eunice instead of another one," his mother said.

Theirs was a turf-conscious world where hand signs signify unspoken allegiance and a passerby on the wrong half block stands to die.

A former Los Angeles gang detective, Steve Strong, said the rough streets of Brown's neighborhood breed kids "who don't really care because they never believe they're going to live to 25."

Unarmed but unflappable, June Wade and Winnie McCloud have cruised the streets of Compton and south-central Los Angeles for a combined 40 years as Los Angeles County probation officers.

Brown, Carter, Howard and Watson were not among their caseload, but the two women work every week with 100 just like them—young men reared in a sociological cesspool with a gravitational pull so strong that some live their entire lives without ever seeing the Pacific Ocean only a few miles away.

"You work with these kids," McCloud said, "you've got to keep it simple. Simple. They're stupid. Why wouldn't they be? They don't go to school and who's at home to teach them?"

McCloud and Wade, her supervisor in the gang unit, drive by a case in point.

"There it is," McCloud said, pointing at a bright blue building at the corner of Alameda and 114th Street on the edge of Compton. Huge letters on the side of the building said Santana Tire and Wheels.

The rival Crips and Bloods gangs have existed in Los Angeles for generations. Crips and Bloods distinguish themselves by color. Crips are blue, Bloods red. The name of the tire store became the name of the Santana Block Crips, the probation officers explained, only because the building was blue.

"That's pretty smart, huh?" Wade said, shaking her head. Paul "Potato Head" Watson and Alphonso "Bup" Howard were Santana Block Crips, according to interviews. Paul Brown, known on the street as "Taco," and Tracey "Trey Dog" Carter were Kitchen Crips, named for Kitchen's liquor store.

Police estimate that there are about 180,000 gang members in Los Angeles County. They say that Compton, 10 square miles southeast of downtown Los Angeles, has more than 6,400 gangsters among its 90,000 population.

The probation officers point out the old haunts of Brown, Watson, Carter and Howard, and there's ubiquitous, tangible evidence of gang presence in this city in decay.

Virtually every surface on which paint can be sprayed—trees, walls, street signs, sidewalks, windows, houses—has been tagged with graffiti by rival gangs.

On Magnolia Street, a block from Compton police headquarters, a man on a bicycle leans into an open window of an apartment, a known crack house that thrives in daylight.

On Compton Boulevard, a Los Angeles County sheriff's deputy uses binoculars to monitor children as they leave an elementary school.

And on a sunny September day, blinds are closed and drapes are drawn in fear of drive-by shootings.

Remarkably, in a small city in which 64 gangs have been identified, the streets are devoid of obvious gang members.

"They're roaches," McCloud said. "They don't like light."

Flower gardens in well-manicured yards of blue-collar families blossom next to shuttered, weed-plagued crack houses that appear abandoned until night falls.

Entrepreneurs who sell ornamental iron burglar bars sell to both. McCloud said decent people bar their doors to keep from being robbed and killed; others use the bars to hold off police until they can flush their drug stashes.

GROWING UP WITH A GANG: A gang member known as "T" displays the sign for his gang, the Santana Block Crips on Rose Street in Compton, Calif. He said his "mentor," Paul "Potato Head" Watson, was like a father to him during his preadolescent years growing up with the gang. Watson is on death row at San Quentin.

Only a few miles from the glitz of Hollywood but light-years away by any other measure, Compton is a city in which one in four residents lives below the poverty line. According to government statistics, its residents suffer roughly three times the violent crime rate of the rest of the country and are three times more likely to be out of work.

About a quarter of the households in the city are headed by single mothers.

Neither Wade nor McCloud will eat in Compton. The president of the Chamber of Commerce doesn't even live here; she maintains that the city's runaway drug problem makes it almost impossible to raise an honest kid.

As timely proof, the latest gang war victim, a 9-year-old, was gunned down earlier this month while waiting for a school bus in front of the chamber offices.

Rose Street, near where Watson grew up, is marginally controlled by the Santana Block Crips. The uneasiness of their hold on the block is evident in the spray-painted threats left by other turf-hungry gangs.

Street signs in the neighborhood are marked with the blue initials SBC, for Santana Block Crips, which counted Watson and Howard among its members. The graffiti stakes out their territory, McCloud said, marking their area "like a dog."

In the 1800 block of Rose, the probation officers point out seven drug houses on the east side of the street alone. A night earlier, in front of the lime-green stucco with the weeds, someone shot a man and left him bleeding in the street.

Only five months ago, 40 police and probation officers sealed off the same block and arrested a small army of gangsters and drug dealers.

"It was like picking roaches," said McCloud. "And like roaches, they came right back."

A few miles north in south-central Los Angeles, near the epicenter of the Watts riot, is Kitchen Crips territory. The Kitchen Crips, which at one point included Paul Brown and Tracey Carter, favor Kansas City Royals ball caps because they're blue and bear the initials KC.

Whether Compton or south-central, the probation officers say there are two sets of laws: one for the courthouse, another for the street. Courthouse law makes it a crime to use force to take another person's property. Street law says that if a gangster puts a gun against your temple, you hand over your property.

One of McCloud's probationers recently killed a woman when she didn't hand over her purse quickly enough. The probation officer asked him why he killed her.

"What was I supposed to do?" he asked. "She wouldn't give it up."

"He thought it was her fault," McCloud said. "She didn't follow the rules."

The two probation officers pull up in front of a 17-year-old's house to find out why he's missed his last two appointments. He stands on the porch, promising, under threat of jail, to appear the next day.

A prayer plaque hangs behind him that reads: "Please Lord, teach us to laugh again, but God . . . don't let us forget that we cried."

Only weeks earlier, three people were killed during a gang battle in the alley behind the youth's house. And nearby, a family of three was killed in their car after making a wrong turn down an unfamiliar street.

Violence on these streets is a deadly cliché among some who live here. It's also glamorized by some. *Straight Outta Compton*, a nihilistic rap album by N.W.A, is a belligerent acknowledgment of that violence:

MARKING THEIR BORDERS: Graffiti at a corner on Rose Street in Compton marks the start of the Santana Block Crips territory.

Taking a life or two

That's what the hell I do.

You don't like how I'm living,

Well, [expletive] you.

This is a gang and I'm in it,

My main man Trey will

[Expletive] you up in a minute.

Ailene Jackson, who befriended Paul Watson as a child, may condemn gangs, but she says she understands them.

"It always comes back to the same old things," Jackson says. "They have to do something to survive. They're not educated. They think they can't go and get a job. They feel like the only thing they can do is sell drugs. And from selling drugs, they always get into something."

Roy Roberts III heads the Watts Willowbrook Boys and Girls Club, where Tracey Carter used to hang out. He knows that the lure of gangs—and the drug proceeds that buy nice clothes, gold jewelry and cars—often is too powerful to resist.

"Those youngsters want excitement," Roberts said. "Gangs offer something—people with education may not want to admit that— especially for a young man who doesn't have a father at home and have all the niceties they want."

William Packer Jr., a friend who pleaded futilely with a judge to keep Paul Brown off death row, compared young Brown's pock-marked background to the poverty and hopelessness of the 19th-century France of *Les Misérables*.

"A soul in darkness sins," Victor Hugo wrote, "but the real sinner is he who caused the darkness."

These are the stories of four childhood friends who ended up together on San Quentin's death row.

The accounts are based on interviews with one of them, their friends and family, and court and school records.

"Taco"

At birth, Paul Madison Brown Jr. had at least one thing going for him: the father for whom he was named. The elder Brown, now retired, was a successful career military officer who, as a civilian, would earn a doctorate in electronics.

But the single edge that would have made young Paul unique in his neighborhood—a father—lasted only "a very short period of time," the senior Brown said.

"I must admit something," Brown said during an interview. "I really don't know the man, and he's my son."

Paul was raised mostly by his mother, who, by several accounts, lived in a decaying neighborhood near a junkyard in south-central Los Angeles.

Paul's sister, Thyra Denise Williams, said their childhood was one of deprivation.

"I don't remember a Christmas. I don't remember a birthday. I don't remember . . . my brothers and sister even having a party."

The dominant male figure in the house was the oldest brother, Allen Butler, a gang member, now 39, who is serving a nine-year drug sentence at a California prison.

Paul and brother Eunice idolized Allen, as did some of Paul's friends. Allen's life as a gangsta appeared glamorous and romantic. "What they did seemed attractive, made it seem fun," Williams said. "If that's what all the other men are getting involved with in your neighborhood, what do you do? You get involved because you don't know anything different."

When his older brother got into trouble, his mother said, Paul "kinda got wild. He had to experience being in jail. He'd straighten up, then he'd go right back to it.

"I don't care how much support you give them, most of them do get into trouble. And once they get into trouble, the police are after them all the time."

By age 10, Paul was smoking marijuana. He graduated to speed, heroin and PCP. He was still in grade school when he watched Eunice die.

The shooting at Allen's birthday party apparently was part of an ongoing struggle between the Kitchen Crips and a rival gang. Eunice and Allen were Kitchen Crips.

About the same time his brother was killed, Paul joined the Kitchen Crips.

"I remember him being excited and coming home telling me his gang name, 'Taco,'" said Williams, his youngest sister.

According to juvenile records used in his murder trial, Paul Brown was first sent to a California Youth Authority camp in 1980, at age 13, for threatening another boy with a knife.

Shortly after he was released in 1981, he shotgunned a rival gang member in the face, telling police he acted in self-defense and that the other gang thought he was "mad at them because my brother got shot."

Released again in 1984, he was free just 13 days before he was arrested again for pulling a gun on a woman and her child. Ordered back into custody for another three years, he was released a final time in 1987.

Freedom, as it had been in the past, was short-lived. Brown was arrested on charges that he murdered Walter Dejuan Lyles and Sherry Lee Gee, who were killed during unrelated robberies on May 30 and June 1.

Brown's record of juvenile violence was introduced during the punishment phase of his murder trial. In November 1990, having already spent close to half his life in custody, Mr. Brown was sentenced to death.

He arrived on death row at San Quentin on November 26, 1990, at 23 as inmate No. E77700.

"Trey Dog"

Tracey Lavell Carter, the youngest of the four friends on death row, lived much of his early youth with his grandmother in south-central Los Angeles. His father was shot to death when he was 3.

The women in his family—his mother, sister and grandmother—tried to steer Tracey to religion, taking him on Sundays to a local Church of Christ. For a time, he was a regular at the Watts Willowbrook Boys and Girls Club, headed by Roy Roberts III.

Roberts remembers Tracey as a fine young man until he succumbed to the lure of gang life.

"I knew him when he was doing fairly well," Roberts said. "When he was a younger kid, he told me he wasn't going to get involved in gangs. But at some point, I guess the streets won over what we were doing here."

In a brief conversation, Tracey's grandmother—who did not want to be identified—said the boy she raised until he was 14 or 15 was a good kid who worked hard in school.

Her grandson, she said, is afraid to talk about his life because he's "living up there with those people" on death row, and he "doesn't want to be killed."

"I cry every night," the grandmother said. "I pray every night. He's my oldest grandson, my daughter's only son."

Tracey was 11 when he was first arrested. In the seven years between 1980 and the day he was accused of capital murder, he was arrested 19 times for car theft, robbery, burglary and an assortment of drug, sex and alcohol charges.

In 1987, he was accused of killing two people in two hours. David Eugene Thompson, a minister in Tustin, Calif., was shot to death after Carter and two companions stole his car; Leo Salgado was killed as he witnessed a friend being robbed.

At 21, with an extensive rap sheet including two murders, Carter arrived on death row on April 25, 1990, as inmate No. E54002.

"Bup"

Mary Williams was 15 when she gave birth to Alphonso Howard, one of nine children she would bear. Young Alphonso grew up on Oaks Street in Compton. Two of his childhood playmates, brothers Rus and Derrick Robinson, said the boy they called "Bup" avoided trouble until his teens.

At 13, Alphonso started stealing and exhibiting wild behavior, once hurling a brick through the Robinsons' window for no apparent reason.

"He was a disturbed person, psychologically disturbed," Rus Robinson said.

As a teenager and young man, records show, Alphonso was arrested four times for burglary and theft between 1982 and 1987. He was enrolled in a program for delinquent youths but attended only a few sessions.

A below-average student in junior high, he was suspended for attitude problems. In spring 1987, the troubled loner abducted an 11-year-old girl, Wendy Bustamante, who lived up the street.

He dragged her into a vacant house and raped her. He dressed her, gagged her, then shot her through the heart with a .380-caliber, semiautomatic pistol.

The Robinsons were present a few days later when Wendy's body was found in the abandoned house.

"We looked at each other and said, 'You know who did this? Bup,'" Derrick Robinson recalled.

They said Alphonso was a "wannabe" gangsta in the Santana Block Crips, which controlled his neighborhood.

Awaiting trial, he fell more deeply into gang life and appeared in court with Santana Block Crip tattoos on his arms and hands. After more than four years in jail, the 25-year-old Howard was sentenced to die.

He arrived on death row on October 28, 1992, and was assigned California Department of Corrections No. H54602.

"Potato Head"

Paul Gregory Watson grew up on Spring Street, in southwest Compton, not far from Kelley Park, where he would eventually kill two people in a drive-by shooting.

His mother, Mary Cooper, worked as a maid. His stepfather worked at staying high, sometimes sending Paul into the streets to score heroin.

To earn spending money, Paul washed cars, mowed lawns and worked for a custodial service. He liked to ride his skateboard and his bike. When he stayed in school, his mother said, she "got good reports on him." He liked to write poetry.

A family friend, Ailene Jackson, remembers Paul as a happy kid, "mannerable and very respectful," even though "he didn't have too much of a life to be happy for."

"His daddy was using drugs," Jackson said, "and his mother was waiting on the daddy."

To break the monotony of his impoverished life on Spring Street, Jackson said, she took Paul to Disneyland and her husband hired him to help out with the gardening.

His stepfather's death and his mother's health problems left 13-year-old Paul the head of his family, and he grimly set out to make a living from the streets.

"He was serious about that," Jackson recalled. "His mama and his sister came before anyone."

Said his mother: "I think when Devon his stepfather passed, he just started looking for something somewhere, probably a male role model."

He apparently found what he was looking for in the Santana Block Crips.

"Things just started getting worse," Cooper said, "and I guess he just got caught up in it."

The pressure to support the family was immense, and Cooper said she sometimes "caught Paul crying in his room."

"I kept telling him he needed to go to school," Jackson said.

The lure of selling dope as a gangbanger was more than he could resist. He countered Jackson's admonition to get an education with the economic theory that he had learned as a crack cocaine dealer.

"I am making $300, $400 and $500 every day doing that," he told her.

Watson was twice convicted for drug possession. While incarcerated, he beat another inmate.

He had his gang's initials tattooed on his back and arms. Along the way, he also got shot seven times in his abdomen.

On April 2, 1989, he fired an AK-47 assault rifle from a white Cadillac into a crowd of more than 100 people attending an Atlantic Drive Crip party. He killed Earl Solomon, a rival gang member. But he also killed Ava Williams, who died holding her 1-year-old child in her lap.

As he was about to be sentenced to death in 1991, Watson, handcuffed and shackled, leapt from his chair and attempted to attack the prosecutors.

"You white [expletive] aren't going to put me to death," he reportedly screamed.

Watson arrived on death row December 18, 1991, and was assigned California Department of Corrections No. H20100. He was 25.

Waiting at San Quentin

The California State Prison at San Quentin, a 145-year-old facility not far from San Francisco, is home to the nation's largest death row with about 470 inmates. Like the four men in this story, one in every seven condemned inmates is a black man convicted in Los Angeles County.

Though they are housed in separate cells, Brown and his three friends stay in contact inside the prison. At one time, Brown and Carter lived four or five cells apart on the same tier and Watson was on the same prison block.

Sometimes, the men see each other when visiting with families or in the recreation yard.

On death row for only a few years, none of the men is close to being executed. There are inmates at San Quentin who have awaited execution for 18 years.

Death row changes men, and these are no exception, according to people who know them.

A friend of Watson's said he's no longer the hothead he used to be.

"Being up there will cool you down," she said.

Relatives of the four sometimes carpool for the six-hour trip to San Quentin. During one recent visit, Cooper said, Watson wondered aloud about the path of his life.

"He asked me why this thing had to happen to him," Cooper said. "I said, sometimes it goes with the people you hang around with. Sometimes you pay for playing."

CHAPTER 7

・・・

Crimes of the Father

Son placed for adoption follows his parent to death row. A killer gene?

TUCKER, ARK., OCTOBER 1997—Darrel Hill last saw his son 35 years ago. Hill was a young junkie, locked up on a burglary charge. His son Billy was a baby on a jailhouse visit, nestled in his mother's arms.

Soon after, Billy was adopted into a more stable, affluent family. He was given a new name—Jeff Landrigan—and what seemed to be a chance for a better life.

Hill, a third-generation criminal, continued his family's legacy of lawlessness. In 1980, after several stints in prison, he murdered a state game warden during a gas station robbery and wound up on Arkansas's death row.

Though he grew up as Jeff Landrigan, Billy remained his father's son. A self-described misfit in the middle-class life he was given, he turned to a life of alcohol and drugs. And 1,100 miles and three decades removed, he sits on Arizona's death row, a two-time killer just like the father he never really knew.

The possibility that a tendency toward violence might be inherited—a kind of "killing gene"—raises fundamental questions about human nature and human nurture: Do chromosomal cards dealt at birth determine whether a person becomes a sociopath or a productive member of society? Or does the world in which a child is reared cast the mold that forms the adult?

In the *Morning News* survey, almost nine of 10 death row inmates across the country said they think environment plays a far larger role in shaping an individual than any genetic factor. Only one in 20 thinks people are born good or bad.

But many also reported that they came from families well acquainted with crime and violence. Almost four of 10 said that at least one other member of their families had been convicted of a felony. And of those, one-quarter said their fathers had a serious criminal history.

Those who know Hill and Landrigan are struck by the similarity in their nature and their crimes.

"They look alike, talk alike, sound alike and think alike," said Hill's ex-wife and Landrigan's birth mother. "It's mind-blowing."

Defense attorney Dale Baich argues in court documents that Landrigan was "genetically predisposed to land on death row."

Landrigan was sentenced to die in Arizona for the 1989 killing of a Phoenix bartender. At the time, he was an escapee from an Oklahoma prison where he had been serving a 40-year sentence for killing a childhood friend.

From his cage on Cell Block 6 in a prison near Florence, the 37-year-old has been known to boast that he wants "to be like his father." His father sometimes wonders whether he, or his son, actually had a choice.

Hill, 57, wonders whether his own criminal tendencies were inherited from his father, a robber and drug addict, "like cancer, heart trouble or alcoholism." And he fears that he may have passed his criminal nature to the son he didn't raise.

"We grew up in totally different environments," Hill said. "The people who raised him had everything in the world. They had money. They gave him what he wanted." And still, his son "got off into drugs, alcohol and crime."

"It don't take anybody too smart to look at three generations of outlaws and see if there's not a deviation. There's a link of some kind. There's a pattern," Hill said.

The best indicator?

Among scientists, the possibility of a genetic link to crime has often been deemed too explosive for public debate. As recently as 1994, the National Institutes of Health forced the cancellation of a planned conference on genetic factors in crime because the topic was considered by some to be inherently racist.

Medical science has slowly inched toward the conclusion that

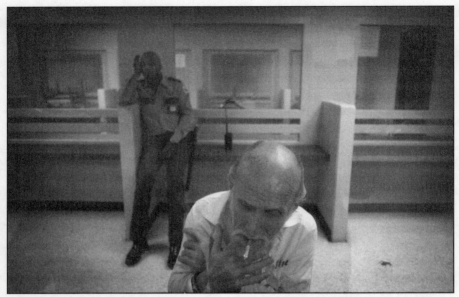

APPROACHING DEATH ROW FROM DIFFERENT ENVIRONMENTS: Darrel Hill has said he wonders whether he inherited his criminal tendencies from his father, and, in turn, passed them on to his son, whom he didn't raise.

there is a link from mental illness and substance abuse to violence. Although most people who suffer from addiction or mental illness do not become violent, research shows they are more likely than others to have a history of violence.

According to experts, the most compelling evidence of a genetic link to violence has been uncovered in studies focusing on adopted children, including twins separated at birth. In those studies, children fathered by criminals were far more likely to become criminals themselves—regardless of their upbringing.

Dr. Sarnoff Mednick, a professor of psychology at the Social Science Research Institute at the University of Southern California, said virtually all research on the topic supports the straightforward notion that "the best indicator of crime in the boy is crime in the father."

James Q. Wilson, widely recognized as the nation's preeminent criminologist, says it is difficult to determine the precise role any one factor—environmental or genetic—plays in the outcome of a particular individual.

"We're all the product of all the aspects of our lives, of some combination of genetic and cultural factors," said Dr. Wilson, a professor of management and public policy at the University of California at Los Angeles. "But clearly something is being passed on."

TIES TO THE PAST, LACKING A FUTURE: Darrel Hill, on Arkansas's death row, wears a crucifix that was worn by friends on the row who were executed. In the background is a corrections officer.

The father's story

At the Arkansas Department of Correction's Maximum Security Unit in the fertile farmlands around Tucker, SK877—Safe Keeping Prisoner No. 877—is a gaunt heart patient with thinning hair. He has a neatly trimmed white beard and twinkling green eyes, and he fingers a crucifix at his neck—a medallion that several death row friends have worn when they were executed.

Darrel Wayne Hill—according to court documents, interviews and his unpublished autobiography, *Destination Death Row*—grew up in a world of poverty, drugs, violence and crime.

Born in 1940, a "poor Okie" on the outskirts of Tulsa, Hill said his first home was a "two-room shack" that looked like a "run-down toolshed in a junkyard." His grandfather, Hill said, was a bootlegger when "bootlegging was kinda like selling drugs." At the time he was born, Hill said, his father was on a five-day "running drunk."

"He was a drunk and an outlaw," Hill said of his father, William Leonard Hill. "He wasn't made out to be a family man."

Heir to a paternal legacy of lawlessness, Hill had a criminal proclivity that blossomed early. He had a well-established record of theft by the time he could legally drive. At age 7, he joined the Hellcats, a gang that prowled the neighborhood stealing from fruit stands, cars and a March of Dimes donation box.

At 9, he saw his father off to prison for a five-year burglary sentence. At 10, he was arrested for attempted burglary. At 11, he was shot in a burglary and committed to a reformatory, from which he repeatedly escaped.

In 1956, he was arrested for car theft and became, at 15, one of the youngest prisoners at the Oklahoma State Penitentiary.

In prison among far more experienced and violent adults, the seasoned thief became a killer—stabbing another inmate with a homemade "shiv" in an act he said was self-defense.

In an interview, Hill said the other inmate made an unwanted sexual advance. The inmate, he said, "thought I'd make a nice little girl, which didn't fit into my program at all."

Released at age 17, he moved into an apartment with his father, and the two plunged headfirst into the gutter.

"Before long I was solidly fused into the criminal element," Hill wrote. "My only friends were thieves, fences, hookers and drug connections. It was during that time that I became addicted to hard drugs. Acquiring an oil-burning drug habit was the beginning of the end. My dad had become addicted, too. Like father, like son."

Driven like sugar mill mules, father and son scrounged for drugs and money for drugs in a cycle of illicit highs and criminal high jinks that ended in Leonard Hill's death.

Killed in 1961 during a shootout after a high-speed chase, Leonard Hill died only a few feet from his son. But three decades later, Hill barely remembers the emotional particulars of his father's death.

"I can't tell you what I was thinking except getting my ass out of there," Hill said. "When you got somebody shooting at you, you don't think a lot except that you might return the favor."

Hill escaped the shootout but was arrested at his father's funeral. In the next few years, he was arrested on a variety of charges and once served part of a three-year drug sentence at the Oklahoma State Penitentiary in a cell with his brother, Bill.

His mother remarried while Hill was in prison. Her new husband, a widower, had a teenage daughter. And when he returned home, Hill wrote, he fell in love and married the 15-year-old girl.

"Something just clicked between us," he wrote. "Lust and love take on a lot of the same characteristics when you are 21 and just out of prison and looking at a doll in a miniskirt."

In court records there is a darker account of their relationship. Though the marriage lasted more than a decade, it began with an act of violence; the young ex-con raped her shortly after they met, records show.

His teen bride—referred to as "Linda" in Hill's manuscript—has since remarried and established a stable life with a new family. "Linda" was interviewed by the *Morning News*. She said she was married to Hill for 11 years "out of ignorance and loyalty."

On March 17, 1962, Linda gave birth to Billy Wayne Hill, and Hill said the event caused him to try to turn his life around. But like his father before him, he had a strange way of celebrating a moment of joy.

Hill had developed a taste for the severe hallucinations attained by injecting an over-the-counter nasal inhalant known as Valo. He liked it so much that sometimes he did it as many as five times a day. And shortly after Billy was born, court records say, Mr. Hill "slipped into a hospital restroom and shot up."

Within a few months of his son's birth, Hill, then 22, returned to prison on a burglary sentence. It was during that stretch that he lost contact with his son.

"While I was gone, she had him put up for adoption," Hill said. "I didn't find out till I got out."

When he was released from prison, Hill said, he conducted a fruitless search for Billy. Linda heard a rumor a few years later that Billy had died in a fire at the house of his adoptive parents. She gave the boy up for dead.

Hill said he began to hear voices and hallucinate. He checked himself into a hospital and told doctors that his dead father was speaking to him.

"This isn't real," the voice said. "You going to be killed anyway, you should kill yourself."

Mental history

In years to come, doctors said Hill had an abundance of psychiatric problems. One saw a "sociopathic personality, antisocial type, with alcoholism and drug addiction." Another said tests "indicate both sociopathic tendencies with schizzy underpinnings" plus the "potential of unpredictable, possibly at times violent behavior." Yet a third said Hill had abused a virtual pharmacy of illegal drugs: "LSD, amphetamines, heroin, cocaine, opium, marijuana and others."

The boy burglar became an armed robber. He held up liquor stores and fought running gun battles with police. He was sentenced to five years in prison for robbing a liquor store, then 18 years for robbing a grocery store. And eventually, he was released to a halfway house.

Battling addiction and other demons, he was sent to a state hospital in Tulsa for evaluation. But in January 1980, he escaped.

Less than two weeks later, and following a drug-addled crime spree spanning three states, Hill arrived in Arkansas behind the wheel of a maroon Thunderbird.

On February 7, 1980, Hill robbed a service station in Pencil Bluff. He took two witnesses—owner E. L. "Bug" Ward and another customer, Arkansas game warden Donald Teague—and shot them in a field near the service station.

Ward was shot four times but lived to identify Hill at trial. But Teague died, leaving behind a wife and a 7-year-old son.

Hill said that he's not sure where he was the day Teague was murdered but that he doesn't believe he killed him.

"Although I have always had an exceptionally good memory, I was so poisoned by drugs and liquor that I'm not exactly sure," he wrote in his manuscript. "There are at least four days that I cannot account for."

His first lucid memory was "sitting in a small room at the police station in Hot Springs, Ark., handcuffed to a chair, naked."

Carl Smith remembers that day, too. The night police arrested Hill, he was on duty as a jailer.

Hill discounts the story, but Smith said that he asked Hill, "'Why would a man do that?' You've never seen a prettier smile on an infant's face. He stuck out both hands, palms up, shrugged and said, 'Just one of those things.'"

Smith, now a real estate agent, said he was chilled.

"He had about as much feeling and tone in his voice as you would if I asked you why you didn't stuff a nickel in the parking meter," Smith said. "He's the only man I can say that I've met who truly seemed to be totally indifferent to having taken a human life."

The son's story

In Bartlesville, 41 miles from Tulsa, Nick and Dot Landrigan and their daughter lived in a world that the Hill family might only dream of—or prey on.

When they adopted the infant Hill child, they had a spacious home in an upper-middle-class neighborhood, befitting Landrigan's work as an oil company geologist. They named him Jeffrey Timothy Landrigan.

Jeff got a car as soon as he could drive and had, a relative said, "anything he wanted."

But from an early age, the family noticed that something was disturbingly different about Jeff. Troubled sleep gave way to restlessness and, his sister said in court documents, "uncontrollable outbursts of temper, occasionally violent" that grew worse as he grew older.

Somehow, other children learned vaguely of Jeff's past. They taunted him that his "real" daddy had been a bank robber; he said they shamed him with questions about being "thrown away." He began to question whether he belonged in this middle-class world and pestered his parents with questions about whether they were his real mother and father.

Snooping one day inside a family strongbox, he found documents that mentioned a family named Hill. Although the records stopped short of identifying his birth parents, according to his defense team, they fueled his curiosity about where he came from.

At 10, an age when his birth father was prowling the streets of Tulsa with a gang, Jeff began to drink. Soon he was hanging out in pool halls and hustling quarters with trick shots, beer on his breath.

Like the birth father he did not yet know, he embraced the escape that drugs offered, smoking marijuana and swallowing quaaludes by the handful. At age 14, he managed to stay sober once for 2½ months but only because he was at a boys' ranch.

At 18, he enrolled in an alcohol rehabilitation program in Austin, where he met his future wife.

Three weeks after their marriage, Landrigan was sentenced to a year in an Oklahoma prison for marijuana possession.

While serving time, he learned about his birth family from another convict.

Telling past

Tommy Owens, a thief who once lived near the Hill family in Tulsa, told Landrigan he was the spitting image of a man he once knew named Darrel Wayne Hill. Any relief he gained by learning his father's name vanished when he learned his fate: The father he had searched for all his life was in Arkansas on death row.

Landrigan was released from prison after four months of his one-year sentence. He and his wife moved into an apartment that his adoptive parents rented for them as a wedding present. Like his birth father, prison had little impact on his appetite for alcohol, pot and pills.

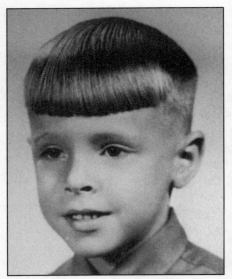

NATURE VS. NURTURE: Jeffrey Timothy Landrigan was adopted and raised by a middle-class family in Oklahoma. Years later, while he was behind bars, he learned about his birth father from another inmate. Landrigan and his father are on death rows in different states.

The following year, when Landrigan learned that his wife was pregnant, he asked Greg Brown, a childhood friend just out of prison, to be godfather to his child.

On a summer day in 1982, at a party to celebrate Brown's release and Landrigan's impending fatherhood, the two ex-cons smoked dope and drank whiskey. Lapsing into prison patter, the two men argued, called each other "punk," and Landrigan stabbed his childhood friend to death. Darrel Hill, who once killed a fellow prisoner after a homosexual advance, said he understands too well how that single epithet could trigger a murder.

"Prisoners have a strange way of classing homosexuals," he wrote in his autobiography. "If you play the female role, you are scorned, degraded, mistreated and abused. If you play the male role, you are accepted, respected or just taken for granted. . . . To call someone a punk in prison and mean it is the worst insult that can be used."

Landrigan was badly outsized by Brown and claimed self-defense. But a jury convicted him of first-degree murder and sentenced him to life. And when his wife gave birth to their daughter, once again a Hill child began life without a father.

The murder conviction was overturned. Instead of a retrial, Landrigan agreed to a 40-year prison term. But he escaped in November 1989.

At 27, Landrigan, like Hill nine years earlier, became a convict on the run. And like his father, he would soon kill again.

Landrigan made his way to Arizona, where he met Chester Dean Dyer, a bartender at a Phoenix club. Dyer was described by friends as perennially drunk and promiscuous. The two men spent the evening of December 12, 1989, together at Dyer's apartment. The following day, Dyer called the club where he worked. He was intoxicated, according to witnesses, boasting that he was having sex with a man he identified as "Jeff."

Friends found him dead in his apartment. A wire used to strangle him was still around his neck and a pornographic playing card had been placed face up on his fully clothed body.

Police were eventually led to Landrigan, who was locked up in the Maricopa County Jail on an unrelated theft charge. A distinctive shoe mark and fingerprints that matched Landrigan's were found in Dyer's apartment.

Landrigan was convicted of capital murder. His wife and his birth mother attended the trial. The two women could have told the story of an adopted child unable to break from his biological past. Landrigan refused to let them, asserting his innocence while taunting the judge.

"I think the whole thing stinks," Landrigan said just before he was sentenced to die. "If you want to give me the death penalty, just bring it right on. I'm ready for it."

Reunion

Landrigan was sentenced to die in October 1990. He arrived on death row about a decade after his father was sentenced to die in Arkansas. Since then, father and son have corresponded—death row to death row. They even play chess by mail.

"I don't know if you want me writing you or not," began Landrigan's first letter to his birth father. "But I am your son."

Arizona prison officials refused to allow reporters to meet with death row inmates. And Landrigan chose not to talk about his family by phone. Except for a short letter, he has not responded to requests for information about his life and case.

"You seem engrossed by my family," wrote Landrigan. "Most of what you may have read is half-truths due to the fact we've never agreed to any direct information about us."

Although he has been on death row only about half the time his father has, Landrigan's appeal has progressed further than his father's. Landrigan, therefore, may be closer to execution than Hill.

Hill's death sentence was overturned in 1994, 14 years after his conviction. Though he was quickly resentenced, the ruling began the appellate process, in effect, all over again.

Landrigan's appeal, meanwhile, has made its way through the state court system in Arizona and is pending before a federal judge.

Nick and Dot Landrigan are dead. Their daughter declined to be interviewed about Jeff Landrigan.

Landrigan's daughter, now a teenager, has visited her biological grandfather. The young girl asked Hill when he was going to get out of prison. It is unlikely he ever will.

And for the families of their victims, the delays are frustrating. They say they are eager to put an end to two generations of killers.

"I believe it was in his genes," said Albert McVay, brother of the bartender Landrigan was convicted of murdering. "But everybody is responsible for their actions, no matter what's in their genes. . . .

"I think they should have done put him to death."

The widow of Donald Teague, the Arkansas game warden, has remarried in the 17 years since his death. She said she has tried to get on with her life—despite having to endure the resentencing of her husband's killer 14 years after the fact.

Though she thinks Hill should be executed for her husband's murder, she said she is not without compassion.

"I feel sorry for him and his circumstance," she said. "But I think he has to accept responsibility for his actions.

"We all inherit a tendency towards something—whether it's mental or physical—passed on from our parents," she said. "But we still have choices."

Landrigan's birth mother said she thinks her son inherited his violent nature, as other Hill men have, "as far back as you want to trace it."

"He has a warped way of thinking," Linda said. "A warped sense of humor. It's sickening and scary. I don't want him around me. Ever. Period. In prison or behind bars.

"He's not mine. He's not the innocent baby I gave away."

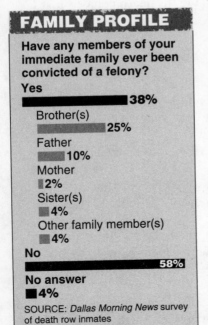

FAMILY PROFILE

Have any members of your immediate family ever been convicted of a felony?

Yes 38%

Brother(s) 25%

Father 10%

Mother 2%

Sister(s) 4%

Other family member(s) 4%

No 58%

No answer 4%

SOURCE: *Dallas Morning News* survey of death row inmates

CHAPTER 8

. . .

Descent into Murder

Devout Mormon turned to drugs, crime despite middle-class life

ELY, NEV., 1997—Edward Bennett's life is the kind of tale that makes parents pace in the dead of night and flinch at distant sirens.

His 28 years are a middle-class, mid-American nightmare.

Old photographs offer insights into Ed's young mind: a charmer at four; an optimistic Little Leaguer; a pickup basketball player with a crooked grin; an obedient Mormon in Sunday school.

This is Ed's teenage mind on drugs: "My nickname was 'Diehard' because I could drink a fifth of whiskey and drop acid and do speed and shoot heroin and snort coke and still be on my feet when the sun came up, asking for more."

Shortly after a Las Vegas sunset in February 1988, Ed Bennett and his drug buddy, Joe Beeson, needed more. They were two sleepless days on the road to Los Angeles from Utah, footloose in Sin City with no cash, no drugs and a bad craving for heroin.

Their solution, decided over two 40-ounce beers apiece, was to rob a convenience store. Bennett passed out before they got to the store and after they left.

But in the frenzied few minutes in between, according to court records, the onetime class president of his Mormon seminary shoved a .45-caliber automatic across the counter of a Stop 'N Go and pulled the trigger on Michelle Moore. The shot hit Moore, 21, a newlywed, in the right eyebrow and exited at the base of her skull. The medical examiner said she died instantly.

A customer walked in on the robbery. Derrick Franklin, 17 at the

LAS VEGAS NIGHTMARE: Edward Bennett was once the class president of his Mormon seminary. According to court records, he fired a .45-caliber automatic across a convenience store counter in Las Vegas and killed clerk Michelle Moore. Photo: Howard Swindle

time, said he didn't hear any words before or after the shot. But he saw a white teenager, whom he later identified as Beeson, coming down the aisle after him.

Franklin said he ran screaming for the door. A blast shattered the plate glass to his side, and as he made it into the parking lot, he heard another blast and felt a sting in his right thigh. He managed to escape with his life.

Inside, Beeson and Bennett had their own troubles. They were too whacked to figure out how to open the cash register. They escaped, but three shots and a dead woman later, they were just as broke as before.

"We weren't even in Vegas 24 hours," Bennett said. "We left by the next sunset."

A month later, another of his drug buddies in suburban Provo, Utah, turned them in and collected $30,000 in rewards.

Prosecutors convinced a jury that Bennett actually fired the fatal shot, and he was sentenced to death. He was 19.

Beeson, at 18, was sentenced to life in prison without parole. He was killed by another inmate during his first year behind bars.

Bennett, who has spent eight years on death row at Ely State

Prison, was one of 700 inmates awaiting execution who responded to the *Morning News* survey.

Bennett, like nearly two of three of those surveyed, was a regular drug user. He started, he said, at age 12.

A 1990 University of Texas Medical School study showed that drug abusers are 35 percent more likely to be violent than the general population.

"Having done what I've done and being where I'm at, it sounds crazy," Bennett said on death row, "but I'm a people person. I've spent years trying to figure out what I did. This is completely against my character.

"I'm not making any excuses because there are no excuses. . . . If you say drugs were the turning point, you've got to ask why I did drugs in the first place. You keep going back farther and farther. There is no turning point. It's the whole piece of everything that happens."

Bennett's early years were a snapshot of mid-America. He was the fifth of eight children born in the bedrock of Mormonism in Lehi, a suburb of Provo. His father, Gordon, was administrator of the computer science department at nearby Brigham Young University, named for one of Mormonism's earliest leaders. Edward's mother, Raima, a local girl from Lehi, was a stay-at-home mother.

The first blemish on the portrait of young Ed, ordinary as it seems, came in the first grade, when the rest of the class learned to count to 100.

"I couldn't do it," he said. "I couldn't get past 19. I felt completely humiliated."

Bennett said one of his teachers arranged her students in order of intelligence as she perceived it. The brightest sat in the front-row seats.

"Whoever was sitting in that last row, right seat, was stupid. And that was me," Bennett said.

"The problem I had was that I looked like a normal little boy and acted like a normal little boy and played like one . . . so what is wrong with me? Why am I so flawed?"

Bennett suffered from dyslexia, a relatively common reading impairment often associated with genetic defects or brain injuries. He didn't learn about his condition until he was on death row.

"I always felt lesser," Bennett said. "Really, you just want to be like everybody else. Your whole life at that age is going to school."

School only got tougher. He found ways to anesthetize himself.

At 12, according to a history he gave psychologists, he was drinking. At 15, a group of lifelong friends asked if he wanted to try marijuana.

"The second I did, wow," he said. "I had found my niche in life. I finally found what I was good at. I could drink and party and do drugs like nobody else."

Soon he was drinking and smoking four joints a day. Over the next year, he was using LSD and hallucinogenic mushrooms regularly, as well as amphetamines.

If Bennett's hidden dyslexia created a lack of self-esteem and a resulting susceptibility to drugs, as some psychologists in his case have said, a near-fatal head injury at 16 only greased his downhill plummet.

"It was a friend's birthday party," Bennett said. "I had drunk a 12-pack of beer, smoked probably five joints, and I had taken some speed. We were at a place where people ride three-wheelers. . . . I went over a cliff."

Friends told emergency room doctors that he was without a pulse and unconscious for four minutes before they were able to resuscitate him. Medical charts show young Bennett suffered a major closed-head injury with lengthy unconsciousness.

Closed-head injuries, according to forensic psychiatrists, have long been associated with impaired judgment and decision making, impulsive behavior and, sometimes, significant personality change.

"At the time I didn't notice any changes," said Bennett, who still bears a gaping scar over his right temple. "I didn't think my philosophy or outlook on life changed."

Others, however, said they saw dramatic changes. Nathan Bennett, his younger brother, told psychologists years later that Ed had complained of headaches, vision problems and hallucinations and "he could not sit still for five minutes."

By 17, Bennett said, he was snorting, smoking and injecting from a quarter to a half gram of cocaine a week, along with the rest of his routine pharmacology.

The drugs triggered more than physical changes; there was a culture that went with it—"a door to the dark side," as he once explained it—signified by black boots, black leather, black T-shirts, spikes, skull rings and crosses.

"Being middle-class doesn't protect you from drugs," Bennett said. "In any culture, you have those who go against the culture."

The change created havoc inside the red brick house in the Mormon heartland.

"The moment I got on drugs, grew my hair long and started acting differently, there was all-out battle," Bennett said of his relationship with his parents. "We argued over everything—my long hair, my earring, my clothes, my friends—constantly.

"They'd ask me if I was doing drugs, and I was bold and arrogant. I told them, 'Yeah.'

"As parents, they tried to do everything, from yelling at me, trying to ground me, to sitting me down and trying to talk to me. Always asking me, 'Why are you doing drugs? What do they do for you?' . . . The argument wasn't going anywhere. I was getting worse and worse. They tried."

Ed Bennett quit trying. He quit high school during his sophomore year after barely making it through the year before.

"In the 10th grade, I got the report card and it was F, F, F, F, F," he said. "I showed it to all my friends. They said, 'Straight Fs. Cool.'"

His life, he said, evolved into heavy metal music and, eventually, to satanic worship.

"I went from going to school and church to listening to music, Ouija boards, to tarot cards, to astrology, to satanic books, to the occult," Bennett wrote to a former Sunday school teacher in September 1989, shortly after he was sentenced to death.

". . . Satan binds you with chain instead of ropes," he wrote. "Each temptation is a link. It happens, oh so slowly, and while he does it, he also slowly pulls a blindfold over your eyes."

Bennett, heavily into the occult, was 18 when he met Joe Beeson, a 17-year-old skinhead from Orem, just a few miles south on Interstate 15 from Lehi.

"Joe played drums, I played the guitar in several bands," Mr. Bennett said. "We hit it off."

Along with a third teenager, they formed a band. They called it Rigor Mortis.

"In the first four hours," Bennett said, "we had our first song written."

Some of those dark lyrics, which Bennett's lawyer Timothy O'Toole said were song lyrics and most of which he said were actually written by Joe Beeson, were left scattered around Bennett's room in Lehi. Some of the writings were also transcriptions of songs recorded by heavy metal bands.

Prosecutors would tell jurors that the lyrics were Ed Bennett's poetry, and that they offered irrefutable truths about his macabre philosophy: "I need to kill somebody or tear somebody apart. I got to satisfy my need, cure this thirst for blood."

"Whether he was writing lyrics or poetry or a theme from

school," a prosecutor said, "anyone who will write this kind of language is depraved."

The verses transformed a tragically botched convenience store robbery by two drug-addled teenagers into what prosecutors described as "a random, ritualistic, satanic execution."

Bennett, who plans to challenge the constitutionality of Nevada's capital-murder statute, recounted his life and his crime, he said, "so maybe somebody can get something from it."

Sitting at a long table under the silent scrutiny of two black-clad guards on either side, Bennett periodically interrupts his story to disclaim the usual alibis: "This isn't an excuse. . . . I take sole responsibility. . . . There is no excuse."

He said he and Beeson had been selling LSD to bankroll their heroin habit. They had been busted on minor drug charges, and the police, Bennett said, were making it tough on skinheads, including his buddy. Los Angeles was to be their sanctuary, a place where they could get a heavy metal band off the ground.

"Joe was a skinhead, and we were going to L.A., where the Crips and the Bloods were killing each other every hour," Bennett said. "We figured it'd be a good idea to have at least a weapon."

Bennett said he bought a .45-caliber automatic.

"The whole problem was that because we were on heroin, our mentalities were so spotty, we didn't even have any money," Bennett said. "We just jumped in the car and took off. Think about it. We're moving to another state, and we don't even have any money.

"By the time we hit Vegas, after we got a hotel room and a couple of beers . . . we said, 'Wait a minute, we don't have any cash.'"

Bennett said he suggested robbing tourists on the Strip, "maybe a foreigner because they'd have more money." His colleague argued for a convenience store, he said.

Michelle Moore, described by family members as an artistic, attractive woman who worried about a weight problem, had a $4-an-hour job on the night shift at the Stop 'N Go on Sahara Avenue, less than a mile from the glitzy hotel-casino for which the street was named. Shortly before she was killed she had married a man who suffered from neurofibromatosis, or the Elephant Man's disease.

Bennett said he remembers very little about that night at the Stop 'N Go. He recalls more clearly the painful aftermath.

After two days without sleep, 80 ounces of beer and a bad case of heroin withdrawal, he said, he passed out on his way to the robbery.

He said he remembers following Joe Beeson through the parking lot toward the store. "In my mind I can see him walking, but it was like my body wasn't working, like I could see a pair of eyes following him."

He said, "I wasn't exactly sure what happened because when I fired the pistol, I wasn't watching."

At trial, Jeff Chidester, the Utah friend who turned him in, said Bennett told him that he had jumped over the counter to examine the gunshot wound in Moore's head, and remembered that he could see the floor through her skull.

"There were some things that never took place," said Bennett, visibly upset as he dropped his head toward the table, "and when they hit the media, it was horrendous. Sick stuff that never even happened. . . .

"I didn't look at the person even once," Bennett said.

After the shooting, he said, he passed out again.

"I kept thinking, 'What did I do? Every time I replayed it, I saw the gun going past the person. First, I thought I must have shot past them, and they must have ducked.

"Every time I'd replay it, the gun would get closer. Until I could see it in my mind, taking a piece of . . ." he said, trailing off and motioning to his forehead.

At the hotel, he said, Beeson kept telling him, "Yeah, you . . . killed this person."

"We turned on the TV set and watched it on the news. And that's when we left."

Back in Utah, Bennett said, he and Beeson went their separate ways: "We didn't argue, we didn't fight or curse each other out. It just kind of dissolved."

Meanwhile, his drug problem escalated, he said, "if that's possible."

"It was like nothing matters anymore," he said. ". . . All hope had washed out of me. It was all over."

Sleep, he said, was impossible: "It . . . was like a bad nightmare. You wake up and your heart's pounding and you're sweating and you're gasping. . . . I knew this was real, but there was still this dreamlike quality.

"I remember standing in the bathroom in front of the mirror," he said, pointing his finger, "and saying, 'You killed somebody! You killed somebody!'

"I knew what I did," he said quietly. "It just didn't seem solid or valid."

A month after the Las Vegas murder, Bennett and Beeson were arrested in Utah. Chidester led police to Bennett and the murder weapon, which Bennett had pawned.

"I was in county jail on my 19th birthday," Bennett said, "and I was happy. . . . Here I am 100 miles from home, charged with first-degree murder and I'm definitely going to prison for the rest of my life and I might be sentenced to death and I'm happy. It didn't make sense.

"Later, I realized that was the point at which the drugs had gotten cleaned out of my system. It had been so long since I had felt normal that I had mistaken it for happiness."

After eight years of state-mandated sobriety, Bennett said he accepts "sole responsibility" for his actions.

In his response to the *Morning News* survey, Bennett wrote:

"I made the unfortunate choices to get high on drugs . . . and then it was that I committed the horrible act of killing a living, breathing human being. . . . Responsibility for having taken a life is the heaviest weight to have to carry.

"The hardest thing for me to differentiate is what is just and fair for victims, giving them what is right, but still leaving room for an offender to repent.

"I am not a murderer. I was a drug addict."

Inmates say alcohol drove them to destiny

Graterford, Pa.—Alcoholics Anonymous teaches that an alcoholic has little chance of quitting until he acknowledges that his life has become "unmanageable."

Kenneth John Williams watched through the bottom of a bottle as alcohol overwhelmed him.

It was late 1983, after a bloody stretch in Vietnam, failed marriages, barroom fights, two children and more jobs than he could remember. Now, too late, he knows that he was out of control.

KENNETH JOHN
WILLIAMS,
Pennsylvania

"What I did was drink," said Williams, a truck driver and onetime army sniper who won four Bronze Stars in Vietnam.

He was arrested at a truck stop in Texas and extradited to Pennsylvania, charged with murdering another trucker, William Miller, 22, and stealing his credit cards.

Williams is among 41 percent of the nation's death row inmates who admit having alcohol problems in the survey by the *Morning News*. Williams still protests his innocence. Though offered a plea bargain, he went to trial, where a Pennsylvania state trooper testified that Williams told him: "I did it. I killed him, but I don't remember doing it."

Williams was condemned to death row, where he has been for 13 years. Three years ago, he was diagnosed with posttraumatic stress disorder, a mental condition whose symptoms frequently include alcohol and drug abuse.

"It's been 27 years since 'Nam . . . many mistakes and many nightmares," he said. "All the drinking, all the pushing people away and all the guilt of coming home, and still Vietnam seems like yesterday. It just won't go away."

Donald Miller is a second-generation alcoholic. He took his first drink before he was 12. Growing up in Tucson, Ariz., he was twice convicted of driving under the influence.

And he wouldn't have ended up on death row at age 30, Miller said, if he hadn't been an alcoholic.

Miller was convicted in August 1995 of helping a drinking buddy, Jose Anthony Luna, kill his girlfriend. Jennifer Ann Geuder, the 18-year-old mother of one of Luna's children, had gone to court to collect $50 a month in child support. A short time later, Geuder was found dead in the desert with six gunshot wounds to her head.

DONALD J. MILLER, *Arizona*

"I would not have had these kind of people around my house if I wasn't an alcoholic," Miller wrote in his survey.

The one thing he would have done differently in his life, Miller said, was "never drunk alcohol."

Both Milo Rose and Robert "Butch" Richardson were "blind drunk" in October 1982, according to court records, when they got into a fight in a Clearwater, Fla., barroom. The men stumbled off together when police ejected them from the bar.

According to witnesses, Richardson fell in a nearby vacant lot. When he didn't get up, Rose smashed his head repeatedly with a 35-pound concrete block.

Prosecutors said Rose had a history of drunken assaults; appeals have kept him alive since he was sentenced to death 14 years ago.

MILO ROSE, *Florida*

Six of 10 death row survey respondents said they grew up in families where alcohol was a problem for at least one family member.

Rose was one of them. The 46-year-old American Indian said he was "was raised by alcoholic parents and a racist stepfather." As a child, he said, he was hospitalized when he was "beaten up by the police after I punched one in a drunken stupor."

Rose was among the 56 percent who identified drugs and alcohol as the most important cause of crime.

Given his record of boozing, it was no surprise that Mitchell Sims's trip to death row began in 1985 in a Las Vegas bar.

Shortly after Sims left the establishment, one of the patrons saw his picture on the bar's TV. Hearing there was a $100,000 reward, the customer phoned Las Vegas police.

The call ended a murderous weeklong coast-to-coast trek when Sims was arrested on Christmas Day.

Apparently angered at Domino's Pizza for firing him, Sims killed Christopher Leroy Zerr and Gary Dean Melke, both 24, as they worked at a Hanahan,

MITCHELL SIMS,
South Carolina

S.C., Domino's. He and a girlfriend, Ruby Padgett, stole $1,300 from the register.

A week later and bolstered by vodka, he lured Domino's deliveryman John Harrigan to his motel room in Glendale, Calif. There he bound and gagged the pizza man, put a pillowcase over his head, choked him with a ligature and submerged him in the bathtub.

After trials in two states, Sims was sentenced to death in both California and South Carolina.

Sims had a drunken-driving arrest and said he tried to stop drinking. Sims said his life would have gone differently had he not been abused as a child and "if I had not abused drugs and alcohol."

CHAPTER 9

• • •

Insane and Condemned

Inmate's case typifies
question of legal sanity

*H*UNTSVILLE, *TEX.*, OCTOBER *1997*—For five years, Corpus Christi police had no idea who slipped into the jewelry store across from the downtown courthouse on a rainy Friday morning in July 1983 and killed Christine "Cricket" Sanchez.

A customer discovered the clerk shortly after the store opened. The store had been robbed and Sanchez, 21 and an inch shy of 5 feet, had been shot a single time in the top of her head. Eventually, police came up with the name Troy Alexander for a mysterious man seen outside the store. It turned out to be an alias.

The case had no suspects until September 1988, when the Nueces County district attorney's office received a letter from California: "I want to clear up the jewelry store robbery homicide in 1983. . . . I know the identity of Mr. Troy Alexander. Contact if interested . . ."

The letter was written by Jermarr Carlos Arnold, who, at the time, was confined in the California Department of Corrections at Vacaville. Arnold had a lengthy record of violence, but two states had declared him legally insane.

In time, Arnold would confess that it was he who killed Sanchez when she went for a .357-caliber pistol hidden in a drawer.

"He knew details down to Sanchez wearing a green dress," said former Detective Sgt. Paul Rivera. "I knew it was good information. . . . I was shocked when he finally said he was Troy Alexander."

At trial, Arnold was equally accommodating. He ignored his attorneys' advice and told a jury that he was "a monster who will kill again." The Corpus Christi jury agreed and condemned him to death.

But the unusual confession isn't that simple, according to Bill May, who at the time was top assistant prosecutor for Nueces County. No crime scene fingerprints matched Arnold's and no murder weapon was ever found, despite Arnold's detailed directions.

Without the help of an insane defendant, the case was unwinnable, said May. He said he refused to prosecute and later resigned.

"I didn't think he was telling the truth," said May, now a Corpus Christi defense attorney. "What he was doing was manipulating the system to get the odd result he wanted. He wanted the state to help him commit suicide."

The premise that a mentally deficient person shouldn't be legally accountable for crimes dates to the McNaughton Rule, a British legal standard set in 1843 and later adopted in the United States.

For May and others, Arnold exemplifies a troubling number of inmates on death row who are insane and, because of their diminished mental condition, understand neither the nature nor the severity of the crimes for which they were condemned.

In the nationwide survey of death row inmates by the *Morning News*, more than a third, including Arnold, said they had been treated for some kind of psychiatric disorder.

"He's crazy," said Catherine D'Unger, a Corpus Christi private investigator assigned by the court to Arnold's defense team. "It's crystal clear. There's another person who lives inside of Jermarr."

But Anne Marie Marshall, who prosecuted Arnold after May's resignation, said she sought the death penalty with a clear conscience and sees in Arnold the distinction between being clinically unstable and criminally insane.

"Jermarr is a classic sociopath, with superficial charm and high intellect," said Marshall. "He showed no more emotion about killing that jewelry store clerk than I would about exterminating a nest of fire ants.

"I think he's legally sane," Marshall said. "But clinically, I think he's crazy as a [expletive]."

Psychotic break

Before mid-1977, according to the foot-tall stack of psychological and background reports in his file, there was no public indication that Jermarr Arnold, a handsome and quiet-spoken 19-year-old, was anything other than a success story in the making.

In high school in Liberal, Kans., Arnold had been an above-average student who dabbled in football and wrestling, but who excelled in photography and debate. With strong recommendations from teachers, Arnold had been offered a journalism scholarship at the University of Kansas. The oldest of three boys, he would have been the first in his working-class family to get a college education.

In 1977, he spent part of his summer vacation in Denver, where his family had once lived. In mid-August his father, a truck driver and welder, phoned to tell him that his grandmother had died of a stroke.

"I just fell apart," the younger Arnold told psychiatrists a few months later. "I already was on the edge of that kind of episode. This just pushed me over. I lost contact with reality. I became quite delusional. I felt angry, confused, hurt, abandoned. I thought I had to take this out on somebody."

That night, Arnold broke into a Denver house shared by two women, grabbed a butcher knife off the cabinet and raped them at knifepoint. When he was arrested a few days later, he slashed his wrists.

Arnold was transferred from a Denver jail to the Colorado State Hospital in Pueblo. His behavior fluctuated from "polite" and "cooperative" to "feelings of persecution," according to psychiatric charts. When he lost control, he would throw chairs and run into walls, and he was placed in restraints.

Arnold's mother, in interviews with psychiatrists, said her son had been unusually close to his grandmother, who had lived with the family the first six years of Jermarr's life. She said his other grandmother had been hospitalized for a mental illness.

Arnold's sexual attacks in Denver were diagnosed by a psychiatrist at the Colorado State Hospital as the result of a "gross psychotic schizophrenia episode." He was found not guilty by reason of insanity and continued to be confined in the state mental hospital.

In May 1983, as he was being transferred between maximum-security wards at the state hospital, he jumped from a van and vanished.

By his own account, Arnold slipped out of Colorado, hitchhiking to Dallas and Houston, then on to Corpus Christi. He acknowledges that he was in Corpus Christi when Christine Sanchez was killed.

But only a month after the murder, Arnold was arrested in Los Angeles, where, without benefit of masks or disguises, he was captured on surveillance cameras robbing two banks.

He pleaded guilty and was sentenced to three years in prison.

California soon discovered what Colorado psychiatrists already had documented: Arnold was deceptively intelligent and spontaneously violent; his rages were uncommonly vicious and occurred without apparent provocation or warning.

His prison files show a steady stream of unprovoked violence. While at Folsom Prison, he mutilated himself repeatedly, he set himself on fire, and he attacked other prisoners. The violations added 16½ years to his sentence.

After recurring attacks on other prisoners at Folsom, officials moved him to another prison unit at Chino, then to the California Medical Facility at Vacaville for psychiatric evaluation.

"One of his most striking personality dynamics is the incredibly pronounced splitting in which he engages," wrote Dr. Cynthia J. Neuman, a staff psychologist. "People are seen as either idols on a pedestal (primarily women are seen in this light), or as objects of contempt, whose pain and suffering invoke worse than indifference to him.

"On the one hand, Arnold is a bright and insightful young man. . . . On the other, without treatment, the combination of long-bottled-up emotions and utter hostility . . . make his proven violence potential quite likely to reoccur in the future."

In March 1987 at Vacaville, after being refused transfer to a lower-security unit, he used a "shank," or homemade knife, to slash another inmate. Arnold slashed the prisoner's throat and genitals and cut off his eyelids. The prisoner survived, and Arnold was charged with attempted murder.

Prosecution of the incident fell to Jackson F. Harris, an ex-cop who heads Solano County's Prison Prosecution Unit.

"Something was definitely going on with Jermarr," Harris said. "If it's psychological, I don't know. But if you look at his file, his attacks are always on other inmates, never staff."

A Solano County clinical psychologist said that although Arnold didn't "appear to be delusional" when interviewed, the prisoner "does appear to be psychiatrically ill with a diagnosis most likely of schizophrenia, chronic paranoid type."

A psychiatrist, calling Arnold a "time bomb," also noted: "He needs to be in a therapeutic setting, for his sake and the sake of those around him, all of whom are at risk."

A judge found Arnold not guilty of the attack by reason of insanity.

Vacaville couldn't continue to "single-cell" Arnold, the prosecutor said, and he was transferred, first to the maximum-security

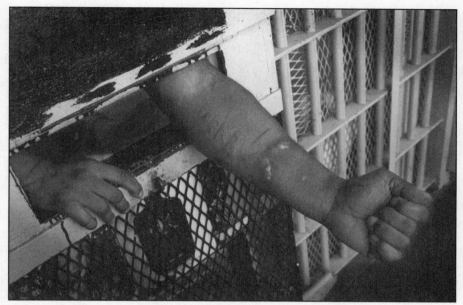

SCARS AND BARS: Jermarr Arnold has slashed his wrists, mutilated himself repeatedly and set himself on fire. The scars on his arm include one that says "dark blood."

Atascadero State Hospital and then to the Special Housing Unit at Pelican Bay State Prison. And it was there that Arnold said he decided to end his "hellish" existence.

Confession or "delusion"?

On this day at Texas's Ellis I Unit in Huntsville, on the most efficient death row in America, Jermarr Arnold is unmedicated. He is pensive and rational, even tranquil, a far cry from the self-inflicted violence suggested by the white scars that litter his forearms and wrists.

A year earlier in the recreation yard outside death row, a fight erupted between Arnold and another condemned inmate, Maurice Andrews. As prison guards watched, Andrews fell dead to the pavement, a sharpened bolt lodged in his left temple. Arnold was locked up in administrative segregation and indicted on a charge of murder.

Arnold has been out of solitary confinement only a few days, and prison guards treat him like a grenade missing a pin. By prearrangement, they steer him to the visiting cage nearest the guard station. The chair in this heavy mesh cage is bolted into concrete, ensuring that it won't be used as a weapon.

Arnold, a bear of a man at 6-foot-1 and 250 pounds, is known among prison officials as "the meanest man on death row."

He knows what they call him.

"I don't lose any sleep over it," he said. "It's more their need to create an image of a stereotypical death row inmate—someone without feelings, someone prone to violence, someone with no moral principles—to support their lawmakers and their bigger prison budgets. But I don't like being used that way."

His voice is flat and emotionless as he describes stabbing Andrews with the sharpened bolt about 20 times.

"I've seen so many people here get killed or hurt, so if I'm put in a situation where I perceive I can get hurt, I have to take care of business," said Arnold. ". . . I observed him, and he acted suspicious. I saw he had a knife out there. I saw what I saw."

The murder of Christine Sanchez is now another matter.

Arnold said he confessed to being Troy Alexander to escape the "hellish environment" at Pelican Bay, the tough California prison where he ended up after the incident at Vacaville.

Pelican Bay is a maximum-security prison where inmates are locked in isolation and monitored by cameras around the clock.

While at Pelican Bay, Arnold filed and won a landmark lawsuit. He alleged that he was shocked with Taser guns, shot with gas guns, dragged down a flight of stairs and choked with a towel by guards who filed a bogus assault charge against him to cover their abuse.

Though terms of a settlement were sealed, a source familiar with the litigation said Arnold received a "substantial" award from the California prison system.

In a January 1995 decision that Arnold says vindicates him, a federal judge ruled in another lawsuit that officials at Pelican Bay had condoned the use of excessive force and created prison conditions that crossed the "constitutional line."

"That kind of experience," Arnold said, "will cause a person to become unstable, or unhinged, if you will."

He said, "I became very disoriented, confused and started committing very impulsive acts, very violent acts. . . . I didn't see any way out. I eventually wrote to authorities in Corpus Christi and gave them a little information on the crime [Sanchez's murder] because I wanted them to come and get me and take me back to Texas."

Arnold said the details he used in his confession in the Sanchez case came from newspaper reports in *The Corpus Christi Caller-*

Times. The clips were sent to him in prison by Bill Jensen, a former Nueces County sheriff's deputy who began corresponding with Arnold after his letter to prosecutors became common knowledge.

"He'd write and ask for stories," Jensen said recently, "and I'd send them. There's no question that he had all the facts in the case."

The clippings, according to Arnold, came at a particularly chaotic time in his life, a period in which he estimates he assaulted himself and other inmates as many as 50 times.

"I started believing I had committed this crime," Arnold said. "That was part of my delusion. . . . There were times I didn't even know who I was."

On a death row where claims of innocence are as common as legal appeals, Arnold fell momentarily silent as he contemplated the question: "Did you kill Christine Sanchez or not?"

"I really don't know," Arnold finally said. "I don't have a clear memory of it. In the past, I've had episodes where I thought I was somewhere else and I was someone else that seemed very real to me."

Three months after he confessed to the Corpus Christi murder, Arnold wrote California Attorney General John Van de Kamp complaining about conditions at Pelican Bay.

A deputy director of the prison system responded that Arnold was too unstable for his complaints to be trusted:

"Inmate Arnold is not mentally stable and is considered a very dangerous psychotic. Most likely, his allegations are products of his imagination."

D'Unger, Arnold's investigator, has a master's degree in psychology. She said the diagnoses in California and Colorado ought to have some weight in Texas.

"No one to this day has been able to explain to me how you can be insane in Colorado, insane in California, come to Texas and not only be sane, but sane on a day way in the nebulous past," D'Unger said.

"How did the jury know on the particular day that he supposedly killed that girl, that on that day, he was sane? He's insane everywhere else, but suddenly he had this one big moment of sanity in Corpus Christi, Texas?"

Mary Sanchez, who watched the jury convict her daughter's killer, said that during the trial Arnold didn't appear insane to her.

"No, not to me he didn't," she said. "Even being down there on death row, he's killed somebody else."

Jekyll-and-Hyde episode

Returning Arnold to Corpus Christi from Pelican Bay was not easy. He had to be flushed from his cell by guards in riot gear and flown from California by the U.S. Coast Guard.

"He is a mean son of a bitch," said Rivera, the former detective sergeant who is now head of the Nueces County Sheriff's Department's criminal investigation division. "As far as being crazy, no. I call him dangerous crazy. He's a very unpredictable person."

Marshall, the prosecutor, warned jailers to isolate Arnold. Still, he managed to brutally stab another inmate shortly after his arrival in Corpus Christi. Ultimately, he was housed in isolation in a cell block designed for eight men.

To talk to her client, D'Unger said, she normally sat in a folding chair next to the bars. It was during one of those visits, she said, that she became convinced that the voluminous psychiatric reports about him were on target.

Arnold, she said, had told authorities he had no living relatives and "created the impression he was an orphan." When D'Unger told him she had located his mother and two brothers, she said, Arnold "just changed."

His expression became taut, making his face appear thinner, his eyes went cold and he broke out in a sweat, she said.

"He changed like that," she said, snapping her fingers. "He didn't say anything, he just made a guttural sound. And there was this smell. . . .

"The hair went up on the back of my neck and my first thought was to get the hell out of there."

A trial of insanity

Anne Marshall and Catherine D'Unger admit to strong predispositions about the death penalty. Curiously, the Jermarr Arnold case has twisted each to the opposing side of long-held beliefs.

"I've always been a liberal," Marshall said. "I worried as a prosecutor that I'd have trouble asking for the death penalty."

But she found, in Arnold's massive psychiatric records, that he once bragged about his ability to deceive psychologists and psychiatrists, she said. And during questioning, when she asked about a prostitute's body found under a bridge, she found Arnold's answer elliptical and troubling.

"Jermarr said, 'Let's deal with this, Sanchez's murder, right now.' He didn't deny it. I didn't think that was a normal reaction. I suspect there are a lot of shallow graves out there in his path.

"I had no problem seeking the death penalty for Jermarr Arnold because he's exactly the person the death penalty was designed for," Marshall said. "There's no hope for redemption; he's a killing machine."

For D'Unger, Arnold's investigator, the death penalty poses no philosophical problems.

"I'm not a liberal, and I'm not easily conned," D'Unger said. "Most of my clients, I hate to say it, are pond scum."

Furthermore, there is another Texas death row inmate, she said, for whom she would be happy to "pull the plug." Alberto Valdez is awaiting the death penalty for murdering a Corpus Christi police officer. At the time of his death the police officer, Daniel Joseph Bock, was D'Unger's fiancé.

"But I look at every case as an individual," D'Unger said. "And Jermarr is a different story. I don't think you need to execute a man who is desperately mentally ill. I don't think Jermarr can control that other person within him.

"I think if there were a medication that would keep the real Jermarr here, he would probably spend the rest of his life making reparations for the stuff he's done.

"What should have happened to Jermarr was that he be sent back

VIOLENTLY UNSTABLE: Texas death row inmate Jermarr Arnold, according to the lawyer who prosecuted him, "is exactly the person the death penalty was designed for. There's no hope for redemption; he's a killing machine."

to the mental hospital from which he escaped in the first place. There shouldn't have been a trial anywhere."

At trial in Corpus Christi, Arnold insisted on picking his own jury, which had a palpable law-and-order bias, D'Unger said.

"It was obvious he wanted to die," she said.

Against Arnold's wishes, his lawyers pursued an appeal, basing the bulk of their arguments on his history of mental illness. They maintained that there wasn't sufficient proof that he was sane at the time of Sanchez's murder, that the court failed to hold a competency hearing and that Arnold's confession, therefore, should have been suppressed.

The Texas Court of Criminal Appeals upheld Arnold's conviction, despite the testimony of Dr. Kathy Morall, a psychiatrist who treated him for four years at the Colorado State Hospital and had reexamined him before trial.

Noting that at least two psychologists rebutted her testimony, the court concluded that Arnold was sane "beyond a reasonable doubt."

Arnold, in the interview on death row, said that because of his history of violence and mental illness he had tried to commit suicide and "was trying to get the state to do it for me."

He said he was surprised that the state of Texas was so willing to help.

"I just can't believe they couldn't see the implications of a man who has an extensive history of psychiatric episodes," he said. ". . . I think they were very anxious—maybe overly anxious—to resolve this case. And I just stepped right in and confessed."

Over the years of waiting, he said, he has grown and changed. He has developed, he said, a "moral inhibition" to suicide. He has also changed his ideas about the death penalty.

"Since I've been here in Texas, I've been sickened and disgusted in the way I see the death penalty carried out. It's obviously not deterring anything. I think it's not morally right or justifiable either."

But for Mrs. Sanchez the maneuvers and delays come as no revelation. Two years before her daughter Cricket was murdered, her son was also killed. His killer served time and was released.

"The guy who did it served maybe three years. Maybe," said Mrs. Sanchez. "They said he found the Lord in prison.

"We were aware of the system. This has gone on too long. But I'm not surprised."

Crime provides thrill of a high, inmates say

Harry Charles Moore is a specter, even on death row. Condemned in Oregon for a double murder, he virtually begged to be executed, threatening to sue anyone who tried to intervene. He said he believed that most death row inmates deserve to die.

Many death row inmates search for new ways to blame others for their actions, but Moore—like a third of death row inmates who responded to the comprehensive survey by the *Morning News*—said he believes criminals enjoy crime.

HARRY
CHARLES MOORE,
Oregon

"Not yes, but hell yes," he wrote in response to the survey. "And you can never change any of these animals. . . . They love to see sobbing and crying."

Moore, who twice had married his own nieces, was convicted of the 1992 shooting deaths in Salem of his half sister, Barbara Cunningham, 53, and her former husband, 60-year-old Thomas Lauri.

"These insects talk to me about what young women will be next, after they get out," he wrote about his fellow inmates. "I just listen to the beasts and how they love the raping and killing of women."

Many of the inmates who said crime is fun cited a thrill they felt from reckless behavior.

Charles Rhines, a South Dakota death row inmate with prior convictions for burglary, robbery and murder, abused speed in the free world but said nothing beat getting high off crime.

"Adrenaline becomes the best drug of all," wrote Rhines, who was sentenced to die for killing a man during a 1992 donut shop heist. "I once heard a 17-year-old boy say, 'Almost getting caught is better than sex.'"

A South Carolina death row inmate who didn't want his name used—a man who had also abused amphetamines—said a life of crime has the same highs and lows as drug abuse.

"Getting away with it is a power thing," he wrote. "Knowing you're in a dangerous position [i.e., getting caught] makes the adrenaline flow. It's a rush. Getting caught is the hangover and withdrawals."

Charles Roche Jr. grew up in a poor family and dropped out of the 10th grade. He started using drugs in grade school and developed a taste for marijuana, heroin and acid. An admirer of Fidel Castro and Che Guevara, Roche as an adult said he took particular pleasure in preying on the affluent.

"I always got a rush from doing armed robbery on the upper-class society," said the man who was convicted of the 1990 killings of Ernest Graves and Daniel M. Brown in Indiana. He was one of five inmates who attempted an escape from death row in 1994.

CHARLES ROCHE JR.,
Indiana

James Eugene Bigby is on Texas death row for the 1987 murder of a friend, Michael Trekell, and his son, Jayson Trekell. He was almost wistful in his recollections of a youth spent vandalizing and stealing anything with wheels.

"When I was a car thief, it was a blast," said the 10th-grade dropout. "Excitement was my thrill. Every type of crime provides some type of need for the criminal."

And while it may seem strange to think of crime as fun, Moore awaited his own execution in Oregon like a child counting the days to Christmas.

"I hope that in time I will be happily executed and all of these sick animals will be right behind me," he wrote. "Just my way of putting the beast in the chamber vault and then into the pit."

On May 16, 1997, a few days after his 56th birthday, the beast in Moore was executed by lethal injection.

PART THREE

Meting Out Justice

CHAPTER 10

• • •

States of Execution

Texas, California contrast reality of capital punishment

I N a just world, Aaron Lee Fuller and John Lee Holt would share the same fate.

Both men were 23 years old in 1990, when they were sentenced to die for robbing, raping and killing women old enough to be their grandmothers. Both had troubled childhoods. Both had problems with marijuana. And both had been behind bars before.

But Holt, who killed in California, is years away from execution. And Fuller, who killed in Texas, was executed November 6, 1997.

In a final interview before his execution, Fuller readily admitted his guilt. The 30-year-old former diesel mechanic, one of about 440 Texas death row inmates, predicted that the final appeal of his seven-year-old death sentence would fail.

"What I did was inexcusable. It was wrong," said Fuller, the 141st man executed from the nation's deadliest death row. "I've been through the whole process—all the way to the Supreme Court. I always knew it would come to this."

Holt, one of 488 condemned men on the nation's largest—and least lethal—death row, lingers in the early stages of his appeals. Since 1976, California has executed four men. Holt is in no immediate danger of joining the list. About 250 prisoners have been there longer than Holt, his attorney said.

Twenty-five years ago, when Fuller and Holt were just starting school, the U.S. Supreme Court, in a landmark decision called *Furman v. Georgia*, declared the death penalty unconstitutional

THE END IN SIGHT: Aaron Lee Fuller, a 30-year-old former diesel mechanic who was executed November 6, 1997, in Texas, predicted that the final appeal of his seven-year-old death sentence would fail. "In the near future, we're going to see the death machine really crank up."

because of its arbitrary use against minorities and the poor.

Four years later, the court approved new standards for the death penalty and put the nation's executioners back in business.

Much about capital punishment has changed since the Furman decision, but actual executions, at least in their geography, remain as inconsistent as many of the arbitrary practices the Supreme Court sought to end.

To explain the disparity between the two states, *The Dallas Morning News* analyzed hundreds of appeals filed by the 1,162 people condemned to death in Texas and California in the last 20 years.

A computer analysis of those cases, combined with interviews and the results of the death row survey by the *Morning News*, revealed:

- In California, death row inmates often languish at the California State Prison at San Quentin for years before a lawyer is appointed to file their required appeal. In Texas, lawyers are appointed soon after conviction to begin the same process, speeding up the first level of appeal.

To illustrate: The judge who presided over Fuller's case appointed a lawyer to handle his appeal to the Court of Criminal Appeals on

February 12, 1990, the same day that he was sentenced to die. But Holt waited almost three years after his conviction before the California Supreme Court named an appellate lawyer for him.

While Holt's case gathered dust for three years, Fuller's appeal was considered and rejected by the highest Texas court.

Holt's case is not an aberration. About one-third of California's death row inmates are waiting for a lawyer. Some, like Holt, have waited for years.

- State and federal appellate court judges with California jurisdiction advance cases more slowly than jurists on Texas cases. In the seven years since his death sentence, Holt's appeal was heard by a single appeals court, and Fuller's was considered—and repeatedly rejected—by judges on five courts stretching from the Texas Panhandle to Washington, D.C.

If executions in Texas are being carried out at what some consider a gruesome pace, California officials complain that judges sit on death penalty appeals for as long as nine years.

- Throughout the appeals process, judges with jurisdiction over Texas death penalty cases have tended to side with the prosecution. Judges of California cases have been more likely to side with the prisoners.

According to the computer review of published cases in the U.S. circuit courts of appeals, the 9th Circuit Court of Appeals has heard far fewer California death penalty cases than its Texas counterpart, but ruled in favor of prisoners in two-thirds of the cases. Some jurists on

APPEALS

Texas vs. California

	Texas	Calif.
People with death sentences 1978-96	625	537
Number appearing before federal appeals courts 1978-96	103	17
Number obtaining relief	19	11
Percent obtaining relief	18%	65%

SOURCES: *Dallas Morning News* review of all death row cases of inmates received on California and Texas death rows beginning Jan. 1, 1978, and ending Dec. 31, 1996. Information for the review was obtained from various sources, including: the Texas Department of Criminal Justice, the California Department of Corrections, case files and published appellate decisions recorded by WESTLAW. Analysis by Shawn McIntosh. Jean Chance, Charles Davis, Jeanette Prasifka, Tim Wyatt and Allen Pusey contributed to this report.

TEXAS VS. CALIF.

	Texas	Calif.
Number now on death row	439	488
Number executed since 1976	141	4

that court were deemed so philosophically opposed to capital punishment that California resumed executions only after the U.S. Supreme Court temporarily stripped them of its power to halt them. Writing for *The New Yorker* earlier this year, 9th Circuit Court Justice Alex Kozinski said the appeals process has turned "judges into advocates."

"There are those of my colleagues who have never voted to uphold a death sentence and doubtless never will," wrote Justice Kozinski, who has voted to uphold California's death penalty.

Meanwhile, the New Orleans–based U.S. 5th Circuit Court of Appeals, with a much more conservative reputation, issued rulings favorable to prisoners in fewer than one-fifth of the Texas cases, according to the *Morning News*'s examination of published cases.

A similar disparity has existed at the state appeals level. During the early 1980s, when the Texas Court of Criminal Appeals was affirming death penalty convictions, it was virtually impossible to obtain approval for a death penalty case from the California Supreme Court. Of the first 80 or so cases heard after the death penalty was reinstated, only four were approved, according to the California attorney general's office.

Although Texans and Californians disagree on many issues, the death penalty is not one of them. Public opinion surveys show that capital punishment is supported by three-quarters of the population in both states.

But the attitudes and expectations of death row prisoners reflect the differences between the two states, according to the *Morning News* survey of death row prisoners.

In California, about 15 percent say they expect to be executed. In Texas, more than 30 percent say they expect to be put to death.

The threat of execution is so distant in California that four of five inmates in the survey there said they have never been given an execution date. In Texas, more than half said they had received at least one execution date during their years on death row.

And while executions may have become commonplace in Texas, records show that an inmate in California is more likely to die by his own hand than by execution. For every death row inmate who has been executed in recent California history, three have committed suicide.

The appeals process

The journey from the courtroom to the death chamber can last a few months—or a few decades.

Gary Gilmore, the first person executed since the death penalty was reinstated, was killed by a Utah firing squad on January 17, 1977, three months after his conviction. A few others, such as Fort Worth courthouse gunman George Lott, are executed within a few years of their convictions.

Perhaps a dozen—such as Montana's Duncan McKenzie Jr., who was executed in 1995 after 20 years on death row—stretched their appeals over two decades. And some—such as Kerry Max Cook of Tyler, Tex., who was released on bail in 1997 pending a fourth trial in a 20-year-old murder—are tried, retried and tried again. (Cook was later freed after pleading no contest to a reduced charge for time served.)

However, most death row inmates, such as Fuller and Holt, fall somewhere in between. The average stay on death row for the more than 400 people executed nationwide since 1976 is about 8½ years, according to the Death Penalty Information Center in Washington, D.C.

Appealing a death sentence is usually a two-step process involving a hierarchy of judges that stretches from the trial court to the U.S. Supreme Court.

The first step, mandatory in most states, is the direct appeal,

BUILDING A CASE: William Mason, 42, has been on death row at the Ellis I prison unit near Huntsville, Tex., since 1992. Like many inmates, he spends a great deal of time working on his case. Mason, who was convicted of kidnapping and killing his wife, is working on his federal appeal.

which deals with what happened during trial. Did the judge issue proper rulings? Was the evidence used to convict legally admitted? Were the instructions to the jury appropriate?

The direct appeal is heard by the highest criminal court in the state, such as the Texas Court of Criminal Appeals or the California Supreme Court. But sometimes, issues raised at this level of appeal also are taken up by the U.S. Supreme Court.

In the second step of the appeal—optional, but nearly always pursued—a condemned prisoner challenges the death sentence on constitutional grounds with a writ of habeas corpus, a Latin term meaning "you may have the body." Dating to 13th-century England and the Magna Carta, this procedure allows a prisoner to raise issues that did not come up during the trial. Were the defense attorneys ineffective? Has new evidence been uncovered? Did prosecutors hide evidence? Is the state's prescribed manner of execution unconstitutional?

This phase of the appeal starts out in state courts and then can proceed through the federal court system—from district judge, to appellate court, to the U.S. Supreme Court.

Appeals can obtain relief that is either temporary—such as a stay of execution or a fact-finding hearing on a key issue—or permanent—

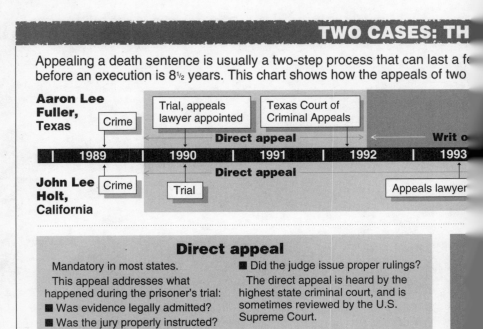

TWO CASES: TH

Appealing a death sentence is usually a two-step process that can last a fe before an execution is 8½ years. This chart shows how the appeals of two

Aaron Lee Fuller, Texas | Crime | Trial, appeals lawyer appointed | Texas Court of Criminal Appeals

Direct appeal — Writ o

| 1989 | 1990 | 1991 | 1992 | 1993

Direct appeal

John Lee Holt, California | Crime | Trial | Appeals lawyer

Direct appeal

Mandatory in most states.

This appeal addresses what happened during the prisoner's trial:

■ Was evidence legally admitted?

■ Was the jury properly instructed?

■ Did the judge issue proper rulings?

The direct appeal is heard by the highest state criminal court, and is sometimes reviewed by the U.S. Supreme Court.

such as being sentenced to life or being set free. Until recently, there was no limit on the number of successive habeas corpus appeals that could be filed—or a time limit for filing them.

Of the approximately 6,000 people who have been sentenced to death since 1976, about one-third have attained some relief through appeals, according to the Death Penalty Information Center.

In most cases, only the sentence was overturned or the prisoner was sent back for another trial. Many escaped the death penalty but remained in prison. But in 73 cases, the center says, individuals once sentenced to death walked away free.

The Holt and Fuller cases are not identical. Holt, for example, is black; Fuller is white. But their cases—coupled with the history of executions in Texas and California—demonstrate how two similar crimes can produce such dramatically different results.

Early executions in Texas

The earliest executions in Texas were local affairs—a killer tried in a county courthouse was often quickly strung up on a nearby tree. In 1924, the state took over the business of executions and replaced the hangman's noose with the electric chair—a relic

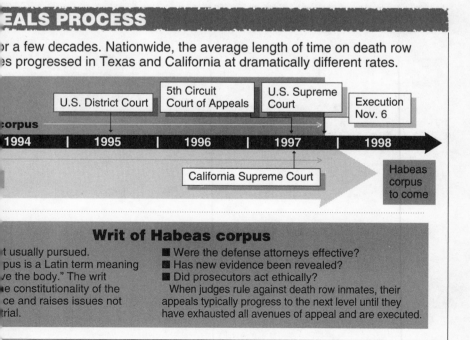

EALS PROCESS

or a few decades. Nationwide, the average length of time on death row es progressed in Texas and California at dramatically different rates.

| U.S. District Court | 5th Circuit Court of Appeals | U.S. Supreme Court | Execution Nov. 6 |

:orpus

| 1994 | 1995 | 1996 | 1997 | 1998 |

California Supreme Court

Habeas corpus to come

Writ of Habeas corpus

t usually pursued.
pus is a Latin term meaning
e the body." The writ
e constitutionality of the
ce and raises issues not
rial.

■ Were the defense attorneys effective?
■ Has new evidence been revealed?
■ Did prosecutors act ethically?
   When judges rule against death row inmates, their appeals typically progress to the next level until they have exhausted all avenues of appeal and are executed.

known as "Old Sparky" now preserved in a museum in downtown Huntsville. During the next 40 years, 361 people were electrocuted in Texas—an average of just over nine a year, according to state records.

Old Sparky's last victim was Joseph Johnson Jr., a 30-year-old Houston robber who went to death praising Jesus and proclaiming his innocence. Johnson was convicted of killing Joseph Ying Chiu, 38, during a 1962 robbery. His appeals kept the executioner at bay until July 30, 1964, when the state sent 2,000 volts of electricity through his body.

Johnson, like most of those who died in the electric chair, was black. Increasingly in the late 1960s, the death penalty was being attacked as racist—a view adopted by the Supreme Court in the 1972 *Furman* case, which invalidated about 600 death sentences in 39 states.

Four years later, the Supreme Court approved new guidelines for the death penalty—and state legislatures began to recast their death penalty statutes. Texas resumed executions in 1982, making national news—and starting a national trend—by being the first state to execute by lethal injection.

Eighteen years after the state electrocuted Johnson, condemned

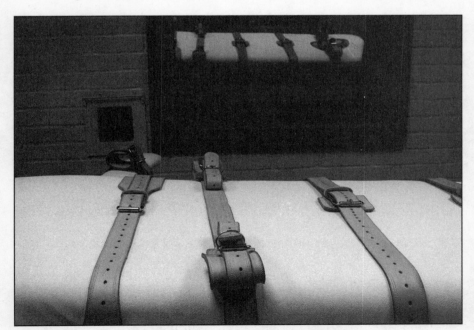

FINAL REST: Texas's lethal injection table is next to a window, which executioners stand behind when they monitor and perform the procedure.

killer Charlie Brooks Jr. was strapped to a hospital gurney in Huntsville and put to death in what some called the first "humane execution."

Brooks, convicted for the 1976 murder of David Gregory, a 26-year-old mechanic, had been on death row for five years—twice as long as Johnson. His final statement was a proclamation of love for his girlfriend, who witnessed his death. Like Johnson, the convicted killer was black.

The life and death of Aaron Lee Fuller

During the last 15 years, 141 men have been executed in Huntsville, the same nine-per-year average as before the *Furman* decision. Aaron Lee Fuller was among 37 inmates executed in Texas in 1997.

In an interview the week before his execution, Fuller was the picture of health. A muscular man just shy of 6 feet, he had a full head of light brown hair cropped high at the sideburns and combed straight back in a pompadour, hazel eyes, solid white teeth, bushy reddish eyebrows and a strong chin. He smiled a lot.

He said he underwent a spiritual awakening on death row, and he professed disinterest when asked about his impending death. "I have no concern for this," Fuller said, touching the flesh of his right forearm with his left hand for emphasis. "This goes back into the ground and turns into dust. Right now, I only have spiritual concerns. I know this may sound messed up, but as each day it grows closer, I grow more peaceful inside. I have no fear at all."

On death row for seven years, Fuller recalled how he felt lured to the outlaw life even as a child. Small acts of rebellion, he said, "felt good at the time—just being bad."

He bounced between the police station, the probation office and state prison for a series of thefts. Released from prison in 1988, the thief turned killer in less than a year.

Arrested for the March 1989 murder of Loretta Stephens, a 68-year-old Lamesa woman, he was convicted and sentenced to die the following year. On Valentine's Day 1990, Fuller arrived at the Ellis I prison unit and was assigned Texas death row No. 964.

During the first stage of his appeal, Fuller argued that his conviction should be set aside because of the damning testimony of a controversial psychiatrist, the revelation of his alleged links to a neo-Nazi prison gang and the exclusion from his jury of a woman with reservations about the death penalty. The Texas Court of

Criminal Appeals rejected all of Fuller's arguments, noting the senselessness of Stephens's death. Fuller, the court wrote, could have easily spared Stephens's life. He had been able to break into her house and steal $500 while she was sleeping and could have left, "no one the wiser."

Instead, the court said, Fuller was "overcome by a sudden, inscrutable impulse to take a human life," and he began to beat and suffocate his victim. As a final affront, the court said, Fuller then "raped her dying body."

Asked about his crime during the interview, Fuller said he robbed Stephens for money to buy drugs and killed her to eliminate a witness. He had no easy answer for why he raped a dying woman.

"I'd like to know the answer to that question myself. It's one of the things that's made my time hard down here. Tried to erase it from my mind for years. It keeps coming back to haunt me."

The Texas Court of Criminal Appeals upheld Fuller's death sentence in March 1992. The U.S. Supreme Court refused to examine the case in June 1993, ending the mandatory phase of his appeal.

Fuller's attorneys began the second phase of his appeal, using many of the same facts to argue that his constitutional rights had been violated.

A writ of habeas corpus was filed with the judge who presided over Fuller's trial—and rejected in October 1994. The Court of Criminal Appeals heard the new appeal, and also rejected it five months later.

Rejected by a federal district court judge a year later, the appeal then moved to the 5th Circuit. Fuller argued that his constitutional rights had been violated because he was denied state funds to hire expert witnesses during trial, specifically a psychiatrist and pathologist of his own.

The court said Fuller should have been permitted to demonstrate his need for those witnesses but ruled that the mistake was a "harmless error, not the denial of a constitutional right."

Rejecting his appeal in 1997, the court wrote that "the contemptible facts of this case need not detain us long."

A request for the U.S. Supreme Court to take up the case was made on September 22. While that request was pending, the trial judge issued a death warrant ordering Fuller's execution on November 6.

About an hour before his execution, Fuller's attorneys received by fax a final notice from the U.S. Supreme Court: "The application for stay of execution of sentence of death is denied."

As his last words, Fuller uttered a prayer to Jesus: "Thank you for saving me." Seven years after arriving on death row, Aaron Lee Fuller was executed.

"Most people," said Ricky Smith, the district attorney for Dawson County who prosecuted Fuller, "here or anywhere else, think that's a long time."

Death in California

Before the 1972 federal moratorium on the death penalty, California's record of capital punishment rivaled that of Texas. Between 1893 and 1967, the state of California executed 501 prisoners, almost seven per year.

Hanging remained the preferred form of execution until 1938, when it was replaced by the gas chamber.

The last man executed before the federal moratorium was Aaron Mitchell, a seasoned car thief executed April 12, 1967, for the murder of a Sacramento policeman during a robbery. His final words after 2½ years on death row: "I am Jesus Christ."

Whereas Johnson's death marked only a pause in executions in Texas, Mitchell's death in the California gas chamber marked an end to anything other than an occasional execution in the Golden State.

In 1977, under the new Supreme Court guidelines, the California Legislature put a new death penalty on the books. And a new generation of death row inmates started showing up at San Quentin in 1978.

In 1978, Robert Alton Harris was a 25-year-old thief and killer. Just released from prison, where he had served time for fatally beating a roommate, Harris kidnapped and murdered John Mayeski and Michael Baker, both 16, who had stopped at a Jack-in-the-Box in San Diego while on a fishing trip.

Harris was sentenced to die in 1979. But his execution—California's first in 25 years—did not occur until 1992. By that time, 19 other states had resumed executions in the country, having killed 168 prisoners.

Harris's execution became a battle of wills between the 9th Circuit Court of Appeals, which seemed determined to block his execution at all costs, and the U.S. Supreme Court, which wanted it to proceed.

With Harris scheduled to die in the gas chamber just after midnight on April 21, 1992, the 9th Circuit issued a series of last-minute orders blocking the execution—one of which arrived after Harris was strapped into the gas chamber and on the cusp of death. Each order was overturned by an increasingly exasperated Supreme

Court, which finally issued an unusual order blocking any additional delay.

"No further stays of Robert Alton Harris' execution," the high court decreed, "shall be entered by the federal courts except upon the order of this court."

Harris was returned to the gas chamber at 6 A.M. Ten minutes later, cyanide pellets were dropped into a sulfuric acid and water solution. Pronounced dead at 6:21 A.M., the three-time killer's last words were: "You can be a king or a street sweeper, but everyone dances with the grim reaper."

California has since executed three more prisoners, the last two by lethal injection. All four of those executed were white.

The life of John Lee Holt

John Lee Holt, according to court records, was a menace early in life. Brain-damaged at birth, he engaged in acts of self-mutilation and, records show, "gave a cousin pesticide to drink."

As a 13-year-old, he knocked an elderly woman to the ground and snatched her purse while masquerading as a helpful Boy Scout. A few years later, he raped a 90-year-old woman and robbed her of $500.

In 1988, he was convicted of an apartment burglary that netted a cash haul of $1.57.

Medical testimony indicated Holt suffered from a brain injury. But his parents claimed the teenage rapist was "born from the devil." And, according to court records, they wished that he, and not his twin, had died as an infant.

Holt's probation for the 1988 burglary was revoked for smoking marijuana, and a warrant had been issued for him when he was arrested for the July 1989 rape, robbery and murder of 66-year-old Marie Margie Axtell in her home in Bakersfield, Calif.

At the time, Holt had been working as a salesman peddling cleaning supplies door to door. Holt told police he "snapped" after Axtell rebuffed his sales pitch. He forced himself inside her home, pocketed loose jewelry, downed a root beer, and sodomized and choked her. She died from her injuries in a hospital nine days later.

A jury took 60 minutes on May 30, 1990, to sentence Holt to death. He was sent to California's death row as inmate E58200. For the first three years, his mandatory appeal went nowhere because an attorney had not been appointed to represent him.

In the appeal that was eventually filed with the California Supreme Court, Mr. Holt's lawyer challenged numerous aspects of his trial—ranging from jury selection to questions about evidence. In an unusual twist, Mr. Holt also argued that the three-year delay in appointing a lawyer denied him a right to a speedy appeal.

In a 163-page ruling in July, the court rejected every element of Holt's appeal—including his complaint about the delay in appointing a lawyer. The delays, said the court, are necessary to give the court time to screen lawyers to "ensure that competent representation is available" for death row prisoners.

Although his appeal was rejected, Holt is in no immediate threat of execution. The second stage of his appeal, one that frequently takes years to be heard by a succession of judges, is just beginning.

Appellate attorney Robert M. Myers, who said he believes Holt is "legally innocent" of the crime, declined to speculate how much longer his appeal might take.

A look to the future

As different as the history of executions in Texas and California might be, officials in both states have taken steps in recent years to expedite appeals.

In Texas, the law has been changed to allow both the direct appeal and the habeas process to start at the same time. And the state has recently made money available to pay attorneys handling some of the optional, second-stage appeals.

In California, officials have taken a step they hope will speed up the appointment of lawyers for death row appeals—increasing the pay for private lawyers appointed by the California Supreme Court.

Congress, too, has attempted to simplify the appeals process, setting deadlines for end-stage appeals and limiting the number that can be filed.

Fuller, nine days before his execution, said he knew what such changes will bring to death row. "In the near future, we're going to see the death machine really crank up," he said in his final interview. "It's no holds barred on the death penalty—on executions anyway."

CHAPTER 11

. . .

Twists in the System

Administration of capital punishment marked by inconsistencies

WHEN the U.S. Supreme Court allowed the reinstatement of the death penalty in the 1976 case of *Gregg v. Georgia*, it did so with the hope that capital punishment would be applied in a way that was "evenhanded, nonselective, and nonarbitrary."

"Under these laws no standards govern the selection of the death penalty," Justice William O. Douglas had written in *Furman v. Georgia*, the case that brought a four-year halt to executions in 1972. "People live or die, dependent on the whim of one man or of 12."

After 21 years and 421 executions, there are those on both sides of the death penalty debate who believe that capital punishment has become too often "arbitrary and freakish" in ways that the Supreme Court sought to avoid.

In Washington, a man avoids the gallows because he is too obese.

In North Carolina, an accomplice is sentenced to die, while the triggerman lives.

An Iowa killer is put to death because he drove his victim to Missouri, five miles to the south.

In Pennsylvania, a condemned killer eludes a jury's death verdict by making a deal with prosecutors.

So inconsistent has the administration of the death penalty become in recent years that the American Bar Association in February 1998 called for a moratorium on executions until state practices can be standardized.

"Today, administration of the death penalty, far from being fair and consistent, is instead a haphazard maze of unfair practices with no internal consistency," said the ABA in its report.

In the *Morning News* survey of death row inmates, many expressed views similar to those of the bar association.

Here are a few examples that illustrate the vagaries of capital punishment.

Geography of death penalty

As brutal and outrageous as his crime was, Andrew Six—kidnapper, rapist and killer—could have escaped the death chamber had he not driven his victim five miles south. In a bloody rampage in 1987, Six and his uncle, Donald Petary, abducted Kathy Allen, a mentally handicapped 12-year-old, from her home in Ottumwa, Iowa. After Six, 32, cut her mother's throat and raped her pregnant 17-year-old sister, he and Petary killed Kathy and dumped her body in a ditch in northern Missouri.

ANDREW SIX
Executed in Missouri

Iowa has no capital punishment statute. But in Missouri, across Iowa's southern state line, a murder committed during a rape, kidnapping or robbery can trigger the death penalty. Six was executed by injection on August 20, 1997.

Despite the geographic anomaly, officials in the rural Missouri farming community where Kathy's body was found proved determined to prosecute the capital cases despite what was, for them, an exorbitant cost. At the time, the region was in the grip of a devastating drought, and Schuyler County was more than $100,000 in debt and anticipating a $40,000 shortfall for the coming year. Voters already had voted down three tax increases, and the county was on the brink of bankruptcy.

In a cost-cutting move seven years earlier, the local jail had been closed. Schuyler County officials had to pay a neighboring county to house Six and Petary. And the estimated $30,000 it would cost to try the two men on capital murder charges was something the county could ill afford.

In addition, the two men already had been convicted in federal court on kidnapping charges; each was sentenced to 200 years, making them eligible for parole after serving only 66 years.

DONALD PETRY
*Awaiting death in
Missouri*

County Commissioner Eldon Tallman said he changed his mind three times before voting to borrow the money to try the death penalty cases.

Before his execution, Six responded to the *Morning News* survey, noting that the one thing he would have done differently with his life was to "keep away from my uncle."

Six's uncle, Petary, now 62, awaits execution on Missouri's death row at Potosi Correctional Center.

In his appeal, which was denied, Petary contended that the trial judge erred when he allowed jurors to hear evidence that he had sexually assaulted his daughter and stepdaughter and that he attempted to escape and assaulted another prisoner while awaiting trial.

Stella Allen, Kathy's mother, bears a 60-stitch scar on her neck from Six's slashing. In August, she finally witnessed her attacker's execution.

"Dirty, lousy creep," she uttered, as she watched through the witness window.

Cheating the hangman

When Mitchell E. Rupe stood trial in 1982, accused of killing two bank tellers, his lawyers argued that he had been a productive member of society until the U.S. Army discharged him for being overweight.

After the jury sentenced him to death, the 6-foot Rupe, who weighed nearly 410 pounds, cheated the hangman by convincing a Seattle federal judge that he was too obese to go to the gallows.

Some condemned killers, such as Rupe, have managed to elude their death sentences, exploiting narrow legal issues and situations that keep them alive, despite their acknowledged guilt.

Rupe contended that, because of his weight, hanging would almost certainly decapitate him, violating his Eighth Amendment right against cruel and unusual punishment.

At the time of his conviction, Washington's primary method of execution was hanging, or, at the request of the inmate, lethal injection. Rupe refused to choose lethal injection, but he challenged his execution by hanging.

The U.S. Supreme Court decision that allowed reinstatement of the death penalty held that the Eighth Amendment "must draw its meaning from the evolving standards of decency that mark the progress of a maturing society."

Execution by hanging, in which the condemned inmate loses consciousness within six to seven seconds of a "fracture dislocation" of the spinal cord, is not cruel and unusual, according to lengthy legal precedent.

However, the possibility that his extraordinary weight would cause him to be decapitated, Rupe argued, is cruel and unusual, notwithstanding the fact that he would probably lose consciousness in the same amount of time and would probably feel no more pain than others who have been hanged.

Washington's execution protocol is excruciating in its detail. Adapted from British army studies, it prescribes a soaked and stretched manila hemp rope ¾ to 1¼ inches in diameter; the knot in the noose is treated with wax, soap and clear oils so that it slides smoothly.

The condemned man's body weight is used to calculate the length of the rope. Washington's scale ranged from 120 to only 220 pounds.

Rupe's hearing in U.S. Judge Thomas S. Zilly's court produced macabre testimony from a variety of experts, including two pathologists, a neurologist and a biomechanical engineer.

The defense also introduced photographs of the 1901 hanging in Clayton, N.M., of "Black Jack" Ketchum, a train robber who killed two lawmen.

Shortly after uttering his last words—"I'll be in hell before you start breakfast, boys"—Ketchum fell through the trap door and was decapitated by the noose.

An engineer estimated that Rupe could be executed by a rope three feet, six inches long without fear of decapitation. But a biomechanical engineer testified he couldn't predict what would happen with a shorter rope.

Judge Zilly said Supreme Court rulings "make it clear that decapitation and similar mutilation, even if accomplished after death without unnecessary and wanton infliction of pain, offend basic human dignity."

Rupe has since won a third sentencing trial for killing the women during a 1981 bank robbery in Olympia, based on prosecutors' failure to produce polygraph results showing that the state's key witness lied about his own part in the robbery.

The issue of Rupe's legal fate, however, may be moot. His attorney, Todd Maybrown, has told officials that Rupe is gravely ill with liver disease and is not expected to live 18 months.

Rupe's case, while perhaps among the most bizarre, is not the only one in which a man condemned to death has held off the hangman.

In Florida, Carlos Bello, who killed one Tampa narcotics detective and wounded another, has dodged the electric chair for 16 years. Ruled to be sane at the time he killed the officer during a drug bust in the summer of 1981, Bello has since been declared insane.

Because Florida, like other capital-punishment states, requires a condemned inmate to be sane at the time he is executed, Bello has been on a perpetual shuttle between death row and state mental hospitals. Doctors, who have prescribed drugs for the convicted killer, thus far haven't kept Bello legally sane long enough for the state to execute him.

In Philadelphia, Willard "Junior" Moran, a confessed mob hit man, had already been sentenced to death in 1984 when he agreed to become a federal witness against organized crime.

The 47-year-old former porn store operator, who killed a union executive in front of his wife, testified against two leaders of the Philadelphia–South Jersey mob family who hired him. He did it in return for a commuted life sentence, which ultimately would make him eligible for parole.

The Pennsylvania Supreme Court has refused to overturn the jury's death sentence against Moran despite strong recommendations by the prosecutors who helped convict him. Meanwhile, state officials don't even have access to Moran, who is being held by federal authorities in the Witness Security Program at an undisclosed federal prison.

Prosecutors say they need Moran to testify once more in the retrial of two mobsters. Moran has threatened not to testify unless his sentence is commuted to life with possibility of parole.

Race discrimination

In a precedent-setting 1979 case, a federal court declared that even the hint of racial discrimination "destroys the appearance of justice and thereby casts doubt on the integrity of the judicial process."

Brian J. Kinder, a black man on Missouri's death row, like 84 percent of black inmates who responded to the *Morning News* survey, believes racial discrimination helped condemn him to death in 1992.

Kinder, an unemployed handyman in overwhelmingly white Jefferson County near St. Louis, was indicted for raping and fatally bludgeoning Cynthia E. Williams, a distant cousin and a 32-year-old mother of three who lived within a mile of his home.

A witness claimed to have seen Kinder carrying a length of pipe shortly before the murder. But despite a bloody murder scene, police

BRIAN J. KINDER
*Believes race
influenced trial*

produced no fingerprints or other physical evidence to put Kinder in the dead woman's bedroom.

Kinder denied raping and killing Williams, and he passed a polygraph examination, the results of which are not admissible in the guilt-or-innocence phase of Missouri trials.

In addition, witnesses said Williams's estranged husband, against whom she had obtained a protective order for threatening her with a pistol, had been at her house hours before her murder.

Six days before Kinder was to be tried on capital murder charges, the judge in the case, Earl R. Blackwell, issued a news release announcing his switch from the Democratic to the Republican Party.

"The truth," Judge Blackwell wrote, "is that I have noticed in recent years that the Democratic Party places far too much emphasis on representing minorities such as homosexuals, people who don't want to work, and people with a skin that's any color but white."

Jefferson County, just southwest of St. Louis, is a working-class county where less than 1 percent of the residents are black.

Kinder's attorneys, arguing that Judge Blackwell couldn't be fair and impartial in a trial involving an unemployed black man, asked the judge to recuse himself. Judge Blackwell refused to step aside, saying: "As far as this court is concerned, every individual and every citizen of this country is absolutely entitled to their individual constitutional rights, whether they are yellow, red, white, black or polka dot. I think people get off the track when they start talking about color."

When the jury pool was impaneled, no blacks were seated. According to court records, one black man, Robert Russell, said he had been summoned for jury duty the week of Kinder's trial, but he said a sheriff's deputy or court clerk contacted him and told him not to appear.

Russell said he had been called as a prospective juror on eight previous occasions but was told six of those times he need not appear.

Kinder, now 37, was convicted and sentenced to death. Judge Blackwell was a Missouri state senator who had been a key figure in efforts to ban busing to achieve integration. According to court records, a member of a key group supporting his efforts said group members "don't have to be white, but you can't be black."

Judge Blackwell, in a postconviction hearing, testified that he opposed busing because of financial considerations, not because of racial issues.

In January 1997, the Missouri Supreme Court affirmed Kinder's death penalty conviction. Judge Blackwell's public announcement, the court held, "did not call into question the judge's impartiality in the trial of the indigent African-American defendant; statements merely expressed the trial judge's dissatisfaction with affirmative action and government entitlement programs."

Supreme Court Judge Ronnie White, the court's first black justice, dissented, characterizing Judge Blackwell's comments as "race-baiting" in an attempt to win an election.

Defense attorneys are preparing Kinder's federal appeal.

Apparatus of death

Emmitt Foster should have died in the time it takes to boil water. But the condemned killer gasped for half an hour on a gurney in the Missouri death chamber, his abdomen convulsing. His prolonged execution in May 1995 triggered criticism from lawyers and medical experts concerning lethal injection—presumed by many the most humane form of execution—and dragged into the spotlight the controversial designer of Missouri's death machine.

Before his death, Foster, 42, was among the condemned convicts who participated in the *Morning News* survey. The St. Louis man, convicted of killing a friend during a robbery, was among the 48 percent of death row survey respondents who listed lethal injection as the most humane method of execution.

Foster's prolonged execution is often cited by death row appeals lawyers throughout the nation, who say lethal injection is a violation of the Eighth Amendment prohibition against cruel and unusual punishment.

EMMITT FOSTER
30 minutes to die

Deadly chemicals, which often include mixtures of sodium Pentothal, a sedative; pancuronium bromide, a muscle relaxer; and potassium chloride, a heart arrester, are viewed by many state legislatures as a humane way to kill.

Executions by injection have replaced or provide options to firing squads, hangings, gas chambers and electric chairs in 32 of the 38 states and two federal jurisdictions that have capital-punishment statutes.

Officials in most states say execution by lethal injection should take from five to seven minutes.

Only minutes into Foster's execution, prison officials pulled the blinds in the death house to shield the condemned man from the handful of public witnesses. One, who had witnessed two previous executions, said he heard "a noise" in the lethal injection machine. Because the witnesses didn't actually see Foster's execution, a mandatory requirement in all execution protocols, two refused to sign the death documents.

The debate has been enlivened by the controversy surrounding Fred A. Leuchter Jr., the self-described engineer of execution equipment who designed the apparatus that killed Foster so clumsily. Leuchter, a 54-year-old resident of Malden, Mass., a Boston suburb, was unavailable for comment. But international reports show that Leuchter, whose father was a corrections officer in Massachusetts, was arrested in both Germany and England on charges of inciting racial hatred.

His 1988 paper, "The Leuchter Report: End of a Myth," was embraced widely by far-right, revisionist groups who say that the Holocaust is a Jewish hoax to fuel international guilt and win support for Israel.

And court records show he performed research on Nazi death chambers for Ernst Zundel, who stood trial in Toronto for distributing false information in his booklet, *Did Six Million Really Die?* Zundel was later convicted.

Illinois, believed to be the only state other than Missouri to use Leuchter's lethal injection machine, canceled its contract after he expressed his scientific opinions discounting the Holocaust.

In 1990, Alabama's attorney general wrote other states that Leuchter was not properly qualified to assist in executions. Later, Leuchter was sued in Massachusetts for practicing engineering without a degree. Missouri prison officials blamed Foster's painful death on veins collapsed from intravenous drug use. Pathologist Dr. Edward R. Friedlander, chief of pathology at the University of Health Sciences in Kansas City, blamed it on Leuchter's machine.

"The problem with the infusion was caused by obstruction of the flow somewhere between the drip chamber and the heart . . . a kink or clog somewhere in the tubing."

Because medical ethics prevent physicians from administering the lethal drugs, doctors are present in the death chamber only to certify the inmates have died. Obtaining the chemicals, locating the veins and injecting the dosage are left to prison staff members who aren't doctors.

Dr. Friedlander, a self-described proponent of the death penalty, said he believes that lethal injection "administered by people who don't know what they're doing" is both cruel and unusual.

Foster's problematic execution was not unique. Other cases of prolonged or unusual deaths, according to court records, have occurred in Texas, Arkansas, Indiana and Illinois.

Texas, March 13, 1985: Technicians spent 45 minutes probing veins in three-time killer Stephen Peter Morin before locating a vein they could use for injection.

Texas, December 13, 1988: The syringe popped out of the arm of Raymond Landry two minutes into his execution, causing a "blowout" of toxic chemicals in the death chamber. It took 14 minutes to reinsert the IV and a total of 40 minutes for Landry, convicted of robbing and killing a Houston restaurant owner, to die.

Texas, May 24, 1989: A fainting witness knocked over another witness when Stephen McCoy—a convicted rapist and killer—began choking, gasping and arching his back off the gurney in a violent convulsion. Officials said McCoy's violent reaction may have been due to drugs "administered in a heavier dose or more rapidly than required."

Arkansas, January 24, 1992: In a process that took 50 minutes, Rickey Ray Rector had to help five execution technicians find a suitable vein in his arm. Witnesses said they couldn't see Rector, who killed a policeman and shot himself in the head, causing major brain damage, but they could hear the inmate moan.

Texas, April 23, 1992: The search for a strong vein in Billy Wayne White took 40 minutes. White, convicted of robbing and killing Martha Spinks in a Houston furniture store, ultimately helped technicians locate a vein in his hand. Death came nine minutes later.

Texas, May 7, 1992: Reporters for the Associated Press and *The Huntsville Item* reported that killer Justin Lee May "gasped, coughed and reared against his heavy leather restraints, coughing once again before his body froze."

Illinois, May 19, 1994: The execution of serial killer John Wayne Gacy was delayed by a crimp in an IV tube caused by inexperienced prison technicians. Gacy was executed for the murders of 33 young men and boys.

Indiana, July 18, 1996: It took an hour and 20 minutes to execute Tommie Smith because prison officials couldn't locate a suitable vein. Smith remained conscious on the gurney while technicians spent 35 minutes inserting a catheter into his heart.

The accomplice

KENNETH ALONZO
KAISER JR.
*Implicated brother
for deal*

STEVEN MARK BISHOP
*Accomplice, not
triggerman*

Kenneth Alonzo Kaiser Jr. had a slain woman's bank card in his shoe when police arrested him, and his fingerprints were found throughout her car. The physical evidence was, in prosecution terms, a "slam dunk."

But the way Kaiser explained it to police, Nan Martin Schiffman, a well-known Greensboro, N.C., socialite and businesswoman, actually was shot to death by an accomplice, his half brother, Steven Mark Bishop.

The brothers, both convicted felons from Florida, had worked on a crew that had painted the Schiffman home earlier in the year. After losing their jobs, according to Kaiser's testimony, they decided to burglarize the Schiffman home. Schiffman, 32, left work early and surprised them during the burglary.

More than $17,000 in ATM withdrawals were made on Schiffman's account after she was abducted. Authorities found her body seven months later, in a gravel pit a few miles north of Greensboro. The threat of the death penalty proved stronger than blood ties. Kaiser, offered a life sentence that makes him eligible for parole in 2010, became the key witness against Bishop. He swore not only that his half brother was the triggerman but that he also sexually assaulted Schiffman shortly before killing her in an abandoned farmhouse. In April 1994, a jury sentenced Bishop, now 35, to death.

But according to court records, it was not Bishop who killed Schiffman, but Kaiser, the state's key witness. Before trial, Kaiser failed a polygraph test and admitted to prosecutors that it was he who had killed the victim. Had they backed out of their plea agreement with Kaiser, according to the court record, prosecutors could not have used any of his statements at trial.

Bishop is among 18 percent of death row inmates responding to the *Morning News* survey who never killed anyone but were convicted of being accomplices to a crime.

In virtually every state, an accomplice can be found as culpable as the actual killer, but juries frequently regard a more passive role as a "mitigator" in death penalty cases and levy a lesser sentence.

At trial, prosecutors asked Detective Chris Frazier what evidence they had against Bishop beyond his brother's testimony. "Not much at all," the officer said. The investigator said the state couldn't have linked Bishop to Schiffman's death without Kaiser's testimony. "It really is not that significant who pulled the trigger," prosecutor Gary Goodman told the jury. Although he was asking the death penalty only for Bishop, Goodman also told the jury, "The bottom line is, they did it together."

And Kaiser was not the only criminal to receive a substantial deal for helping to convict Bishop. The state produced two prisoners who had been jailed with the brothers and who, under oath, supported Kaiser's false claim.

The first, who faced a potential life sentence for child molestation, said Kaiser had portrayed Bishop as the triggerman in jail conversations. The other, who faced a potential life sentence as a habitual criminal, said Bishop had confessed to him in prison "once."

Both inmates received total immunity from the possible life sentences in exchange for their testimony.

Twenty years or more

DONALD CURTIS
"BUFFALO" CHAMBERS
21 years on death row

Donald Curtis "Buffalo" Chambers is among the dozen or so condemned men throughout the country who, records indicate, have eluded execution for more than 20 years.

In his 21 years on Texas's death row, the former Dallas resident has been assessed the death penalty by three different juries for the same crime. In his latest appeal, which was denied in 1995, Chambers contended that there was not enough evidence to prove he would be a continuing threat to society, a mandatory element in issuing a death sentence.

In its ruling, the Texas Court of Criminal Appeals noted that the "calculated and cold-blooded nature" of his crime was sufficient proof to show his continued dangerousness.

Chambers was 19 when he was first sentenced to death in 1975. He and three other black teenagers abducted and robbed a 22-year-old Texas Tech engineering student, Mike McMahan, and his date, Deia Sutton, from a Dallas nightspot. They took the couple to the Trinity River bottoms and shot both of them in the predawn hours of April 11, 1975. As they were leaving, they heard McMahan yell to Sutton to see if she was alive. The teenagers returned. Testimony also showed that Chambers hit McMahan 10 to 20 times in the head with his gun, then shot Sutton three more times. McMahan died of multiple blows to the head, a punctured lung and two gunshot wounds. Sutton lived through the attack and testified against Chambers in all three trials.

"It's really hard on us and really hard on all of our families, his [Chambers's] included," McMahan's elderly mother, Bennie, said when the latest appeal was rejected. "I'm sure it's hard on them, too, but of course, he's still alive."

"It's not about me anymore," said Chambers during an interview on death row in 1996. "It's about my family. If we'd have had any kind of money, I wouldn't be here. My people's getting old."

Chambers is 42 now, having spent more time on death row than he did on South Dallas streets. The victims' families are older, as are his, and one of the teenagers convicted in the same crime, serving life, has been diagnosed with cancer, he said. "We've all got death sentences," Chambers said. "On death row, they just give you the date."

In the 21 years since the death penalty was restored, Texas has executed 141 inmates, more than any other state. Chambers has stayed alive in the most efficient death penalty state in the nation by winning appeals.

The state set an execution date for Chambers 18 years ago. Appeals courts granted him two new trials because a state-appointed psychiatrist questioned him improperly and prosecutors excluded three qualified black people from his jury.

"Dates average about five years around here now," Chambers said. "The high-profile cases—the baby killers, multiple killers, cop killers—seem to go faster. Election year makes a difference."

During the time between conviction and execution, Chambers said, inmates change.

"The jury knew that man when he committed the crime," he said, "but they don't follow him nine, 10 years down the line to know if he's changed.

"There's some people here, they try to date my sister, I'd run 'em off. Others, they've changed. They're good people. There's some others here who should never get out, but they shouldn't be killed."

Chambers, in the interim, said he is waiting for the courts to appoint him a new lawyer:

"I'm depending on the people who are trying to kill me to get me some help."

Over the years, family members of the victims and the killer have questioned the integrity of the criminal justice system.

Sutton, now married, has spoken about the trauma of testifying three times about the single most horrific day in her life. McMahan's father, Mabry, said he's had to "rationalize" a criminal justice system that keeps retrying a case in which legal questions—not guilt—are the issue.

And before Chambers's last trial, his father, Herman, said trying a man three times for the same crime isn't fair.

"I'm not trying to win," Chambers said from death row, "I'm trying to stay alive."

CHAPTER 12

. . .

Not Guilty, but Not Free

Oklahoma officials, believing man committed murder despite acquittal in new trial, lift death sentence but keep him in prison on 32-year-old charges in other case

CLINTON, OKLA., DECEMBER 1997—Thirteen years and two trials after Alma Hall's body was discovered in a cow pasture in the Texas panhandle, Adolph Honel "Abe" Munson Jr. no longer is on death row. Despite his claimed innocence of the 1984 murder of Alma Hall, he spent 10 years on Oklahoma's death row, watching appeal after failed appeal move him closer to execution.

He was spared from the death chamber by the discovery, nine years after the fact, of unrevealed evidence in a deceased Oklahoma investigator's file cabinet. That evidence—165 crime scene photographs and more than 300 pages of witness statements and other documents—pointed overwhelmingly to another suspect.

Despite court orders that compelled state investigators to turn over such materials to defense attorneys, Munson was nearly sent to death without seeing the evidence that would eventually acquit him. "I couldn't prove that I didn't, and they didn't have to prove that I did," Munson said. "They just put it on me."

When he won a new trial in 1995, an Oklahoma jury watched as the evidence against Munson, which had seemed so compelling in his first trial, withered away. The case, which the first trial judge

STILL DOING TIME: Adolph Honel "Abe" Munson Jr., 51, has left death row for a medium-security prison in Lexington, Okla. He has spent 32 years behind bars.

once described as near-perfect, took the second jury only two hours to dismiss.

But the controversy around the Munson case continues. Oklahoma officials still maintain that Munson killed Hall. And they continue to hold him on a 1965 conviction for which he could have been paroled more than a dozen years ago. Late last month, the Oklahoma attorney general's office released a 59-page report on the Munson affair to *The Dallas Morning News*.

In that report, Attorney General Drew Edmondson cleared Oklahoma investigators and prosecutors of any wrongdoing or mistakes in the case.

"The miscarriage of justice lay in the subsequent acquittal, not the original conviction," the attorney general said.

But lawyer Melrose "Trey" Minton III, who defended Munson in 1985, said local and state investigators collaborated against Munson, a black man with a criminal record. In doing so, he said, they ignored their own compelling evidence that Hall was likely murdered by a white man arrested a few days later in Texas.

Said Minton: "Abe was framed, pure and simple."

On June 28, 1984, around 2 A.M., Alma Hall and $330 from the register disappeared during her overnight shift at Love's Country

Store No. 2 in Clinton.

A customer told local police that she had seen Hall, a 46-year-old wife and mother, shortly before her disappearance. The normally outgoing and friendly Hall, Deborah Swigart said, "was not herself . . . she was nervous."

There were two white men in the store, Swigart told Clinton police, and they appeared "very nervous-acting and antsy, and there was eye contact between the two of them." Swigart had seen one of the men, who was wearing "oilfield clothes," cashing checks in the Safeway where she worked. She didn't know him by name, she said, "but I remember faces." Later, Swigart would pick his picture from a photo lineup.

There was no surveillance camera in the Love's where Hall worked, but film from another Love's across town showed the same two suspicious men had been there earlier that night; the clerk there had been so unnerved that she had called police after the pair left. Police, according to records, retrieved the film from the camera.

Clinton Detective Lt. Tom Siler and investigators from the Oklahoma State Bureau of Investigation interviewed two other witnesses: a 13-year-old boy who said he saw two white men carrying a woman from the store; and a minister, who said he saw two suspicious white men inside Love's when he paid for gas.

Additionally, witnesses at Love's that night told police they had seen a two-tone Chevrolet pickup.

Within hours of Hall's disappearance, a farmer near Elk City, about 30 miles west of Clinton, found her store-issued smock lying beside a dirt road. The tan smock bore Hall's name tag and what appeared to be bloodstains. By early afternoon, Oklahoma authorities issued an all-points bulletin for a man named Ralph Judson Yeary.

But before Yeary could be found, a maid cleaning Room 103 at the Glancy Motel in Clinton discovered blood on a mattress and a .22-caliber shell. According to later testimony, the motel manager gave Siler an earring the maid had found. The desk clerk said the room had been registered to a black man who used the name Joe or Joel Johnson, whom she described as smelling like alcohol, having bloodshot eyes and looking "tired."

At the time, Yeary, a troubled Vietnam combat vet, onetime package deliveryman and sometime oilfield roughneck, was a man on the fly. He was wanted in Texas for raping a 16-year-old girl he had followed from a convenience store in Austin and for kidnapping and raping a convenience store clerk in Round Rock. Florida authorities also wanted to question him in the disappearance and murder of a 15-year-old girl, who last was known to be using a pay phone outside a convenience store.

Round Rock detective Chris Bratton knew that Yeary had once lived in Weatherford, Okla., about 12 miles east of Clinton on Interstate 40. Playing a hunch that Yeary might return to his oilfield haunts, Det. Bratton wired an arrest warrant and a description of Yeary to authorities in western Oklahoma. It was two days before Hall's disappearance, June 26.

On June 29, a day after the girl was abducted, Yeary was arrested in Texas, and Bratton immediately notified Siler in Clinton. Yeary, according to police reports, apparently was trying to abandon his two-tone Chevrolet pickup truck for another vehicle.

Though Clinton and OSBI officials had issued a bulletin for Yeary, they made no attempt to contact Texas authorities, Bratton said.

On July 2, the Texas detective sent another teletype, according to records, telling Oklahoma authorities that he had transferred Yeary to Round Rock, where he was charging Yeary with kidnapping and raping the convenience store clerk there.

The Round Rock detective, now a captain in charge of the criminal investigation division, said it was clear Oklahoma authorities no longer were interested in Ralph Yeary.

At midday on July 4, a rancher feeding cattle near Shamrock in the Texas panhandle discovered a woman's body lying on a folded blanket in his pasture. The woman, later identified as Hall, had been shot in the head two times; an unknown blunt force had split her lips and dislodged four teeth. The pathologist who autopsied the body, Dr. Ralph Erdmann, would later testify that he removed the woman's jewelry, including a seashell-shaped earring that matched the one Lt. Siler said he had from the room at the Glancy Motel.

The new subject of Oklahoma authorities' attention was Adolph Munson, a 38-year-old prison lifer who had walked off from a work-release center near Muskogee in eastern Oklahoma three days before Hall disappeared.

Using toll records from a pay phone at the Glancy Motel, police determined that it had been Munson, using an alias, who had been in room 103, where they found the blood, the .22 bullet and the earring. The calls he had made were to a former prison employee and to the halfway house from which he had disappeared.

When Munson was arrested in August in Venice Beach, Calif., he said, he thought he was being extradited back to Oklahoma on charges of fleeing the work-release center. But instead of being taken to Muskogee, where the warrant was issued, he was flown by private plane to Clinton. After he awoke from his first night in jail, he said, a police officer was standing outside his cell dangling a noose.

"Things didn't get any better from then on," Munson said.

Munson's prison record apparently made him an attractive suspect to Siler, despite testimony already gathered pointing to two white men.

In 1965, at age 19, Munson had lived for six months with a 26-year-old woman who, he said, never bothered to tell him that she was married until her husband confronted him at a Tulsa bar. A fight ensued, according to Munson, and by the time it was over, his girlfriend and her husband were dead of stab wounds. Munson was critically wounded.

"We both had knives," Munson said. "The medical examiner said that the dude and the girl weren't stabbed with the same knife. He pulled the knife on me first." But there was never a trial. Munson said his lawyer convinced him to plead guilty, and he received two life sentences.

A few years later, Munson bumped into his lawyer in a chow line at the Oklahoma State Penitentiary in McAlester. The lawyer, Curtis Lawson, according to court records, had been convicted of embezzlement in 1968. Lawson, a former state representative, also admitted to Munson that he had falsified records to get his law license, a fact substantiated by Oklahoma Bar records.

But the fact that he had pleaded guilty on the advice of a phony attorney made no difference to the state of Oklahoma. Munson stayed in prison until 1984, when a virtually unblemished prison record won him a transfer to the work-release program in Taft, Okla.

Although he was within months of being paroled from prison, Munson said he fled from the work-release program because he had had an argument with his girlfriend during a weekend furlough. She had called the police, he said, and he feared that a return to the halfway house meant a return to hard time.

Following his arrest in California, Munson acknowledged to police that he had spent the night "in some little town in Oklahoma," but he was too drunk, he said, to remember the name of the town. He was adamant, however, about not killing anyone. He said he asked to take a polygraph exam, but officers refused.

Trey Minton had been a practicing lawyer three years when he was appointed to defend Munson on capital murder charges. There were crime scenes in three locations—Clinton, Elk City, and Shamrock, Tex.—and the young lawyer asked the court to appoint an investigator and a forensics expert to help him investigate. The judge refused, saying the defense could rely on experts from the OSBI.

Minton also asked the judge to examine the prosecutor's files for exculpatory evidence—facts favorable to Munson's defense. The judge also denied that motion, but instructed the prosecutor to make the evidence available to the defense.

"Tom Siler happened to be there," said Minton, "and the prosecutor said, 'Trey's going to come down and go through your file.'"

Siler died in February 1990 of cancer at age 60. The attorney general's report quotes Jackie Duncan, the original prosecutor in the Munson case and now a judge, as describing Siler as "an honorable man, set in his ways, but true to his duties."

Minton held a different view: In an earlier case, Minton said, he had caught the veteran detective trying to conceal a witness. "I don't care if they erect a monument to Lt. Siler," the lawyer said, "he was a bigot, he was a racist to the nth degree in my opinion. He would do whatever it took. And the OSBI was goose-stepping right along with him."

Minton said he was shown about 10 crime scene photos, and little else. When he ran across the APB on Yeary, he said, Siler told him that Yeary had been investigated and cleared. "We go through the process of discovery with the DA saying you have our whole file, the Clinton Police Department saying you have our whole file as well, and basically, we had nothing," Minton said.

At the first trial there were plenty of questions about the evidence, said Minton. Although the body of Hall was taken and dumped more than 100 miles away in Texas, an OSBI expert testified that no blood and only a single hair, one matching Hall's, was found in Munson's car.

"So we are supposed to believe that Abe wrapped the lady up in a blanket and towel, stuck her head down, as big as she was, in the front seat and drove her to Texas . . . yet there was no blood, no body matter in the car," Minton said.

The forensic pathologist, Dr. Erdmann, testified at a preliminary hearing that a "large-caliber gun" created the wounds to Hall's head. At trial, however, he testified that the wounds could have come from a much smaller .22-caliber.

"The sticking point was the earring," Minton said of the state's circumstantial case. The pathologist's testimony, coupled with the discovery of the .22 shell and the seashell earring, put the murder scene in Munson's motel room. "The trial judge, in an interview, said the state's case went together so well, he'd never seen a case go together that perfectly. Well, no kidding."

Almost 10 years later, however, an investigator for the Oklahoma Indigent Defense System, Cliff Everhart, found a set of files in

Siler's file cabinet. And with the discovery of those files, the state's case unraveled.

The strand of hair—the only physical evidence linking Hall's body to Munson's car—came from a synthetic wig worn by Munson's former girlfriend.

After the first trial, Dr. Erdmann, the forensic pathologist, created headlines of his own. In Texas, the pathologist was found to have fabricated autopsies and perjured his testimony. By the time he was brought back to Oklahoma to testify on Munson's petition for a new trial, he had been convicted of seven felonies, had surrendered his medical license and was serving a 10-year probation.

Seventy-six times during his testimony in the Munson hearing, Dr. Erdmann invoked his Fifth Amendment privilege against self-incrimination.

Clinton police denied having a surveillance film from the second Love's store depicting two suspicious white men, but Love's officials produced a receipt showing they had seized it.

A criminologist testified that tire tracks shown on photographs of the site where Hall's body was found did not match the tires on Munson's car. Other photos depicted red dirt on Hall's shoes, a clear indication that she had been forced to walk outdoors before her death—not in a carpeted motel room. And though no murder weapon was ever produced, a bullet shown in the Siler photos near Hall's body was identified by an expert as .38-caliber, rather than the .22-caliber the state claimed killed Hall.

Finally, the earring so critical in Munson's original trial was not listed on any of the evidence inventories, not in the motel maid's statement and not in Siler's own reports. A report written by a Texas Ranger, however, noted: "The seashell earring was shown to the Hall family and they could not identify the earring as one owned by Alma Hall."

"I don't think that earring was ever in that room," Minton said.

Dr. Erdmann's contention in the first trial that he removed a matching earring from Hall's body was among those matters he refused, under oath, to discuss. "That was the only real link, this earring that matched the earring on the body," Minton said.

Saying that he was "saddened" that officials hadn't complied with the law, Judge Charles L. Goodwin ordered a new trial.

Prosecutors appealed to the Oklahoma Court of Criminal Appeals. The state's highest criminal court agreed that Munson deserved a new trial, saying "the state did not allow a complete picture . . . to be painted at Munson's original trial." "Of particular importance," the court said in its opinion, "were the reports regarding suspect Ralph Yeary."

The man seen with him was never found, but Munson's defense team later tried to talk to Yeary, who was by then in prison near Huntsville. Told they had come for information about an abduction, according to testimony, Yeary replied: "I didn't have anything to do with killing that woman."

The acquittal in the second trial, however, has not freed Munson from the criminal justice system, nor has it reinitiated the investigation into Hall's murder.

Munson remains incarcerated today in a medium-security prison in Lexington on the 1965 stabbings. Imprisoned at 19, he is now 51. He has spent 32 years, 63 percent of his life, behind bars, 10 of them under imminent threat of execution for a crime he didn't commit.

As prisons go, the lockup at Lexington, halfway between Oklahoma City and the Texas state line, is night-and-day better than "Big Red," the decrepit maximum-security unit in McAlester. Since he was acquitted on the death sentence, Munson spends his time training dogs for handicapped people. The dogs spend nights in his cell. He carries snapshots of them in his denim uniform.

"Thirty-two years is enough," he said. "But this, man, the reason I'm here isn't about what happened in '65. It's about the case that a jury found me innocent on."

A week after Munson's acquittal, Gov. Frank Keating described him as "an individual who does not have clean hands," referring to the 32-year-old stabbing charge.

"This individual is not getting out. I will not pardon him, and I will not parole him," the governor said.

"He thinks I just beat the system," Munson said.

Two months after Ralph Yeary was arrested in June 1984 and taken back to Round Rock, he overpowered a Williamson County sheriff's deputy, disarmed him and fled. He was arrested about 72 hours later. The escape added 10 years to the 20-year sentences he was assessed for the rapes in Austin and Round Rock.

He was questioned about, confessed to, recanted, then cleared of the murder of a 15-year-old girl in Florida. The records on that case have been sealed. In two letters requesting leniency from Texas judges, Yeary wrote that he suffered from an "illness from the Vietnam war." "Even if I did those things that people say I did, I did not know it at the time," Yeary wrote.

Military files from the National Personnel Records Center show that he joined the army in Coral Cables, Fla., five days after his 17th birthday. He served in both combat engineering and aviation battalions in Vietnam. The circumstances of his discharge, according to the records center, are not releasable without Yeary's consent.

Judges denied both requests for leniency. Released under normal supervisory parole on May 15, 1996, Yeary, 47, vanished two months later. A warrant for his arrest was issued July 30, according to police computers.

He remains a fugitive.

PART FOUR

Living with Death

CHAPTER 13

• • •

Carrying On in the Face of Death

Condemned prisoners carve out
an experience while working

*D*ECEMBER *1997*—A killing. A trial. A death sentence. Then the
wait.

Assigned a number and a cell, they become prisoners of a process
neither swift nor sure, existing in obscurity in warehouses for the
damned—for years, even decades.

Still, even on death row, life goes on.

Some make music, create artworks, write life stories from solitary cells of concrete and steel.

A few marry. More divorce. Children grow; parents die. Some go
insane. Some kill while waiting to be killed.

Most dream of freedom. A handful obtain it. Everyone waits. In
1997, there were 74 executions in the United States, 37 in Texas
alone—a record for recent years, but far from the record of 199 executions in 1935.

"Death row" in the United States is actually a collection of about
60 disparate prisons scattered across 38 states. There are death rows
in ultra-high-tech facilities and century-old stone fortresses. Some
are almost comfortable; others, severe. California has the largest.
Texas's is the most lethal. Death rows in New York, Wyoming and
New Hampshire are empty. Placed side by side, the cells in which
death row inmates live would stretch for 33½ miles.

In their responses to the *Morning News* survey, condemned men
and women describe their lives in terms of wretched, boring days
and routines born of deprivation. Vending machine hamburgers are

warmed in "ovens" made from split aluminum cans fastened to lightbulbs. Typewriter ribbons are reoiled for extra life. Scraps of metal are sharpened on concrete into lethal weapons.

From a condemned man's arrival on death row to another's departure, these stories reflect the daily routines of men and women living on death row in the United States.

A handshake

ELLIS I UNIT, HUNTSVILLE, TEX.—Sentenced to die and pulled from the Dallas courthouse, Genaro Camacho Jr. was handcuffed, hooded and hauled through a gauntlet of cops to a waiting car.

"The first thing that came to my mind was they were going to shoot me," said the beguiling 43-year-old killer with an immaculate ivory smile.

Sentenced to die for the 1988 murder of David L. Wilburn, 24, during a kidnapping, Camacho is suspected of other gory crimes that include feeding a woman's dismembered body through a blood-splattered tree shredder.

But in the aftermath of his 1990 conviction, as Camacho recalls events, he had no idea where he was being taken or what was about

WAITING FOR DESTINY: Texas death row inmate Genaro Camacho Jr. is sentenced to die for the 1988 murder of David L. Wilburn, 24, during a kidnapping. He is suspected of other crimes that include feeding a woman's body parts through a tree shredder.

to happen. The *whump-whump-whump* he heard outside was unmistakable, even to a hooded man. A Texas Ranger on each side, Camacho was locked to the floor of the helicopter, which rose and headed south for the flight to Huntsville.

Landing on a basketball court a short while later, he was led to an office in a nearby building, where he was greeted by a Texas prison captain.

"He shook my hand," Camacho recalled in an interview, "and said, 'Welcome to death row.'"

Living meal to meal

LOUISIANA STATE PENITENTIARY, ANGOLA—Cotton and soybean fields tessellate this former slave plantation, a sprawling 18,000-acre prison farm by the Mississippi River. It is tended by 5,000 inmates who live here, watched by horse-mounted guards in camouflage carrying rifles.

Though it is among the nation's largest prisons, Angola's death row is home to only 58 men and two women. The movie *Dead Man Walking*, based on a nun's ministry to a condemned killer, made Angola's death row among the nation's best known. But whatever glamour Hollywood might have bestowed is long since gone.

Death row is a small structure behind the prison administration building. Huge fans move cool, moist air through concrete corridors, and the floors are damp with condensation.

Abdullah Hakim El-Mumit, a convicted cop killer known in the free world as Tommy Sparks, has spent more than a decade in Angola, marking off day after repetitive day.

He rises each day around 5 A.M., as guards begin their morning rounds, for an hour of prayer, then waits for the first meal of the day, which arrives about 6 A.M. Breakfast, he said, is "just like McDonald's," typically consisting of eggs, biscuits and jelly. "The food is good," he said.

Like many death row prisoners around the country, Louisiana's condemned are confined to their cells for all but an hour a day. During that hour outside, they can walk up and down the hallway, take a shower or go outside, escorted in heavy leather and steel manacles, to the recreation yard.

Three of 10 death row inmates in the *Morning News* survey said they suffered from long-lasting physical or mental illnesses or diseases, such as high blood pressure, diabetes, heart disease and personality disorders.

JUST PART OF THE ROUTINE: Louisiana corrections officers discuss whether they can remove handcuffs from death row inmate Abdullah Hakim El-Mumit, also known as Tommy Sparks. He has spent more than a decade in the Angola penitentiary.

The recreation yard has five dog runs fanning out from an entrance like slices of pie, each with a basketball hoop, a patch of grass and a perimeter of razor wire. The yard is designed for solitary recreation, but on a warm fall day last year, two inmates were seen tossing a prison-made ball—a stuffed sock—back and forth over the razor wire. "There's plenty of life here," Hakim said. "It's just the same every day."

In his remaining hours, Hakim said, he watches television, writes letters or talks to fellow death row inmates. When inmates talk to each other on opposite ends of a wing, "you have to have a good set of lungs," he said.

Other times, he and another inmate might pass a game of checkers back and forth. But mostly, he said, he and his companions wait in their cells to be fed.

"We live from meal to meal."

A solitary confinement

From her cell at Pocatello Women's Correctional Center, Robin Lee Row ponders in solitude what her judge called the "final betrayal of motherhood."

Inmate No. 040171 and the only female on Idaho's death row, Row is one of only 48 condemned women in the United States. She was sentenced to die for setting a house fire in 1992 that killed her two sons and husband, a crime prosecutors said was fueled by new love and life insurance.

"I feel that being on death row that I should be allowed visitors that are not members of my immediate family.

"My family lives 2,000 miles away, so I receive no visitors. The worse thing for me being on death row is the isolation. Since I am the only woman in Idaho on death row, I get housed by myself. The men can communicate amongst themselves."

A death row proposal

Andrea Hicks Jackson, a death row inmate at the Broward Correctional Institution in Pembroke Pines, Fla., was convicted of killing Gary Bevel, a Jacksonville police officer, in 1983. She set conditions for an interview in a letter:

"I received your most welcomed letter a few days ago and I was blessed and overjoyed to hear from you. It is my hope and prayer that these few lines will reach you and your family in good health and in perfect peace. . . . I would love to do your interview but I don't do free interviews. . . . Please understand that I don't have a job and no one supports me so I have to try to make a dollar where I can. . . . I have two sons who I do my best to help out when I can so that is why I ask to be paid for all interviews of any kind.

"If your paper wishes to pay me $800 for the interview, I will do it. If they agree I ask that you please send an American Express money order to me. . . . Please make sure that the money order gets here before you all do. . . . I've been burned before and didn't like the way it felt.

"Thank you and have a Jesus filled day, Sincerely in Christ, Andrea." Jackson was not interviewed; the *Morning News* does not pay for interviews.

A death cell's smell

MAXIMUM SECURITY UNIT, TUCKER, ARK.—Darrel Wayne Hill had been in and out of jails and prisons all his life. But his first day as condemned prisoner SK877, the 57-year-old Hill recalls in his unpublished autobiography, *Destination Death Row*, was unlike anything else the seasoned thief, drug addict and killer had experienced.

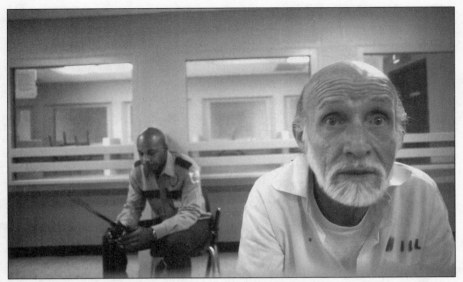

"THEY SMELL OF FEAR": Darrel Wayne Hill, on Arkansas's death row, writes in his unpublished autobiography: "All cells, prison or jail, have a distinct smell that disinfectant can't erase. They smell of fear, hopes, broken dreams and depression."

"The cage I was supposed to live in until the executioner pulled the switch on me was big for a prison cell. Nine feet long and seven feet wide. With a steel bunk, mattress, sink, toilet and wall mirror. All cells, prison or jail, have a distinct smell that disinfectant can't erase. They smell of fear, hopes, broken dreams and depression. I had spent many years in solitary cells, always with the hopes and dreams for the future."

Survey respondents report an average of seven years on death row. One in four said they had been on death row for more than 10 years.

"The feeling of hopelessness set in now the minute I heard the door lock behind me. I had finally come to the end. The death chamber with the electric chair was only a few feet away. The reality of things hit me in the pit of my stomach. Life is a strange sensation when you are dealing with only truth. Money, booze, drugs, whores and the party life lose all meaning. As my mind reflected in the reality of my situation, I had mental flashes of what I missed, what I would never experience again. No more walking in the rain. Never smelling another flower or fresh mowed grass. No more watching the stars at night or the changing of the moon. Never watching the innocence and beauty of children playing. Never telling anyone I love them or hearing them say, 'I love you.'"

"Bloody Harlan" legacy

KENTUCKY STATE PENITENTIARY, EDDYVILLE—Robert C. Foley pulled up the red T-shirt to his throat, exposing a hard-body chest and abdomen with so many scars that they run together in places.

"Prosecutors make it sound like a one-sided thing," said Foley, who is from Harlan County in eastern Kentucky. "Does it look like I ever messed with anyone who wasn't armed?"

Six of the scars are from gunshots, he said. He doesn't recall how many times he's been stabbed.

Foley is a 42-year-old enigma. Polite, dark-complexioned and rough-cut handsome, he also carries within the century-old walls of the Kentucky State Penitentiary the reputation of being the meanest man from the toughest county in America: "Bloody Harlan," as it is known in folklore.

He is considered tough enough that in two trials in Laurel County, Foley has been condemned to death for killing six people. And though not charged, he is also suspected by officials of killing a seventh, a Kentucky state trooper.

Foley narrowly escaped the death chamber in November 1997, winning a reprieve the day before he was to be executed.

His death warrant describes what awaited him: "before sunrise . . . death by causing to pass through his body currents of electricity of sufficient intensity to cause death as quickly as possible, and such currents to be continued until he is dead."

Some prisoners live knowing the time and date of their death. Others are moving targets, arguing that their future is determined by their past. Such is Foley's appeal.

"There's kind of a code down there where I grew up that people carried guns, knives," Foley said. "If somebody's threatened you with a knife or gun, you were pretty well justified in everybody's eyes."

His grandmother bootlegged moonshine, and his father, according to his appeal, was "charged with killing at least seven men." His grandfather and stepgrandfather both were convicted of killing a deputy sheriff and sentenced to prison.

"I think maybe if I had stood trial back in Harlan County, I'd never received the death penalty. People would have been more understanding."

A cure for prison pallor

At the nation's largest death row in California, prisoners can purchase a wide array of snacks, toiletries and cosmetics at the San

Quentin State Prison commissary. A Condemned Canteen Price List dated 1995 reads like an inventory for a small convenience store:

Marlboro cigarettes, $2.30.

Proline Hair Food, $2.60.

Cocoa butter lotion, 70 cents.

Nonalcoholic aftershave, $1.25.

Hemorrhoidal ointment, $3.70.

Taster's Choice coffee, $5.45.

Gallo salami, 60 cents.

Picante sauce, $1.65.

Sliced jalapeños, $1.85.

Protein Powder, $6.30.

This being California, death row prisoners who want to work on their tans can purchase a bottle of sunscreen for $4.70.

The most expensive item on the list is $17.15, Opti-Zyme Cleaner for contact lenses. The least expensive: "kill candy," three for 10 cents.

Christmas condemned

In a series of collect phone calls from the Menard Correctional Center in Illinois, Edward Moore talked about the daily frustrations of his cell life for the last six years.

Moore said he lives in a steel cell about five feet by seven feet that has been painted blue and white and watches television six or seven hours a day.

"Everybody looks forward to getting mail, everybody looks forward to visits. And you can't wait to go to sleep because then you start a new day," he said. "Even though it's the same as today, it's a new day."

About half of death row survey respondents say an execution date has never been set for them.

Moore, a housepainter who maintains his innocence, was sentenced to die for the 1991 murder of Judy Zeman, one of his customers. Zeman was robbed, raped, bound with duct tape, then set on fire with gasoline.

Thanksgiving and Christmas are days just like any other on death row. During a phone call last Christmas Eve, Moore said the next day's celebration in the free world had lost all meaning on death row.

"It ain't nothing," he said. "It's just another day in hell. They'll feed you generic turkey, fake stuffing, you get a piece of pumpkin pie."

No rush to kill

ELY STATE PRISON, NEV.—From this high sierra desert death row, Richard Canape, sentenced to die for killing a vacationing hunter, says he and his fellow 80-odd inmates enjoy relatively spacious cells, friendly relations with guards and generous access to telephones and exercise equipment.

However, the most generous benefit, according to Canape, is that Ely State Prison is not in Texas.

Nevada has executed six men in the last 20 years. This year alone, Texas has executed six times that many.

More than one in three death row respondents said they were allowed to work outside their cells—in maintenance, food service and prison barber shops.

"The only time Nevada executes people is when they drop their appeal. Texas is on a path of their own. No other state wants to be like Texas, killing two to three people a week," he said.

"Nevada ain't in no rush to kill nobody."

A letter from death row

"Dear sirs,

It's a darn shame to be trapped in a place like this. White niggers, black racists, people with brain damage. Corrupt guards, drug selling guards, and inmates. People on death row, who think they are better than other people on death row. Hate mail, an over-burdened and burnt-out court system. And the news whores who think they are so clever. They send out a questionnaire like they care, like they are trying to make a difference. You need to come up with a new line of lies. But thanks for trying just the same.

Happy Holidays to you.

Rhett G. Depew."

Depew is on death row at Southern Ohio Correctional Facility in Lucasville for a triple murder committed during a 1984 burglary.

Liner notes

When Robert Sidebottom was executed, Eric "Cockeye" Schneider lost not only a friend, but also a bass player. The two, condemned in Missouri, were the cornerstones of what may be the nation's only death row garage band, Imbalance.

Sidebottom, executed in 1995 for killing his 74-year-old grandmother, played bass. Schneider, executed in January 1997 for killing two schoolteachers during a robbery, worked the drums and sang.

They were joined by Billy Jones, on lead guitar, convicted of killing a man he said was trying to rape him, and Walter Timothy Storey on keyboards, convicted of killing a neighbor. Chris Simmons, convicted of throwing a woman off a bridge, is credited with handling the mixing and recording equipment.

While all five were awaiting execution by injection at Potosi Correctional Center in Missouri, the band sent the *Morning News* a demo tape with two songs. Though the group is unlikely to topple anything on the current charts, the songs are remarkable for having been written and recorded on death row.

In "World of Power," Schneider sings:

Lord, hear his cry

Suddenly it's time to die.

He stands in the street

Broken soul and all alone

He lost his family

He lost his job

He lost his home.

Band members acknowledged the quality isn't great. Jones groused in a letter about having to rush up production and work with a "lack of proper equipment."

They said they weren't trying to "get rich" because of the novelty. Any money the group made, they promised, would go to charity.

The band's future became fuzzy when Sidebottom was executed and downright bleak when Schneider followed.

"I'm not going to lie. It's got me . . . messed up," Schneider said after his bass player's execution. "Ten years living with this guy. I don't know if I can find anyone down here in this house that can play bass again. And I don't know how much time I've got to teach someone again."

A jailhouse lawyer

From B-Block, Cell 58, at the Idaho Maximum Se
at Boise, Timothy Alan Dunlap complained that pr
eavesdropping on prisoners' thoughts.

Convicted of the 1991 murder of bank teller T
Crane, 24, during a robbery, Dunlap sent a copy of a   said
he was filing against President Clinton and others over the matter.

"They can tap into the human mind," Dunlap said in a phone interview. As evidence of what he called "psychic spying," Dunlap in his lawsuit cited the inexplicable and unpredictable shaking of the bed in his 9-by-14-foot white and green cell—all of which, he said, amounts to torture.

"They try to treat the prisoners here like they done something wrong and they're trying to be corrected," he said. "I'm on death row. I'm not here to be corrected. I'm here to finish my appeals and see if I get released."

The loneliest number

Arizona State Prison Complex, Florence—Luis Mata, convicted of raping and killing 21-year-old Debra Lee Lopez in 1977, was waiting for death in white boxer shorts.

NEW CLOTHES: Leather boots and freshly laundered prison blues await Luis Mata, an Arizona inmate, a few days before he was executed August 22, 1996.

He had been moved from the cell that had been his home for almost 20 years into a holding pen that allows guards to better see him as his execution date draws near.

The 45-year-old prisoner was standing, talking on a telephone reserved for men about to die. His dark beard and hair starkly contrasted with the gymnasium white boxer shorts and T-shirt he was wearing.

His execution was still a few days off, but prison officials were busily preparing to take his life. The clothes he would wear to death—freshly laundered denim pants and shirt and brown boots—were laid out on a counter in Arizona's death house, a spotless facility stinking of chlorine and fresh wax. A black chair set inside a glistening white, egg-shaped gas chamber in one room; a gurney for lethal injection in another. A red phone, linking the building to the governor's office, could have rung with a last-minute reprieve for Mata. But it didn't, and on August 22, 1996, he died by lethal injection.

One in five prisoners listed family photographs as their most prized death row possession. One in six listed holy books. Others cited televisions, typewriters, radios, crafts and art supplies, jewelry and legal materials.

Some executed inmates end up in the rough quiet of the prison cemetery, where lizards slither across the surface to dart down burrows near sandy graves.

Richard Rossi, a condemned inmate convicted of killing a Scottsdale man in a 1983 robbery, calls the pauper's cemetery "Potter's Hill" in a poem he wrote on Christmas Eve 1994:

There are no plaques to tell who is in eternal slumber
just a very small marker with a cold lonely number.

Life's what you make it

MAXIMUM SECURITY UNIT, TUCKER, ARK.—Eugene Wallace Perry, a 53-year-old beanpole with bad teeth and a long black ponytail, made something of himself on death row.

In 1988, the onetime building contractor said, he started painting in his 7-by-9-foot death row cell and startled himself with his ability.

"I realized I was and always had been a master artist," he said. ". . . My entire life is dedicated to my artwork, and my life is very meaningful." During an interview, he brought with him a large realistic portrait of an eagle, a symbol of his lost freedom.

AN ARTIST'S SPIRIT: Eugene Wallace Perry, a onetime building contractor, started painting in 1988 in his death row cell and startled himself with his ability. "I realized I was and always had been a master artist," he said.

On Arkansas's death row for 16 years, Perry was convicted in 1981 of killing 50-year-old Kenneth Staton and his 24-year-old daughter, Suzanne Staton Ware, in a Van Buren jewelry store robbery. He insisted that he was innocent.

In 1986, his death sentence was set aside and prosecutors offered him a plea bargain for life without parole. He turned them down and was resentenced to death row. Two years later, another man confessed to the killing for which Perry was convicted. Perry spoke optimistically about being released.

While waiting on the court to rule on his case, he continued to paint—and find meaning in an otherwise dreary existence.

"A painter doesn't reach his stride for 20 or 30 or 40 years," he said in a deep southern accent. "I've found death row to be just like life anywhere. It's what you make of it."

Courts subsequently concluded that the man who confessed to Perry's crime was lying. And Perry, his appeal exhausted, was pronounced dead from a lethal injection at 9:12 P.M. August 6, 1997.

For his final statement, Perry reasserted his innocence and chanted a phrase later translated as "Oh, the jewel has left the lotus."

Already dead

John Gerish, sentenced to die in Ohio, refused to participate in the death row survey, scrawling a cryptic message on a letter he returned to the *Morning News:*

"Leave me alone," he wrote in uneasy block letters, "I died May 2, 1991."

A look at his records revealed that on that date he murdered his aging mother and a woman who had tried to help her.

Shared fate bonds women on Texas' death row

GATESVILLE, TEXAS, DECEMBER 14, 1997—Hundreds of hours of aimless walking have beaten ruts in the caliche outside the single-story Mountain View building that is Texas's death row for women.

Daily exercise along the narrow dog run between the razor-wire fence and the steel-fortified brick building has worn circular paths where grass doesn't grow. Barely more than a year ago, Darlie Lynn Routier would have had little in common with the six women inside the padlocked gate. She was a housewife and mother. She drove a Jaguar and lived in an elegant, brick two-story in suburban Dallas. She favored capital punishment.

AMONG A HANDFUL: Darlie Routier became the seventh woman on Texas's death row, after two of her three sons were fatally stabbed. She says she was afraid that she would be locked up "with people that had actually committed heinous crimes."

Ten months ago she became the seventh woman on Texas's death row, after two of her three sons were stabbed to death.

"I didn't really understand the way our system worked," said Ms. Routier, 27. "We're raised to believe in the system."

Maintaining her innocence, Ms. Routier said she had been frightened that she would be locked up "with people that had actually committed heinous crimes."

"These women have made me see a different side of all that," Ms. Routier said, during a recent interview at the Central Texas prison. "They've proven that they're not a continuing threat to society. It's not what everybody thinks it is."

Ms. Routier said two of the women held at Mountain View the longest—Pam Perillo and Karla Faye Tucker—were particularly supportive when she arrived here at the onetime youth reformatory. "Let me tell you, it's hard, because you live with these women 24–7, 24 hours a day, seven days a week," she said. "You come from different families, different backgrounds, different ways of doing things. But I've never seen anything that made me feel threatened. It's just not there."

When word filtered through the prison last month that Tucker had been given an execution date in late January, it put a pall over Mountain View.

There are 48 women on death rows in 16 states. But only two have been executed in modern times: Velma Barfield, on November 2, 1984, in North Carolina; and Elizabeth Ann Duncan, on August 8, 1962, in California.

No woman has been executed in Texas since 1863, when Chipita Rodriguez was hanged from a mesquite tree near Sinton for allegedly killing a horse trader.

Victor L. Streib, a law professor at Ohio Northern University and an expert in women on death row, said that may soon change. "The actual execution of another woman in the United States seems likely to occur in the next year or two," he said. Some of the Texas women have had execution dates over the years. One year, said Mountain View warden Pamela Baggett, a woman was scheduled to be executed on Mother's Day. But none has come close enough to be transported to Huntsville, where the death sentence is carried out.

Tucker, who turned 38 last month, was convicted in 1984 in Houston of killing two people with a pickax. In almost 14 years on death row, Tucker, an erstwhile drug addict now a born-again Christian, has been a favorite of both inmates and staff.

"When they get a execution date, reality sets in, not only with the one involved, but with the others," Baggett said.

Between them, the seven women in Texas have been accused of killing 13 people.

Betty Lou Beets, of Gun Barrel City, was convicted of killing two husbands; Frances Elaine Newton, a Houston woman, killed her husband and two children. Both women killed for insurance money. Tucker, Perillo and Erica Sheppard were sentenced to death in robberies; Cathy Lynn Henderson for abducting and killing a 3-month-old Austin boy. Routier, convicted in the death of one of two sons fatally stabbed in their Rowlett home, is perhaps the only woman condemned on circumstantial evidence and whose motive is unclear.

At 60, Beets is the oldest. The youngest is Sheppard, 24. Five are white; two are black.

In general, life in prison is decidedly different for women, according to Baggett, a career penal officer previously assigned to men's prisons.

"At Mountain View the fact that they just won't hush is the biggest problem we have," Baggett said. "We baby them in female facilities. Our death row inmates are definitely spoiled."

Inside the bright white individual cells, afghans and fluffy pillows cover the mattresses on the bunks, and artwork and pictures of children and relatives line the steel walls. During an early afternoon visit last year, Beets lay idly on her bunk staring at the ceiling. In the adjoining day room, separated from the cells by heavy mesh wire, Tucker and Sheppard ate sandwiches and potato chips at a table. Tucker wore colored slippers, which she crochets as a hobby.

The room is the size of a large den, with shelves of paperback books, a pair of wooden benches at right angles, a television, refrigerator and microwave.

Through another heavy mesh screen is a cavernous room filled with dolls, the prison industry for condemned women. They paint the faces on the cloth dolls, which the prison sells for $25.

Baggett says the dolls' facial expressions reflect the moods of the women as they painted them. "The ones for my children are all smiling and happy," the warden says.

Baggett doesn't mention women by name when she discusses case histories, but one of them, she said, has a 15-year-old son who was adopted by her attorney.

"He was pulled out of the culture and rescued," Baggett said. While his classmates are unaware of his background, the warden said, he regularly visits his mother.

Another inmate has three young children who are being reared by their grandmother.

Whether an inmate is a teenage runaway like Perillo or an upper-middle class wife and mother like Routier, tight quarters and sharing the same legal fate apparently erodes class barriers on death row. "I haven't judged them for the crimes that they have committed," Routier said. "I think in the beginning I did. . . . The people that I know in here are not the people that committed those crimes a long time ago."

CHAPTER 14

• • •

Inside Story

Condemned prisoner at San Quentin says the key to understanding life on California's death row is the types of men who live there

By Michael Wayne Hunter, Inmate C83600

*S*AN QUENTIN, CALIF., OCTOBER 19, 1997—A considerable amount of mail flows into my cell from people out there in the world asking what it's really like living day to day on San Quentin's death row. I'm always tempted to quip that it's a hell of a lot better than dying here. But then I really don't know if that's true—yet.

I answer every letter even if the writer is rabidly pro–death penalty. It's easy for me to understand the attraction to the concept of killing convicted murderers. In the abstract, the death penalty has an elegant Newtonian symmetry—for every action, there's an equal and opposite reaction—that easily harmonizes with an Old Testament overtone—an eye for an eye. It strikes a reassuring resonance with most citizens.

Editor's note: Michael Wayne Hunter, the abused child of an alcoholic father, shot and killed his father and stepmother in 1981 in Pacifica, Calif. Hunter has written numerous articles about death row for an assortment of publications. At the time this article was written for the *Morning News*, Hunter had spent 13 years on death row and the appeal of his sentence was pending.

Many of them believe California's death row simply consists of men in cells lined up in a neat row, each awaiting his turn to march into the gas chamber, inhale and fail to metabolize cyanide gas. The day-to-day barred existence really can't be appreciated or understood until one is introduced to the sort of men sitting in the cells.

Essentially, there are three different types of prisoners lurching around death row: career criminals, non–career criminals and serial murderers.

The largest category by far is the career criminal. From the moment one of these gangsters hits death row, he already knows all the rules, including the unwritten ones, the ones that keep you alive in the barred world. Immediately recognizing each other, these tattooed, muscular, cigarette-smoking, aggressively in-your-face men band together and compete with the guards for control of the prison. The only reason the guards have any chance at all is their rifles and the fact that they don't hesitate to use them.

Career criminals are the same guys who scared the hell out of everybody in high school. Hard-core unemployable, once introduced to the judicial system, career criminals generally spend only a couple days here and there out in the world in between increasingly longer stretches behind bars. It's called doing life on the installment plan, and they inevitably die before they make their final payment.

I always take it for granted that at least a couple of men on death row are here for crimes they didn't commit. Let's say that the state of California gets it right 98 percent of the time (seems like an impossibly high success rate for government bureaucrats), a 2 percent failure rate would imply about eight prisoners are on death row here for murders they didn't commit, and career criminals are probably seven of the eight.

If the cops don't catch someone dead-bang at the scene of the crime, they don't investigate like Lieutenant Columbo. Generally investigation means they look around for someone who looks good to hang the murder charge on. The detectives pull out the files of career criminals in the area, handcuff them and defy them to prove themselves innocent. If the career criminal doesn't have a rock-solid alibi, it's fairly easy for prosecutors to convince 12 solid citizens sitting in a jury box he's probably involved in the crime somehow.

Once I read a California Supreme Court decision affirming the death sentence for a friend of mine, Jay Kaurish. Catching up with him in the exercise yard, I said, "Can't believe they found you guilty. The cops arrested you for the girl's murder because you knew her mother. But there weren't any eyewitnesses or credible physical evidence."

"Didn't kill her," my friend answered with a shrug, and took another puff on his ever-present cancer stick, "but I've done so much the po-leece don't know nothing about, it don't matter much to me. If you live in the edge, robbing and stealing for a living, you shouldn't go 'round whining when the cops invent some fairy tale and push you off the edge into prison."

Kind of liked Jay's attitude about the whole thing, but it doesn't matter much anymore. The cigarettes finally caught up with him, and he died of a heart attack a few years ago.

With a few exceptions, career criminals don't have much of a clue about the most fundamental aspects of the unbarred world. Once I listened to two career criminals argue, almost come to blows, over what time a football game came on television. They'd both seen a commercial advertising the game for 1 P.M. eastern time and were trying to figure out what time that would be at San Quentin.

Attempting to head off violence, I said, "Ten A.M."

"How's 'zat?" they both wanted to know.

"Well, uh," I started to answer while beginning to suspect that opening my mouth had been a big mistake, "the East Coast is about 3,000 miles away. . . ."

"What does 3,000 miles have to do with it?" one of the gangsters demanded. "Me and my buds rode our Harleys to Seattle. That's at least a thousand miles, and it was the same time there as here."

"Seattle's north of us," I tried to explain. "Time zones go from east to west."

"Why's 'zat?"

Absolutely certain I should've kept my mouth shut, I tried again. "You see, the sun rises in the east, and . . . ."

"Never b'lieve all dat . . . 'bout duh sun bein' millions of miles away," one of them snarled at me while the other nodded his head. "Hell, you can jus' look up and see it in duh sky. No one can see a million miles, can't be more than a hundred, maybe two hundred miles away at duh most."

Shaking my head, I said, "Trust me, 10 A.M.," and walked away.

It always amuses me when I see a television reporter stating that some condemned prisoner has filed a petition with the courts asserting his rights have been denied under the United States Constitution.

The prisoner didn't write the petition and probably didn't read it. The only thing he might have asserted was directed at his attorney and he probably said, "Sounds cool, hope we git action on that there petition. Now that's all done, can yah send me some money?"

Frequently, I hear career criminals say, "I got a real good attorney, he or she sends me money to buy smokes."

The first time I heard those words, I wondered, What does cigarette money have to do with whether they're a good attorney or not? Then I realized that career criminals never expected to have any sort of future, so they don't dwell too much on dying in the gas chamber. Let's light up some cancer sticks, is the attitude, and deal with the future when/if it bangs into our bodies.

The reason the attorneys send the money is easy to understand. If they know the prisoner's appeal is going nowhere, they can't do anything for their client in the courts so they simply buy him things that'll keep the condemned man happy until it's time for him to take those last steps into the gas chamber.

It's rumored that the death penalty is supposed to act as a deterrent to potential murderers. Whatever laws are on the books, career criminals prey on society—what else are they equipped to do? Deterrence is an abstract concept which these wild men understand and embrace just as strongly as they do the concept of time zones.

Although smaller in number than the career criminals, there's a sizable collection of prisoners on death row who were never in trouble until their arrest for murder. Since I'm one of them, it's difficult for me to write objectively about these non–career criminals, men who played by the rules, but for some reason real or imagined their lives didn't go the way they'd expected.

Maybe they lost their jobs or didn't get a promotion. Maybe their wives left or the women they wanted as wives said no. Maybe a member of their families died. It could simply be that their lives didn't measure up to the American success myth depicted on television in beer commercials sponsoring football games. They grew older, and the wonderful house, large automobile, beautiful wife and perfect life weren't on the horizon.

Whatever the reason, they became deeply clinically depressed and looked around their largely middle-class world and tried to find someone to pin their personal misery upon. Ultimately, if they fixed the blame on themselves, they committed suicide, but if they found someone else to blame, they committed homicide.

Often found at murder scenes simply waiting for the police,

non–career criminals almost from the moment the handcuffs are clamped onto their wrists try to justify their actions and let everyone know they led productive lives before prison and shouldn't be treated like common criminals.

Career criminals despise non–career criminals and their attempts to explain away homicide. "Never explain, never complain" is an integral part of the career criminal code, and they bully, rob and occasionally sell the law-and-order virgins to jailhouse rapists for a couple packs of smokes.

Living in a strange new world they find largely incomprehensible, many non–career criminals complete their break with reality and end up in the jail ward of the hospital pumped full of psychiatric medication.

On San Quentin's death row, many of the non–career criminals are so fearful of the other condemned men, they stay in their cells and watch television (condemned prisoners are allowed to purchase a radio and television). The only time these men are ever seen is in the visiting room, easy to spot: Their skin has turned gray from lack of exposure to the sun.

Career criminals don't appear to dwell on their victims. In contrast, most non–career criminals are still furious years after their victims are dead and buried.

"Dig him up and kill him a thousand times," was a comment I heard from a non–career criminal who had killed more than a decade ago.

Another non–career criminal, a bright, articulate man who had worked as an engineer, went to work armed to the teeth and shot and killed several people when a female coworker repeatedly turned him down for a date. Strangely, he wounded but didn't kill her.

"Didn't want her to die," he told me. "Wanted her to live with what she'd done."

"What did she do?" I said, curious to discover what could set off such violence in an otherwise easygoing man.

"You'd have to know her, she's . . ." he paused, and his face turned into a mask of fury, the first time I'd ever glimpsed this emotion in him. "She's a bad person, that's all."

"If she's such a bad person, why'd you keep asking her for a date?"

"You just don't understand," he answered.

I hear those words often from non–career criminals. They may be generally quite amiable but have an irrational murderous rage lurking inside them when it comes to their victims. Although they can never articulate a rational explanation why the person they killed needed killing, they have an inexplicable, but absolute, confidence in the correctness of their actions. These men honestly feel if they were given an opportunity to explain their motivations to a national television audience, everyone in the country would immediately clamor for their release from prison, and they'd receive a ticker-tape parade down New York's Fifth Avenue.

Although they have a lot of trouble accepting that they're convicted felons, if pressed, most non–career criminals will admit they should do some time behind bars. When questioned about how much time, not surprisingly, most peg the appropriate time at about one year less than the amount of time they've already spent in prison.

Generally, non–career criminals don't demand anything material from their attorneys. What they want is for the attorney to buy into the theory that their murder was an aberration which only occurred due to a unique set of circumstances which could never, ever be repeated.

I'm not sure how benign most of these men would be if released from prison. Anyone so angry after 10 years behind bars—he'd kill a thousand times again and again and again—might still be a wee bit dangerous.

Then there are a few non–career criminals who trudge around with a haunted air about them.

"Yeah, he was a poor excuse for a human being, and getting mad at a really lousy person's OK," one of them told me. "You can yell at them, stomp around, but you can't give in to the killing rage. The killing rage doesn't come from the outside, it comes from the ugliness deep inside your soul. Murder has to do with what's inside you, not the sad sack you're killing."

"Why don't these other guys see that?" I gestured at the condemned men surrounding us.

"It's hard," he said slowly, painfully, "real hard to admit to yourself that you stole away a life and ruined your own for no good reason. Makes you a monster or a fool."

"You are . . ." My mocking smile took the edge off my query.

"A moron," he answered with a dark, self-loathing grin. "When I still blamed that guy for everything, I was so full of hate there wasn't room for anything else inside me."

"It's better now?"

"Yeah." But then he shrugged his shoulders, adding, "The man's dead—how I feel about it now really doesn't matter, it's just too damn late." Head down, eyes pointed toward the ground, he shuffled away.

The third and by far the smallest group on death row, although it receives almost all the public attention, is made up of serial murderers. Difficult for the police to catch because they don't have any direct connection to their victims, serial murderers lurk in the shadows, pick out victims, stalk, snatch and kill in order to satisfy some macabre inner need. Many serial murderers deliberately leave corpses in places designed to engender the most public attention and horror. After a couple of dead bodies are found, the media descend like vultures picking over carrion and lend the unknown killer a nickname: the Freeway Killer, the Nightstalker, the Hillside Strangler.

The serial murderers I've met are emotionally self-contained. They peer at you with the same lack of humanity, the same lack of anger as a crocodile. Given an opportunity, they're going to live out their fantasies and kill you. But it's not personal; hunting humans is just what they do to fulfill themselves.

Serial murderers imagine themselves enlightened renaissance men who're misunderstood by a world still stuck in the dark ages. No one has ever been born or will ever be born who's as intelligent as these men think they are, and they often feel great frustration at the ignorant masses who fail to perceive their greatness.

It's difficult to comprehend how they came to have such a high opinion of themselves. But then it's hard to conceive of any other mind-set from someone who thinks it's OK to snatch, torture and kill someone simply because that's what gives them pleasure.

For some unfathomable reason, a segment of the population is fascinated by serial murderers. These groupies write to serial murderers, and their intense interest heightens serial murderers' sense of self-importance. Several serial murderers at San Quentin even sell memorabilia through Rick Staton, a Louisiana funeral director who publishes and circulates *Grindhouse Graphics,* a catalog advertising wares sent to him by serial murderers throughout the United States.

Serial murderers hawk their artwork and writings, which seems fairly legitimate to me, but some serial murderers also sell autographed trial transcripts containing testimony describing the gruesome details of their murders. One serial murderer even autographed and advertised for sale the autopsy reports of his victims. These soulless cretins are despised by the rest of the condemned men.

Most serial murderers don't get along very well with the attorneys (or anyone else) handling their appeals, and they spend a great deal of time at the law library attempting to write their own appeals. This is much like a passenger in an airliner on an angling path into the ground attempting to wrest the controls from the pilot. Of course, an airline pilot would attempt to fight off the passenger and keep control of the plane because his body's also on the line. But attorneys can afford to simply shrug, sit back and let serial murderers crash-land inside the gas chamber.

The death penalty doesn't appear to even slightly deter serial murderers. Government-sanctioned executions actually seem to make them feel their impulse to kill is normal and acceptable. In their twisted brand of logic, they believe that their only problem is with the masses who have stupidly failed to recognize that they have been put on earth to pick out who needs killing.

There's a great deal of tension and even hatred between the three groups of condemned men. Each group feels that it's far superior to the other two groups. Of course, most of society views all of us with emotions ranging from distaste to loathing, but still we continue to draw pejorative distinctions—how human of us.

From the lips of individuals in all three groups of condemned prisoners, I hear a lot of talk about injustice in The System. Seems to me if justice in The System is about the police, prosecutors, judges and guards following all the neat little rules derived from the Constitution and written down in law books lined up in bookshelves; well, yeah, The System isn't even close to the lessons taught in my high school civics class. But if justice in The System is about putting dangerous people behind bars, looking around my death row world, it appears that The System gets it right most of the time.

No matter which category of condemned prisoner, execution dates are something every man on death row potentially has in common. After I'd been on death row for about five years, I was walking into my cell block from the exercise yard, and a sergeant pulled me over. He escorted me to the cell block lieutenant's office, and I was planted in a chair. On the other side of the desk, a woman from the warden's office had a death warrant with my name on it. I was scheduled to die in about eight weeks.

After we updated my next-of-kin notification form, she wrote down the title of my personal mythology, so the correct brand of chaplain would be summoned to ease my transition into the netherworld. Finally, I had the choice of either signing for my copy of the death warrant or staff members would be summoned to witness that I had received a copy.

Shrugging, I decided not to be a jerk. Locked into a cage, unhandcuffed, a pen was thrust into my hands, and I signed. Rechained, I was taken to my cell, ordered to pack my belongings, and the guards moved me down to a filthy death-watch cell on the first tier. With dirty walls tightly surrounding me, I almost said the hell with it and didn't clean the cell.

After all, I thought with some resignation, one way or the other I won't be inside this cell very long. But after a few heartbeats, I piled my boxes on the steel bunk, pulled out a rag and started scrubbing. Oddly enough, once the cell was clean, I felt a lot better about everything.

Every hour while in the death-watch cell, a guard would come by, carefully note what I was doing and then steal away. It was really strange, and I quickly learned to schedule my toilet needs around the hourly visits.

"Have you had a chance to phone your attorney?" a guard asked me from my cell bars.

I shook my head no.

Unlocking my tray-slot, he pushed a phone mounted on a cart in front of my cell. Reaching out, I dialed my attorney's number, then pulled the receiver into the cell, sat on my bunk and listened to it ring. When my attorney answered and accepted my collect call, she told me she'd received a copy of the death warrant and was coming to see me.

"Don't come here," I protested. "You can't get the order stopping my execution at San Quentin. Go see a judge and get an order."

Three men-in-suits materialized at my cell bars. "Mr. Hunter," one of them called to me, "you're going to die in a few weeks. How do you feel about that?"

Lasering hostile eyes toward them, I knew what this was all about. California isn't allowed to execute anyone who's pregnant or insane. Apparently, the warden took it for granted that I wasn't pregnant and sent these men to determine if I was insane. Grimly thinking about how they judged a friend as sane before he hanged himself, I pulled on my headphones, turned in an alternative rock station, pumped up the volume and closed my eyes. When I opened them, the suits were gone.

I received the order stopping my execution about 30 days before I was scheduled to die. But sometimes, late at night, I awaken and think about my own execution, imagine sitting in the gas chamber holding cell waiting for the execution team to escort me into the green chamber, strap my body into a chair, watch cyanide fumes rise from the acid, feel my body frantically attempt to metabolize the gas . . . fail . . . die. I try to tell myself that everyone dies some-time. But I wonder how well that impeccable logic will carry me through.

Death row is about all the things I've described, but most of all it's about isolation. We're walled away from the world, removed from the pain and anger of a public that feels less and less safe in its communities.

One day, I turned on my television, and one of the living victims appeared. A woman spoke of her strong emotions regarding my friend, Bobby Harris, who had killed her brother. In a few days, she would be at San Quentin to view Bobby's execution.

As she spoke about her anger, her frustration with The System which had slowly toiled for 15 years in its quest to kill Bobby, I shook my head and, perhaps for the first time, understood. The intellectual arguments about condemned prisoners being released because the appeals process had unearthed their innocence would not move this woman.

She didn't know and didn't care about those cases; she simply knew that her brother was dead and Bobby was responsible. She'd spent 15 years of her life on the long road to a seat at the execution chamber's window. She wanted the trip to end with justice for her brother, which to her meant the death of Bobby.

After more than a decade of living among condemned men, it's clear to me that the notion that the death penalty provides deter-rence to murder is a myth. Therefore, the only useful purpose I can imagine for executions is to provide a sense of justice and emo-tional closure for the living victims. Watching this woman, I wondered if the execution would provide the solace she'd be seek-ing at the viewing windows of San Quentin's gas chamber. Perhaps it did.

In another case, a condemned man, Dave Mason, waived his federal appeals and asked to be executed. Once his execution date was set, he wrote to the daughter of a woman he'd killed.

When interviewed on television, the daughter said that she wanted Dave put in a place where he could never hurt anyone again but she didn't want him killed.

"Why not?" the reporter asked. "Does it have anything to do with the letter?"

She said, "He wrote: 'Sorry, I killed your mother.'" Tears slowly spilled from her eyes as she looked down and began to shake. Raising her head, she added, "Is that supposed to make me feel better? My mother's still gone."

"Then why don't you want him executed?"

"My mother's dead," she said quietly, "and what they do to him won't bring her back, so it really doesn't matter."

CHAPTER 15

• • •

Turning the Tables

Living with death: Ex-prosecutor uses memory of slain coworker to help toughen parole laws

PUNTA GORDA, FLA., DECEMBER 1997—Kathleen Finnegan crawled and stumbled from Alligator Creek, but she wasn't out of the woods. She was breathless and light-headed as she eyed the fork in the highway, the first possibility of safety.

Glancing left, she studied the tidy frame house silhouetted by an outdoor light against the coal tar night. Where was he? Maybe behind her, still in the swamp? Or ahead, waiting for her to come into the light? She remembered five shots; there could be another. The blood on her clothes and arms was scaring her. It was everywhere. "OK, just don't look down anymore. Just don't look down anymore."

Unless her memory was failing, there was a motel a few hundred yards down the right fork. The lighted house could be empty; a motel had to have people. Norm was back at the creek. She thought he had squeezed her hand before she bolted into the swamp. Now she wasn't sure.

Her shoes were long gone, lost in a black hole that had buried her up to her thighs and almost consumed her. She forced herself into a broken run toward the motel. The shadowy vulnerability of the motel parking lot terrified her. She hobbled to the bushes outside the lobby and crouched painfully in a bed of ornamental cactus long enough to convince herself the gunman wasn't there.

Once convinced, she stumbled and fell into the lobby, pleading for someone to rescue Norman Langston at the creek.

Fifty yards west, on the path not taken, Samuel Andrew Pettit was behind the tidy house, using the glow of the outdoor light to put his pistol back together.

What he wanted was another shot at Kathleen Finnegan.

Finnegan, a felony prosecutor in the Charlotte County district attorney's office, survived the fiery blasts that lighted up Alligator Creek that August night in 1988. Her colleague Norman Langston didn't. Shot twice in the head when he threw his body over Finnegan's in a spray of gunfire, he lived on life support for two days before his parents told doctors to disconnect him.

But fueled by his memory, Finnegan set about to reform Florida's turnstile parole laws. A self-described "bleeding-heart liberal," she turned the Sunshine State into one of the toughest places in the nation to do time. And in the process, she made Sammy Pettit a pariah among Florida cons.

A demented dance

From the placid coastal town of Punta Gorda on the lower Gulf Coast, it's halfway across the state to the Union Correctional Institution in Raiford, a flat, isolated prison town in the upper thigh of the Florida dogleg.

Knowing two reporters were about to visit Pettit there on Florida's death row, Finnegan made a pointed request:

"Would you ask him a question for me?" she said. "Ask him how it makes him feel to know that I take pleasure every day that he's in constant pain."

Long before he abducted Langston and Finnegan from a restaurant parking lot, doctors had diagnosed Pettit with Huntington's chorea, a degenerative and progressively painful nerve disease. The disease is hereditary; Pettit's cousin, brother and father had it. When his father couldn't stand the pain anymore, he committed suicide.

A death row guard rolled Pettit in a wheelchair, which the guard called "The Cadillac," into the cramped interview room at Union, and the inmate twitched and jerked as he finally pushed and pulled himself into a nearby straight-back chair.

His hair is dark and choirboy short. He is not the Charlie Manson look-alike who appeared in his book-in mug two days after killing Langston and wounding Finnegan.

He wore the standard-issue death row orange V-neck pullover and blue pants with an orange stripe down the sides. Tattoos that read L-O-V-E and H-A-T-E covered the top knuckles of his fingers. A tattoo across the back of his right hand said LOONY. It was one of his two aliases, according to his rap sheet; the other was Wild One.

When he was barely into his chair, Pettit's mouth contorted as he sucked in air, momentarily trapped it, then used it to propel his words.

"I want to die," he gasped.

He speaks in salivary bursts through a jack-o'-lantern mouth; he has as many blanks as teeth, and his words are distorted and frequently incomprehensible.

Huntington's chorea is a progressive disease that destroys nerve cells, and it owns Pettit's body. Chorea is a Greek word for dance, and his body is an incessant jig of involuntary jerking, twitching and snorting.

Experts say that Huntington's chorea produces personality changes that range from moodiness to paranoia and dementia. But doctors who examined Pettit in 1989, when he pleaded guilty to murdering Langston, said the disease had not progressed to the point that he was mentally incompetent.

The deterioration over the last eight years has been dramatic. His is the first cell on death row, a place where guards can watch him more easily. Pettit said he gets medication twice daily.

"Sometimes it helps a little," he said. "I can't sleep at night. I toss and turn all night. I have to take medication to sleep."

But he doesn't want to be moved to a medical cell.

"I don't want to be moved because I can go outside here," he said. "I can still walk."

He described going to the yard for 2½ hours a day, wearing a football helmet and knee pads to keep from hurting himself. He acknowledged that the violent shaking and jerking made it almost impossible to feed himself.

It was during a previous sentence at Union, according to Pettit, that his Huntington's chorea was diagnosed.

"I started shaking a lot and lost a lot of weight," he said. "And I fell down. They took blood and did a CAT scan and found it."

He was released on June 13, 1988; two months later, on August 17, he abducted and shot Langston and Finnegan.

"I couldn't commit suicide," Pettit said. "See, my dad committed suicide. . . . I was going to kill them. I thought the cops would kill me, but they didn't."

Pettit was arrested two days after the shootings as he slept in a patch of sea oats on the beach near Naples, Fla. The murder weapon was in his jacket pocket along with 90 shells.

He pleaded guilty to the capital offense, he said, because he wanted to die rather than live with Huntington's. And though the court appointed him two appeals attorneys, Pettit stammered, "Told 'em don't want no appeal."

Except for the occasional, involuntary grunt, he's quiet as he contemplates Kathleen Finnegan's wrath.

"I should have killed her," he said, jerking violently.

He's asked about the tattoo of the devil on his biceps.

"I don't believe in God," he said.

He suffers from a terminal disease, and he faces the electric chair. What will happen when he dies?

"Gonna come back as an animal," Pettit said. "A bulldog."

A bulldog? His mouth widens into a checkered grin. "So I can kill that girl. . . . That's the thing that terrorizes."

The survivor

Random violence knows no bounds. Kathleen Finnegan and Norman Langston were state's prosecutors who had been celebrating a success in the criminal justice system the night Sammy Pettit abducted and shot them.

Finnegan had spent eight months pursuing an old, unsolved and particularly brutal murder case; she was on the brink of winning an indictment against a pair of men who were accused of murdering a man and sending one of his ears to his widow.

"It I was my first presentation to a grand jury and I kind of patted myself on the back for that one, because I really did a good job that day," Finnegan said. "I left there feeling like it was probably one of my best." Langston, a 27-year-old graduate of Purdue and Nova University Law and the newest prosecutor in the Charlotte County district attorney's office, joined Finnegan, two other members of the staff and two detectives for drinks at the local Howard Johnson's restaurant.

"We were getting these two cold-blooded killers who were just menaces to our society—we had them off the streets already—but this was going to take care of getting a conviction," she said.

In the parking lot outside, Pettit, a career thug only two months into an early-out parole, said he had already determined that someone would die. His cousin had negotiated with a 16-year-old for a revolver, which he turned over to Pettit to use in the robberies already planned. The pistol was a shoddy throwaway that misfired as often as it worked. Pettit had spent the day at the trash dump in his front yard, firing it into the rubbish, scattering the milling pigs.

Around 10 P.M., when the prosecutors and detectives were about to move their party to Finnegan's house, Pettit had been in the parking lot two hours, stalking potential victims. He would later say he planned all along to leave no witnesses.

Langston had offered to drive Finnegan, who told the others to give them a 15-minute head start so she could get dirty dishes out of the sink and walk her dog.

"Norm went to open the car door for me," she said. "That's when Pettit approached with the gun. He stuck it in my side and said, 'Get in the car.'"

Langston was at the driver's side, next to a parked van.

"He could have darted behind that van, but he didn't," Finnegan said. Pettit pointed with the gun, motioning Mr. Langston beneath the wheel and Finnegan into the front seat.

"I even said things like, 'Look, I'm never going to fit. We can't make it. I'm a big girl.'"

Finally, Pettit shoved her onto the console, which she straddled, while he climbed in beside her, resting the barrel of the pistol on her arm. Periodically, he pointed the direction, always with the pistol.

Pettit robbed them of their money and jewelry as Langston drove.

"I gave him my watch and earrings," Finnegan said. "I didn't have much money, $12 or $22. It was a very little amount. We were prosecutors. You don't get paid too well."

She noticed at some point that Langston must have palmed his Purdue class ring because he hadn't given it to Pettit. Earlier in the night, the young prosecutor had passed the diamond ring around the table; it was clear he was proud of it.

"I thought, 'Cool, he kept it.'" As they drove, Finnegan watched the comfort of familiar places flash by in the window: the courthouse where she'd made her presentation that day to the grand jury, the building that housed the prosecutors' offices and the turnoff to the Sheriff's Department.

They ended up at Alligator Creek Dam, a nearby hooky hole and lovers' retreat. The small park there is surrounded by 60-foot pines and was so dark that Finnegan couldn't see the back of her hand.

Pettit, Finnegan said, emerged from the passenger's side and, as he did, the dome light automatically came on.

Samuel Pettit

"He got really angry," she said. "'I told you, don't turn on the lights.'

"As I'm starting to slide over, thinking, "Phew, God, this is finally over,' just at that moment, Norm said, 'Look out!' Then it just started.

"He just stood in the doorjamb, and he just stood right there and just opened fire."

Langston tried to shield Finnegan, draping his upper body over hers in the seat, but Finnegan still could see five bolts of light against the darkness. "But then after the flames stopped coming out," she said, "he kept pulling the trigger. Click, click, and it was like he was getting mad. It was getting faster and faster."

Then there was quiet. For how long, she wasn't sure. Nor was she sure where Pettit had gone. She squeezed her friend's hand, thought she felt him grip hers, then ran bloody into the night for help.

Not until after she had undergone surgery to repair nerve damage in her arm did Finnegan learn her friend had died. Her parents were in the room when Langston's came in.

Finnegan's father, she said, is a tough, stoic Irish Catholic not given to emotion. That changed when he saw the Langstons. "Because of your son," he cried, "my daughter lived."

A victim's legacy

Finnegan was stunned when she pulled Pettit's criminal file from the district clerk's office. His recidivist record was reminiscent of the kind that had transformed her three years earlier from "social worker" public defender to prosecutor.

"You could look up 'bleeding-heart liberal' in the dictionary, and my picture would have been there in 1977," Finnegan said. "I just believed that people are basically good and that given a chance, maybe it would bring that out in people.

"But what I found out was that some people, there's no good there. You can't bring out something that isn't there."

Pettit's file was a case in point: His first arrest was at age 12. He had been convicted 14 times by age 26, each time for a more serious crime.

The file documented the saga of a hardened criminal who had fallen softly through the cracks of the system back into society's lap.

Pettit, according to his file, had last been convicted in April 1986, this time of attacking two Punta Gorda police officers. At the time, he had a 12-inch knife in his pocket.

REMEMBERING A COLLEAGUE: Kathleen Finnegan frequently lays flowers at the crime scene, near Port Charlotte, Fla., where she and a fellow prosecutor were shot by Samuel Pettit, now on death row.

And though his record more than qualified him for Florida's habitual criminal statute—and a corresponding life sentence—he had been sentenced to six years at Union. Less than a year later, a judge reduced his sentence to 3½ years. And notwithstanding six disciplinary actions in prison—for assaults and a prohibited weapon—he was released in June 1988 on parole, something called "provisional release credit."

"They have so many names for it, when people got tired of it being called one thing, they would bop back and call it something else," Finnegan said. "You know, creative name changing."

In the aftermath of the shootings, Finnegan said, she found herself taking her role as a prosecutor too personally.

"You have to care about victims as a prosecutor," she said, "but you can't get too personally involved, and I was finding myself doing that. I was getting somewhat vindictive with defendants. Rather than accepting I could get 10 years, I'd want 15.

"Suddenly I couldn't handle the murder cases. . . . Everything just changed. I couldn't look at the crime scene photos anymore."

She tried a private civil practice, but it wasn't a reprieve: "I found out about divorces and wills, and, oh my God, that was worse. . . .

"I was on that downward spiral. I was in deep depression. I was seeing a psychologist. I was taking antidepressants, angry at the world. My personality had changed."

Then she met Charlie Wells, the sheriff of nearby Manatee County.

He had recently been on one of his sojourns to the Florida Legislature to request more jail space to accommodate the longer sentences for which he lobbied.

"He said that while he was testifying, the legislators were busy talking to the guy next to them or writing notes or whatever," Finnegan said.

"After he testified one day, somebody from Mothers Against Drunk Driving got up and testified. . . . It was this little old lady in sneakers and socks, just a regular person. . . . All of a sudden, they were all listening because she was one of the voters, a real person instead of another politician."

The incident was the genesis of Stop Turning Out Prisoners, a grassroots movement organized by Sheriff Wells in Manatee County, that has spread through Florida like kudzu. In January 1993, Finnegan closed her law offices and became the executive director of STOP. Nearly five years later, she's still a full-time volunteer operating out of a nondescript storefront in Port Charlotte.

Initially, STOP targeted violent offenders about to be considered for parole, organized their victims and appeared at their hearings to argue against early releases. Finnegan and Sheriff Wells became familiar faces to Florida's elected officials, arguing for more prison beds and "truth in sentencing" legislation.

By the end of 1993, Florida had more than 20 STOP chapters. In April 1994, 17,000 new prison beds, the biggest increase in state history, were allocated.

But the organization's biggest coup came in 1995 when the STOP bill—perhaps the toughest sentencing law in America—was made law in Florida.

Bottom line, felony offenders must serve 85 percent of their sentences before becoming eligible for parole, and a life sentence genuinely means incarceration for the rest of an offender's life.

Even though the new, tougher laws don't apply to Pettit on death row, he's felt their impact.

"The inmates all get mad at me because they see it on TV," he said.

Finnegan terms her commitment to STOP a "double-edged sword."

"It's very helpful and therapeutic at times," she said, "but then it keeps me in this world of dealing with these people. There are days when I think about throwing it all in and saying forget it, I've had enough.

"Then we get a phone call from a victim who's crying about her son who was murdered. 'Can we please help keep his killer in jail?' And then suddenly I need to stay. . . .

"But I'm back now," she said. "And I think it's a better version. I've learned to have fun again and enjoy life again.

"And you have to realize that Norm didn't save my life so I'd be miserable. He thought it was worth saving.

"I think he'd be glad that I'm where I am."

Authors' Note

• • •

As this book goes to press in the early spring of 1999, 50 death row prisoners who shared details of their lives with us—in writing, over the telephone, or face to face—have been executed. Two more prisoners, Roberto Miranda of Nevada and Abe Munson of Oklahoma, saw their death sentences overturned. Though executioners most frequently used lethal injections, a few relied on the firing squad, the gas chamber or the electric chair. The names of the executed prisoners, the states that carried out their executions, and the dates of their deaths follow. Except where noted with an asterisk, the condemned were put to death by lethal injection.

—Dan Malone and Howard Swindle
March 14, 1999

1995

Kermit Smith Jr., North Carolina, January 24
Clifton Charles Russell Jr., Texas, January 31
Noble D. Mayes Jr., Texas, April 6
Richard Wayne Snell, Arkansas, April 19
Keith Zettlemoyer, Pennsylvania, May 2
Emmitt Foster, Missouri, May 3
Duncan Peder McKenzie, Montana, May 10
*Varnall Weeks, Alabama, May 12 (electrocution)
Ronald Keith Allridge, Texas, June 8
John Fearance Jr., Texas, June 20
Vernon Lamar Sattiewhite, Texas, August 15
Dennis Wayne Stockton, Virginia, September 27
Robert Sidebottom, Missouri, November 15

1996

Richard Townes Jr., Virginia, January 23
*John Albert Taylor, Utah, January 26 (firing squad)
Jeffrey Sloan, Missouri, February 21
Daren Lee Bolton, Arizona, June 19
Joseph J. Savino Jr., Virginia, July 17
Fred H. Kornahrens, South Carolina, July 19
Emmet Nave, Missouri, July 31
Thomas Battle, Missouri, August 7
Jusan William Frank Parker, Arkansas, August 8
*Larry Lonchar, Georgia, November 14 (electrocution)
Gregory Warren Beaver, Virginia, December 3

1997

*Billy Wayne Waldrop, Alabama, January 10 (electrocution)
Randy Greenawalt, Arizona, January 23
Eric Schneider, Missouri, January 29
Michael Carl George, Virginia, February 6
*Pedro Medina, Florida, March 25 (electrocution)
Kenneth Edward Gentry, April 16
Harry Charles Moore, Oregon, May 16
Larry Wayne White, Texas, May 22
Joseph Roger O'Dell III, Virginia, July 23
Robert West, Texas, July 29
Ralph Cencil Feltrop, Missouri, August 6
Eugene Wallace Perry, Arkansas, August 6
Donald E. Reese, Missouri, August 13
Andrew Six, Missouri, August 20
Johnny Cockrum, Texas, September 30
Dwight Dwayne Adanandus, Texas, October 1
Ricky Lee Green, Texas, October 8
Aaron Lee Fuller, Texas, November 6
Dawud Majid Mu'Min, Virginia, November 13

1998

Lloyd Wayne Hampton, Illinois, January 21
Terry Allen Langford, Montana, February 24
*Daniel Remeta, Florida, March 31 (electrocution)
Clifford Holt Boggess, Texas, June 11
Lance Chander, Virginia, August 20
Genaro Ruiz Camacho, Texas, August 26

1999

*Walter LaGrand, Arizona, March 3 (gas chamber)

Acknowledgments

. . .

A MERICA'S CONDEMNED: *Death Row Inmates in Their Own Words* is based on a series of 19 articles originally published in 1997 in *The Dallas Morning News.* Those stories were based on an unprecedented survey of death row prisoners, follow-up interviews (in person where possible and by phone where not) with more than four dozen condemned persons, and our own observations on death rows in more than a dozen states.

The stories in this book, with the exception of one chapter by a talented writer who happens also to be a condemned killer on California's death row, are ours. But the labor leading up to the actual writing was the hard work of a group of people perhaps as diverse as those whose lives and crimes we documented.

We and our colleagues at the *Morning News* alone are responsible for the selection and wording of the questions in the survey. But we were greatly influenced by suggestions and criticisms from a number of persons who have special insights into or views on death row. We express our appreciation to former Texas death row warden Bruce Thaler, forensic psychiatrist Dr. Jaye Crowder of the University of Texas Southwestern Medical School, Tarrant County District Attorney Tim Curry and felony division chief Alan Levy, the author and distinguished UCLA professor Dr. James Q. Wilson, veteran death row defense attorney Allan K. Butcher of Fort Worth, death row lay minister Maj. Kathy Cox of the Salvation Army, Dr. James Grigson, a frequent and controversial expert witness in death penalty cases, and John Byron Yarbrough, a former police officer who at one time was a death row inmate.

The questionnaires were put in the mail to inmates twice—first in December 1994, then a follow-up in February to those who didn't respond to the first mailing. The mailings were customized prison system by prison system. Mail room supervisor Maryann Grieser and her staff made sure we met the disparate requirements of both the U.S. Postal Service and death row mail rooms. We were assisted in the unglamorous weeklong chore of stuffing several thousand envelopes by Judy Stratton, Teri Geen, Vaniese Scott and Michael Stratton.

The questions eventually selected for the survey were polished and packaged by Patti Boesch, survey coordinator in the *Morning News*'s Research Department, and her supervisor, Barbara Quisenberry. Patti was responsible for the analysis of the survey, but also made sure that our interpretation of the results remained on target.

In addition to the information collected in the survey, Reference Editor Judy Sall and her staff amassed a mountain of background information on the inmates who returned surveys. If we succeeded in portraying the men and women on death row as three-dimensional human beings, it was because of the extraordinary digging by research librarians Julie Wilson, Darlean Spangenberger and Jeanette Prasifka. Jeanette also examined voluminous public records in various court-houses in Los Angeles County to help us document a story about four childhood buddies who wound up on death row together as adults.

Additionally, professors Jean Chance of the University of Florida and Charles Davis of Southern Methodist University, who per-formed professional internships at the *Morning News*, assisted us in an expansive review of all published federal death row appeals. Their work permitted us to analyze the disparate results of the appellate process within the various state and federal court systems.

The tens of thousands of pieces of paper we amassed—question-naires, letters, yellowed newspaper clippings, police reports, appel-late records—filled a four-drawer file cabinet, two bookcases and a dozen storage boxes. It would have been impossible to make sense of this universe of paper without the aid and ingenuity of assistant projects editor Shawn McIntosh. Shawn, now managing editor of *The Clarion-Ledger* (Jackson, Miss.), merged survey results with reams of documents into a database containing what we believe to be the most information ever collected on death row prisoners in America. Shawn's expertise allowed us to use our laptops on the road to call up reams of information on any of hundreds of prisoners.

We also are deeply indebted to our many talented colleagues who were involved in the image end of this endeavor, foremost among them photographer David Leeson. David accompanied us on many of our travels to death row, and made many more trips on his own. We also are indebted to photo editors Leslie White and Guy Reynolds and photographer Jim Mahoney. Others on John Davidson's staff who made significant contributions to the look of this project include Art Director Kathleen Vincent, designers Marc Gilbert and Douglas

Jones, graphic artist Lon Tweeten, graphic editor Lauri Joseph and, especially, Assistant Art Director Leslie Becker, who melded words, pictures and graphics into a seamless package.

Shawna Seed, the assistant managing editor for Sunday editions, made sure we had the space to tell the story of America's condemned and contributed, as always, suggestions that undoubtedly made those stories better. We are likewise indebted to copy editor Laura Ehret, who, strange as it may seem, juggled running her exquisitely fine-toothed comb through our copy while also awaiting the arrival of her first child. She prevented us from being victimized by our own writing more often than either of us would like to mention.

These stories were edited, gently revised and, on occasion, invisibly rewritten by our colleague Allen Pusey. Most people who know Allen think of him as one of the nation's preeminent investigative reporters, but a few, ourselves included, also know him to be one of the finest line editors in journalism. We know of no finer, more complete journalist.

Special thanks to our friends Tim Wyatt of the projects staff for his unmatched ability to ferret out elusive facts quickly on deadline, Mattie Read for assorted acts of administrative voodoo, and Rick Koster, now with *The Day* in New London, not only for his unheralded scut work, but also for his contributions to our death row vocabularies.

During the almost four years we worked on this project, we encountered every imaginable variety of prison warden and public information officer. A few, whose names shall remain anonymous here, were Precambrian in their outlook. But most were modern professionals who extended us every courtesy as they allowed us access to their death rows and execution chambers. None was more helpful than David Nunnelee, who until recently was a public information officer with the Texas Department of Criminal Justice/Institutional Division. We'd also like to thank, in no particular order, several other prison administrators who extended us courtesies: Texas Mountain View Unit warden Pamela Baggett, Jerry Massie and Lee Mann of Oklahoma, Debbie Buchannan of Florida, Mike Arra of Arizona, Cathy Jett of Louisiana, Linda Moodry of Montana, Barry Bannister of Kentucky and Dina Tyler of the Arkansas Department of Corrections.

We also received a great deal of assistance from lawyers who represent death row inmates. These attorneys are no strangers to defeat, but they continue to ply their practices, generally because they're philosophically opposed to capital punishment. Among them: William Swift of the Missouri State Public Defender System; Geraldine S. Russell of La Mesa, California; Laura Fitzsimmons of

Las Vegas; Leslie Delk, a lawyer who has fought the death penalty in Florida and Oklahoma; Arizona public defender Dale Baich and his investigator, Lisa Eager; Timothy O'Toole, assistant U.S. public defender in Nevada; and his supervisor, Michael Pescetta. And perhaps no attorney in the country has a broader overview of capital punishment or was more helpful than Richard Dieter, executive director of the Death Penalty Information Center in Washington.

Along the way, we were fortunate enough to have encountered other truly remarkable people who, professionally or personally, had a vested interest in death rows or in the inmates who inhabit them. Raymond Feyen, a retired police officer in Rodgers, Ark., and Kathleen Finnegan, a former state prosecutor in Punta Gorda, Fla., survived gunfire in which others were killed. They were decent enough to relive those harrowing attacks with us. June Wade and Winnie McCloud, both Los Angeles County juvenile probation officers, taught us the ins and outs of urban gangs. Kathryn D'Unger, a private investigator in Corpus Christi, Tex., gave freely of her time to demonstrate the vagaries of capital punishment. Kathryn, a victim of violent crime herself whose police officer fiancé was shot to death on duty, nonetheless provided documentation to demonstrate why a man shouldn't be condemned to death in Texas.

We appreciate the interest and enthusiasm of our editors at Andrews McMeel, Nora Donaghy, Dorothy O'Brien and Julie Roberts who gave us wonderful ideas about presenting our information in book form.

We express our gratitude to the convicted killers who shared the often painful details of their lives and crimes with us and, now, with you.

Journalism on this scale is possible only at a handful of newspapers in the United States. We are fortunate to work for editors willing to invest the time, dollars and manpower in extraordinary journalistic undertakings. These stories would not have been possible without the support and encouragement of Bob Mong, Ralph Langer, Gilbert Bailon, Stu Wilk, Walt Stallings, Barry Boesch and Lawrence Young. Thanks for the rope.

And finally, both of us are fortunate to share our lives with two women who also are writers; we're appreciative of Kathryn Jones and Kathy Swindle for their understanding, support and insights.

—Dan Malone and Howard Swindle
October 31, 1998

APPENDIX

. . .

A Survey of Death Row Inmates
How the Study Was Conducted

Results are based on responses from 602 inmates residing on death row across the United States. Survey materials—including a questionnaire, cover letter and return postage-paid envelope—were mailed December 14, 1994, to the entire death row population in the country—a total of 2,851. On February 8, 1995, another questionnaire and cover letter were mailed to approximately 2,400 inmates who had not responded to the first mailing. As part of the second mailing, a Spanish-language version of the questionnaire was sent to all inmates identified on the original sample as Hispanic or Latin.

A total of 602 completed questionnaires were received, representing a 21 percent response rate. Additionally, more than a hundred inmates chose to send us a variety of letters, court records, photographs and audiotapes in lieu of a filling out a questionnaire. The contents of those documents, however, are not reflected in this report.

The only option to distribute this questionnaire to death row inmates was through the mail, making the sample a self-selected one. Therefore, results from this survey cannot be considered representative of all death row inmates. And because it is not a scientific random sampling of the entire death row population, a margin of error cannot be applied. However, a good cross section of inmates by geography, ethnicity, age and gender was collected.

The poll was supervised by Barbara Quisenberry and Patti Boesch of the *Morning News*'s Research Department.

Note: Some of the survey results appear elsewhere in this book. They are repeated here for easy reference.

Geographic Profile

State	Total inmates	Percent of total inmates in U.S.
Alabama	126	4%
Arizona	119	4
Arkansas	36	1
California	384	13
Colorado	3	–
Connecticut	5	–
Delaware	14	1
Florida	348	12
Georgia	108	4
Idaho	21	1
Illinois	155	5
Indiana	50	2
Kentucky	29	1
Louisiana	43	2
Maryland	13	1
Mississippi	54	2
Missouri	87	3
Montana	8	–
Nebraska	10	–
Nevada	60	2
New Jersey	7	–
New Mexico	2	–
N. Carolina	104	4
Ohio	136	5
Oklahoma	129	5
Oregon	15	1
Pennsylvania	170	6
S. Carolina	57	2
S. Dakota	2	–
Tennessee	87	3
Texas	384	14
Utah	11	–
Virginia	53	2
W. Virginia	1	–
Washington	9	–
U.S. Gov't	11	–
Total	2,851	100

Personal Profile

	Survey respondents	Total inmates	U.S. adult population*
Men	99%	99%	51%
Women	1	1	49
White	57%	49%	75%
Black	34	40	11
Hispanic	5	7	10
Native American	3	1	[4]
Asian	1	1	
Undetermined	–	2	–
18–24	7%		14%
25–34	37		22
35–44	37		21
45–54	15		15
55–64	3		11
65+	1		17
Average = 37			
Married	13%		56%
Single	46		27
Divorced	31		8
Separated	5		2
Widowed	4		7
No Answer	1		

*Sources: 1990 U.S. Census; 1995 Lifestyle Market Analyst

		Respondents	U.S. adult population*
Not a high school graduate		50%	24%
1st thru 5th grade	2%		
6th thru 7th grade	6		
8th thru 9th grade	24		
10th thru 11th grade	18		
High school graduate		25	30
H.S. graduate	15%		
Vocational/technical	6		
GED	4		
Some college		20	25
College graduate+		4	21
NA/Refused		1	–

*Source: 1990 U.S. Census

Sexual preference	Percentage
Heterosexual	88%
Homosexual	1
Bisexual	4
NA/Refused	7

Age when respondent first had sex	Percentage
Under 10	13%
10–12	21
13–15	34
16–18	23
Over 18	4
NA/Refused	5

Age when respondent first had sex	Percent of inmates who report being sexually abused as a child
Under 10	53%
10–12	33
13–15	20
16–18	26
Over 18	16

Family Profile

Raised by		Percentage
Your natural mother and natural father		45%
Natural mother/father only	40%	
Natural mother/father, plus others	5	
Your natural mother only		20
Your natural father only		2
Your natural mother and a stepfather		18
Your natural father and a stepmother		5
Another relative		13
An adoptive parent or parents		7
In an orphanage		2
Other		7
NA/Refused		1

Note: Results do not add to 100% due to multiple responses.

Family	Percentage
Poor	56%
Middle Class	40
Wealthy	3
NA/Refused	1

**Have any members of your
immediate family ever been
convicted of a felony?**

		Percentage
Yes		38%
Brother(s)	25%	
Violent crime[1]	11%	
Non-violent crime only[2]	14	
Father		10
Violent crime	5%	
Non-violent crime only	5	
Mother		2
Violent crime	0%	
Non-violent crime only	2	
Sister(s)		4
Violent crime	1%	
Non-violent crime only	3	
Other family member(s)		4
Violent crime	1%	
Non-violent crime only	3	
Don't Know (DK)/		
No Answer (NA)/Refused		2

Note: Results do not add to 38% due to multiple responses.

No	58
DK/NA/Refused	4

[1]Violent crime includes murder, robbery, rape, kidnapping, assault and manslaughter.
[2]Non-violent crime includes theft, burglary, drug- and alcohol-related charges and other non-violent crimes.

Childhood Problems

**During your childhood, what
was the harshest punishment
you received from your family?**

	Percentage
Beaten, whipped, spanked	69%
Restricted, grounded	10
Bizarre, cruel punishment	4

(Ex. "My stepmother made me eat a pack of cigarettes for smoking. When I vomited, she made me eat the vomit." "Being forced to hold the wires on a hand crank telephone while my father cranked it." "Chained to a bed with a dog chain.")

Privileges taken away: car keys, television, phone	3
Rejected, abandoned, ostracized	3
Verbally or mentally abused	2
Kicked out of house, sent to reform school	2
Threatened my life, shot	1

Sexually abused	1
Humiliated	1

(Ex. "Thrown out of house in my underwear.")

Other	5
None	5
DK/NA/Refused	6

Note: Results do not add to 100% due to multiple responses.

What was the worst thing that happened to you as a child?

	Percentage
Physical abuse by family member	15%
Death of family member or friend	12
Accidental injury	10

(Ex. "Hit by a car." "Almost drowned." "Serious bicycle accident.")

Sexual abuse	10
Abandoned, separated from parent	8
Witnessed something bad happen to someone	6

(Ex. "Watched my father sexually molest my two sisters."
"Witnessed my father being cut with knives, shot in fights
and lying dead on the floor with his chest blown open."
"When I saw my father jumped on by someone.")

Lack of love, rejected, neglected	5
Beaten, stabbed, shot (not child abuse)	3
Verbal, mental abuse; humiliation	3
Incarcerated: jail, juvenile home, reform school	2
Parents divorced, separated	2
Illness, disease, other medical condition	2
Pet-related	2
Growing up poor	1
Nothing	6
Other	12

(Ex. "Learning how to steal." "Found out I was retarded." "Being sentenced to die."
"Dented the chrome on my shiny new Schwinn.")

DK/NA/Refused	10

Note: Results do not add to 100% due to multiple responses.

Were you ever sexually assaulted or abused as a child? If so, by whom?

	Percentage
Yes	28%
Acquaintance or friend	9%
A parent	8
Other family member: grandparent(s), aunt(s), uncle(s), cousin(s)	8
A stranger	7
Brother or sister	4

Note: Results do not add to 28% due to multiple responses.

No	69
DK/NA/Refused	3

Were you ever physically abused as a child?

		Percentage
Yes		48%
A parent	39%	
Other family member: grandparent(s), aunt(s), uncle(s), cousin(s)	8	
Brother or sister	6	
Acquaintance or friend	6	
A stranger	4	

Note: Results do not add to 48% due to multiple responses.

No	50
DK/NA/Refused	2

As a child, did you ever spend a night in the hospital because of an injury?

		Percentage
Yes		41%
Illness, disease, other medical condition	11%	
Car accident	10	
Accidental injury	9	
Injury (undetermined origin)	6	
Child abuse by parent or sibling	4	
Beaten, stabbed, shot (not child abuse)	3	
Drug- or alcohol-related	1	
Attempted suicide	1	
Other	1	
DK/NA/Refused	2	

Note: Results do not add to 41% due to multiple responses.

No	56
DK/NA/Refused	3

As a child or teenager, were you ever in trouble with the law?

		Percentage
Yes		71%
Non-violent crime[1]	49%	
Runaway	12	
Violent crime[2]	11	
Drug- or alcohol-related	11	
Truancy	4	
Other	2	
DK/NA/Refused	6	

Note: Results do not add to 71% due to multiple responses.

No	28
DK/NA/Refused	1

[1]Non-violent crime includes theft, burglary, drug- and alcohol-related charges and other non-violent crimes.
[2]Violent crime includes murder, robbery, rape, kidnapping, assault and manslaughter.

Employment

What was your last regular job?	Percentage
Construction	20%
Restaurant, bar	11
Machinist, heavy equipment operator	7
Automotive worker	6
Maintenance	6
Factory, plant, warehouse	5
Retail	5
Agriculture	4
Self-employed, business owner	4
Driver	4
Technical	3
Professional	3
Military	2
Service	2
Oil industry	2
Government employee	1
Law enforcement	1
Health care worker	1
Administrative, clerical	1
Other	7
DK/NA/Refused	8

Note: Results do not add to 100% due to multiple responses.

The last regular job you held, how much money did you make in a week?	Percentage
$250 or less	51%
$251 to $500	25
$501 to $750	9
$751 to $1,000	6
$1,000 or more	4
DK/NA/Refused	5

Drugs and Alcohol

If you have ever used drugs, how old were you when you first tried drugs?	Percentage
Under 9	6%
9 to 12	22
13 to 15	28
15 or older	29
Never tried drugs	13
DK/NA/Refused	2

	Age 18–35 percentage	Age over 35 percentage
Under 9	8%	4%
9 to 12	31	13
13 to 15	32	24
15 or older	18	40
Never tried drugs	10	17
DK/NA/Refused	1	2

Did you ever become a regular drug user? If so, what drug did you use most?		Percentage
Yes		63%
Marijuana	52%	
Cocaine	20	
Meth- or amphetamines	18	
Heroin	12	
Crack cocaine	8	
Other (LSD/Acid)	15	

Note: Results do not add to 63% due to multiple responses.

	Percentage
No	36
DK/NA/Refused	1

	Age 18–35 percentage	Age over 35 percentage
Marijuana	62%	42%
Cocaine	22	19
Meth- or amphetamines	15	22
Heroin	9	16
Crack cocaine	9	6
Other (LSD/Acid)	16	13

Note: Results do not add to 100% due to multiple responses.

If you have ever drunk alcohol, how old were you when you first tried alcohol?

	Percentage
Under 9	17%
9 to 12	25
13 to 15	25
15 or older	26
Never tried alcohol	5
DK/NA/Refused	2

	Age 18–35 percentage	Age over 35 percentage
Under 9	22%	13%
9 to 12	29	21
13 to 15	24	26
15 or older	20	33
Never tried alcohol	4	5
DK/NA/Refused	1	2

Do you believe that you ever had a problem with alcohol?

	Percentage
Yes	41%
No	58
DK/NA/Refused	1

Have you ever been treated for drug or alcohol abuse?

		Percentage
Yes		24%
Drug abuse	8%	
Alcohol abuse	6	
Treated for both	10	
Did you consider the treatment successful?		
Yes	6%	
No	18	
No		75
DK/NA/Refused		1

Have any members of your family been regular drug users?

		Percentage
Yes		46%
Brother/sister	34%	
Mother	11	
Father	9	
Child	1	
Other: aunt(s), uncle(s), cousin(s)	6	

Note: Results do not add to 46% due to multiple responses.

No	49
DK/NA/Refused	5

Have any members of your family ever had a problem with alcohol?		**Percentage**
Yes		66%
Father	40%	
Brother/Sister	26	
Mother	21	
Other family member: Aunt(s), uncle(s), grandparent(s), stepfather	14	
Child	1	

Note: Results do not add to 66% due to multiple responses.

No	30
DK/NA/Refused	4

Inmates who have:	**Percentage**
Family members with both drug and alcohol problems	38%
Family members with just alcohol problems	26
Family members with just drug problems	8
Family members with no drug or alcohol problems	22
Can't determine	6

Physical and Mental Illness

Have you ever been treated for a psychiatric problem?		**Percentage**
Yes		34%
Childhood-related	6%	
Suicide attempt	6	
Depression, anti-social behavior	5	
Case-related, evaluated for defense	3	
Sex-related	2	
Drug or alcohol abuse	1	
Military-related	1	
Physical injury	1	
Other	6	
DK/NA/Refused	4	

Note: Results do not add to 34% due to multiple responses.

No	62
DK/NA/Refused	4

Do you have any long-lasting physical illness or disease?		Percentage
Yes		29%
Back problems	4%	
High blood pressure	3	
Heart problems	2	
Personality disorder	2	
Arm/leg injuries	2	
Asthma	2	
Headaches	2	
Ear/eye problems	1	
Diabetes	1	
Brain-related condition	1	
A.D.D.	1	
Other	11	
DK/NA/Refused	1	

Note: Results do not add to 29% due to multiple responses.

	Percentage
No	69
DK/NA/Refused	2

Case-Related

Even if you are innocent, what did officials say happened in your case?	Percentage
Someone was killed during a robbery	48%
More than one person was killed	22
Someone was killed during a kidnapping	13
Someone was killed during a rape	11
Someone was killed	10
Someone was hired to kill someone else	6
A child was killed	5
A police officer was killed	5
Other	2
DK/NA/Refused	6

Note: Results do not add to 100% due to multiple responses.

Even if you are innocent, tell us which statement describes what you were convicted of.	Percentage
Actually causing someone's death	71%
Being a party or accomplice to a death	18
Both	3
DK/NA/Refused	8

Guilty or innocent?

	Percentage
Guilty	15%
Innocent	23
Can't determine	62

Note: These answers are based on inmates' verbatim comments in their questionnaires. To be counted as "guilty," the inmate must have outright admitted commiting the crime. For example: "I didn't mean to kill the guy, but it was in self-defense." To be counted as "innocent," the inmate must have claimed he/she did not commit the crime. For example: "I shouldn't be here, because I didn't do it." Keep in mind: claims of innocence are just that—claims.

How long have you been on death row?

	Percentage
Less than 2 years	11%
2 to 4 years	25
5 to 7 years	20
8 to 10 years	18
More than 10 years	24
NA/Refused	2

Note: Average = 7 years

Have you ever had an execution date?

		Percentage
Yes		52%
One	23%	
Two or more	27	
DK/NA/Refused	2	
No		46
DK/NA/Refused		2

Prior to your conviction, were you offered a plea bargain?

		Percentage
Yes		36%
Life	11%	
Years ranging from 5 to 99	8	
Life without parole	5	
No. of years to life	3	
100 or more years	1	
Other	1	
DK/NA/Refused	7	
No		62
DK/NA/Refused		2

The Victim(s)

	Percentage
White	78%
Black	15
Hispanic	5
Other	4
DK/NA/Refused	3
Male	60
Female	53
DK/NA/Refused	3
A stranger	59
Someone you knew (not family)	30
A family member	12
DK/NA/Refused	4

Note: Results do not add to 100% due to multiple responses.

Race of the victim	Race of the inmate		
	White	Black	Hispanic
White	90%	61%	52%
Black	5	34	7
Hispanic	3	2	48

The Trial

Race of the judge	Percentage
White	91%
Black	4
Hispanic	2
Other	1
DK/NA/Refused	2

Race of the defense attorney	Percentage
White	88%
Black	7
Hispanic	1
Other	2
DK/NA/Refused	2

Race of the lead prosecutor	Percentage
White	94%
Black	2
Hispanic	1
Other	1
DK/NA/Refused	2

Do you believe discrimination—
either against your race or against
your sex—helped convict you?

	Percentage
Sex discrimination	11%
Race discrimination	40
Neither	50
DK/NA/Refused	5

	Race of the inmate		
	White	Black	Hispanic
Believe race discrimination helped convict them	11%	84%	59%
Believe sex discrimination helped convict them	12	10	–

During your trial, did your lawyer
use any expert witnesses, such as
jury selection specialists, defense
psychiatrists, or private investigators?

	Percentage
Yes	41%
No	56
DK/NA/Refused	3

Criminal History

Besides your current capital
crime conviction, what crimes,
if any, have you been convicted of?

		Percentage
Have been convicted before		69%
Burglary, breaking and entering	24%	
Robbery, armed robbery, bank robbery	20	
Assault, aggravated assault, battery	12	
Theft, petty theft, grand theft, larceny	11	
Murder	10	
Drug possession, drug sales	8	
Auto theft	7	
Weapons possession, weapons sales	4	
Escape	4	
DWI, DUI, public intoxication	3	
Rape, attempted rape	3	
Forgery	3	
Sexual assault, sexual battery, sodomy	3	
Kidnapping	3	
Arson	2	
Manslaughter, invol. manslaughter	2	
Rec'g stolen property, selling stolen prop.	2	

Credit card abuse, bad checks	2
Attempted murder	2
Other	12

Note: Results do not add to 69% due to multiple responses.

Have not been convicted before	21
DK/NA/Refused	10

Have you ever been arrested for driving while under the influence or alcohol or drugs or for public intoxication?

	Percentage
Yes	30%
No	69
DK/NA/Refused	1

Have you ever been arrested for a sex crime?

	Percentage
Yes	14%
No	83
DK/NA/Refused	3

Life on Death Row

Are you allowed to work outside of your cell? If so, what is your job?

		Percentage
Yes		37%
Maintenance	16%	
Food service	4	
Garment factory	4	
Barber	1	
Computer operator	1	
Other	4	
DK/NA/Refused	8	

Note: Results do not add to 37% due to multiple responses.

No	61
DK/NA/Refused	2

In an average month, how many books or magazines do you read?

	Percentage
None	7%
Less than 5	30
5 to 10	30
More than 10	31
DK/NA/Refused	2

What is your most cherished possession on death row?

	Percentage
Family photos	20%
Bible, Holy Qu'ran	16
My life, myself	12
Television	8
My mind, my sanity, memories	7
Typewriter, writing supplies	7
Correspondence: letters, mail, stamps	6
Radio, stereo, headphones	5
Books	5
My faith, relationship with Jesus Christ	4
Nothing	3
Crafts, art supplies	3
Friends, family	3
Jewelry	2
My health	2
Legal materials	1
Visits	1
My heart	1
Other	8
DK/NA/Refused	9

Note: Results do not add to 100% due to multiple responses.

Religion

Which of the following best describes your religious preference?

	Percentage
Protestant	32%
Catholic	12
Muslim	9
Atheist, agnostic	7
Jewish	1
Other	35

(Ex. Christian, I believe in God, Searching, Sinner saved by grace, Moorish American, Yoga/Hindu, Higher Power, Pagan, Church of Peter, New Age, Rastafarian, Thelemite, Unsaved, Realism, Sergian-Orthodox, I worship the sun, Cosmology)

DK/NA/Refused	4

Since you've been on death row, how important would you say that religion is in your own life?

	Percentage
Very important	50%
Fairly important	21
Not very important	26
DK/NA/Refused	3

Is that more, less, or about the same than it was before you were sent to death row?		Religion is . . .		
		Very important	Fairly important	Not very important
More	42%	67%	33%	6%
Less	9	6	8	18
About the same	45	25	57	74
DK/NA/Refused	4	2	2	2

Do you think those death row inmates who turn to religion do so for any of the following reasons?	Percentage
Peace of mind	68%
To save their souls	56
To make up for what they've done	36
To help their case	35
Other	28
DK/NA/Refused	6

Note: Results do not add to 100% due to multiple responses.

		Religion is . . .		
		Very important	Fairly important	Not very important
Peace of mind	68%	74%	70%	60%
To save their souls	56	70	53	38
To make up for what they've done	36	37	38	37
To help their case	35	27	32	55
Other	28	30	27	29
DK/NA/Refused	6	2	4	6

Thoughts and Fantasies

What is the one thing in your life that you are proudest of?	Percentage
Children	31%
Wife, marriage, family	10
Education, college degree, GED	8
Relationship with Jesus Christ	8
Talent, craft, skill (incl. sports)	6
Business, job, trade	5
Nothing	4
Military experience	3
Helping someone, giving to others	3
That I'm good/caring/honorable/moral	2
Some heroic act	2
I'm still alive	1

My mind, my sanity	1
Getting off drugs	1
That I'm innocent	1
Turning my life around	1
My heritage/race/ethnic background	1
Other	10
DK/NA/Refused	8

Note: Results do not add to 100% due to multiple responses.

Who is the one person, living or dead, you most admire?

		Percentage
Parents		34%
Mother	23%	
Father	9	
Both	2	
Other family member		30
Grandmother	7%	
Grandfather	6	
Both grandparents	1	
Aunt or uncle	4	
Sister	3	
Brother	3	
Spouse	3	
Children	3	
Jesus Christ		8
Friend		6
No one		5
Other religious/spiritual leader		4

(Ex. "Pastor." "Mother Teresa." "Joseph of Canaan.")

Historical figure		3

(Ex. "Albert Einstein." "Beethoven." "Hitler." "JFK.")

Celebrity, public figure		2

(Ex. "Loretta Lynn." "Jimmy Carter." "Fidel Castro." "Bruce Lee.")

Other		2
DK/NA/Refused		10

Note: Results do not add to 100% due to multiple responses.

Aside from being on death row, do you think you are significantly different from most other people?

	Percentage
Yes	43%

(Ex. "Most people don't care what happens to the next man where I can't seem to allow anyone getting abused in my presence." "I'm not violent, I believe in God and go to church services weekly." "I'm innocent." "I care about other people." "I believe that most people lie—I don't lie." "I'm extremely intelligent.")

No	54
DK/NA/Refused	3

If you could be free for one day, how would you spend it?	**Percentage**
With family, friends (Ex. "Visit my kids." "With my only child who I've never touched, held, kissed." "Visit my grandfather's grave.")	61%
Going to church, praying, other religious activity (Ex. "Serving God." "Spreading the gospel and preaching the kingdom of God.")	9
Educating or helping others (Ex. "Teach teens that honest work is what life is all about." "Trying to convince people that the death penalty is wrong." "Educating our youth.")	8
Nature/outdoor activity (Ex. "In a park, having a picnic." "Fishing and hunting." "Swim, ride a horse, walk in the park." "Enjoy the beauty of nature.")	6
Sex, finding a woman (Ex. "Get me a lady." "Have sex with my favorite girl." "I'd have to have some sex!!")	6
Leaving the state, country (Ex. "On the first plane out of this country." "I'd leave the U.S. for good." "Disappearing." "Go to another state and fight extradition.")	5
Eating (Ex. "Eating decent food." "Eat something cooked right." "Eating real food for a change." "Eat everything I can get my hands on.")	4
Proving my innocence (Ex. "Proving the judge and lawyer knew I was innocent from the beginning." "Collecting evidence to show I'm innocent.")	4
Visiting victims (or their graves) (Ex. ". . . in homes to bring closure, come to terms with his death, say goodbye." "Quality time with the victim's family." "Pay my homage and shed my tears for my ignorance.")	2
Working or looking for work	2
Driving	1
Something criminal (Ex. "I would rape and kill a woman." "Stealing and getting high.")	1
Other	4
DK/NA/Refused	9

Note: Results do not add to 100% due to multiple responses.

Regrets

If there was one thing that you you could do differently in your life what would it be?	Percentage
Stay in school, go to college (Ex. "Get better educated." "Finish school." "Do better in school.")	14%
Not use drugs or alcohol (Ex. "Never do or be around drugs." "Steer clear of drugs and alcohol.")	13
Stay away from crime, not commit crime (Ex. "Have not felt compelled to kill [victim's name]." "To not have taken a life." "Stay clear of crime.")	8
Be a better father/husband/person (Ex. "A better father and person altogether." "Be a family role model." "Be a better father.")	7
Not go to _____, stay in _____ (Ex. "Stayed in Germany." "Not travel to Missouri." "Not ever come to North Carolina." "Would never have returned to Pennsylvania.")	6
Give life to Jesus Christ (Ex. "Not reject the Lord when he tried to come into my life." "Start over knowing of God's love." "Seek the Lord at a much earlier time and age.")	5
Everything, start over (Ex. "Live my life over, knowing all I know now.")	4
Hang out with different people, avoid certain people (Ex. "Keep away from my uncle." "Disassociate myself with certain people in my past." "Not run around with liars." "Choose friends that won't use me.")	4
Change a specific incident or action (Ex. "Never have gone to work for [company name]." "I wouldn't have gone out with my friends the weekend I got in trouble." "Never have gone hunting that December night.")	3
Have a different family/parents, leave home (Ex. "Be born into a rich-ass family!" "Be re-born to parents, not child-beating religious fanatics." "Live with my grandparents.")	3
Get help sooner (Ex. "Tried harder to get help." "Get counseling/therapy.")	3
Case-related (Ex. "Prove I murdered no one." "Paid for my trial attorneys.")	3

Listen to parents or others	2
Help people (esp. youth) stay out of trouble	2
Not marry young, or marry who I did	2
Enlist, stay in military	2
Stay with my wife, get married	2
Nothing	2
Other	17
DK/NA/Refused	7

Note: Results do not add to 100% due to multiple responses.

What events or circumstances would have changed the direction in your life so that you would not be on death row today?	Percentage
Stayed off drugs or alcohol	14%
Case-related (Ex. "If I had honest defense attorney to defend me at trial." "If the state witness had told the truth.")	14
Had more love, discipline, more stable home	13
Stayed in school, gone to college	9
Never gone to _____, stayed in _____	7
Changed a specific incident or action	7
Had more faith in Jesus Christ	6
Hung around with better people	6
Gotten professional help (sooner or at all)	5
Gotten a job, stayed with my job	4
Stayed married	2
Done what I was taught or told	2
Nothing	2
Joined the military, stayed in the military	2
Made better choices	1
Been born white	1
Other	8
DK/NA/Refused	13

Note: Results do not add to 100% due to multiple responses.

Attitudes Toward Crime

Which of these statements is closest to your view?	Percentage
People are neither born good nor bad; it's circumstances and experiences that make them what they are	89%
People are born good or born bad	6
DK/NA/Refused	5

Under what circumstances do you think violence is okay?

	Percentage
To defend yourself	73%
It's never okay to act violently	27
To punish wrong-doing	10
To protect your standing or reputation	5
To get what you want	2
Other: to protect, defend loved ones; to protect the country, in times of war	16
DK/NA/Refused	3

One-fourth of respondents (26%) who said it's never okay to act violently *also* answered, "To defend yourself."

Note: Results do not add to 100% due to multiple responses.

What do you think are the most important causes of crime in America?

	Percentage
Drugs or alcohol	56%
Breakdown of the family	47
Poverty	37
Lack of values or morals	33
Lack of education	26
Lack of parental supervision/discipline	22
Racial prejudice	18
Lack of religion in people's lives	17
Failure of the justice system	16
Violence on TV or in movies	11
Children or teens joining gangs	10
Availability of guns	9
Pornography	2
Other	10
DK/NA/Refused	1

Note: Results do not add to 100% due to multiple responses.

Do you think people who commit crimes enjoy doing it? Please explain.

		Percentage
Yes		32%
Excitement, thrill, natural high	9%	
Need money, greed, poverty	3	
Enjoy the challenge, to see what they can get away with	3	
Power, control	3	
Way to impress others, to be cool	2	
Some do, some don't	2	
They're mean, enjoy hurting others	2	
They continue, so they must enjoy it	2	
Way to get back at others, express rage	1	

Habit forming, becomes a way of life	1
They're sick, high on drugs/alcohol	1

Note: Results do not add to 32% due to multiple responses.

Yes and no	12
Some do, some don't	6%
Need money, greed, poverty	3
Excitement, thrill, natural high	3
No	47
DK/NA/Refused	8

The Death Penalty and Executions

Do you think executions should be shown on TV?	Percentage
Yes	50%
No	44
DK/NA/Refused	6

If executions were on TV, do you think it would cut down on crime?	Percentage
Yes	16%
No	79
DK/NA/Refused	5

Among those who think executions should be shown on TV:	Percentage
Would cut down on crime	27%
Would *not* cut down on crime	70
DK/NA/Refused	3

Finish this sentence: The death penalty discourages people from committing violent crime:	Percentage
A lot	2%
A little	8
Not at all	87
DK/NA/Refused	3

Life on Death Row

In your opinion, how many inmates on death row in the United States are guilty?	Percentage
Nearly all of the them	32%
More than half of them	28
About half of them	15

Less than half of them	9
Almost none of them	2
DK/NA/Refused	14

Predictions

What do you think will happen to you, personally?	Time Spent on Death Row			
	Total	1–4 Yrs.	5–9 Yrs.	10+ Yrs.
Your conviction will be overturned and you will be cleared of any wrong-doing	21%	23%	19%	22%
Your conviction will be overturned and you will get a new trial	37	38	35	35
Your death sentence will be changed to life in prison	20	17	23	21
You will eventually be executed	30	29	32	28
You will die on death row of other causes before you're executed	7	6	8	7
DK/NA/Refused	8	9	8	6

Note: Results do not add to 100% due to multiple responses.

What do you think will happen to you, personally?		Inmates Who:		
	Total	Admit Guilt	Claim Innocence	Can't Determine
Your conviction will be overturned and you will be cleared of any wrong-doing	21%	5%	48%	16%
Your conviction will be overturned and you will get a new trial	37	22	38	40
Your death sentence will be changed to life in prison	20	25	14	21

You will eventually be executed	30	46	22	28
You will die on death row of other causes before you're executed	7	5	5	8
DK/NA/Refused	8	9	5	9

Note: Results do not add to 100% due to multiple responses.

Permission to Quote

Do you give permission to be quoted?	Percentage
Yes, you may quote me	63%
No, you may *not* quote me	34
DK/NA	3

Conclusions: Lack of Education

- Only 50% of all respondents graduated from high school, making them half as likely as most adults to have a high school diploma. And five times less likely than other adults to have finished college.

- Most respondents last worked in unskilled or blue-collar jobs, earning $250 or less a week—little more than minimum wage.

- 14% said the one thing they would do differently in their lives would be to *stay in school or go to college.*

- 9% said the one circumstance that would have changed the direction of their lives so they would not be on death row today would have been to *stay in school or go to college.*

- About one-fourth of all respondents believe *lack of education* is an important cause of crime in America today

Conclusions: Drugs and Alcohol

- More than 60% of all respondents said they had been *regular drug users* and about 40% believed they had a *problem with alcohol.*

- Almost half had a family member who was a regular drug user, while almost 70% had a family member who was an alcoholic. Almost 40% reported having family members with *both drug and alcohol problems*.

- Respondents appear to be using both drugs and alcohol at a younger age. Inmates age 18–35 were nearly twice as likely as older inmates (over 35) to have *tried drugs by age 12*, while older inmates were nearly twice as likely to say they had *never tried drugs*. 51% of younger inmates had started drinking by age 12, versus 34% of the over-35 age group.

- By the time they were teenagers, 11% of respondents had already been in trouble with the law for a drug- or alcohol-related offense. As adults, 30% said they had been arrested for DUI or for public intoxication.

- *Drug and alcohol abuse* was the No. 1 answer for the most important causes of crime in America. 13% said they should've stayed away from drugs and alcohol, while 14% said if they had, it would've kept them off death row.

Conclusions: Family Environment

- More than half of all respondents grew up in *poor families*. And on average, parents' resources—both financial and emotional—were divided among *five children*.

- Fewer than half grew up in a home with both their *natural mother and father*. In many cases, it was the father who was absent.

- 40% said their father was an alcoholic and about 10% said he was a regular drug user. And 10% said their father had been convicted of a felony.

- About four out of ten respondents reported being *physically abused by a family member*, most often a parent. And two out of ten had been *sexually abused by a family member*.

- About half of all inmates said the *breakdown of the family* was an important source of crime in America today.

- 13% said that *more love, discipline or a more stable home life* would have changed the course of their lives so that they would not be on death row today.

Conclusions: Importance of Family

- When asked what was the one thing in their life they were proudest of, four out of 10 respondents said either *their children or their family*. The majority also named a family member—usually "mom"—when asked who was the one person they most admired.

- About 60% would spend their one day of freedom *with family or friends*.

- 20% said their most cherished possession on death row was *family photos*, the most common response to this question.

- About 70% said *religion was important* in their own lives. And 40% said religion had become more significant to them since coming to death row.

The Questionnaire

INSTRUCTIONS

1. Read all parts of the question and answer each one completely. Some questions need only one answer. For others, you may mark all that apply.

2. Place an "X" in the box to mark your answer. Example: ❏ -1

3. When you have completed the questionnaire, mail it back to us in the enclosed reply envelope.

TELL US ABOUT YOURSELF

1. What is your birthdate? _____/_____/_____   2. Are you: Male ❏ -1   Female ❏ -2
     Month   Day   Year

3. Are you: African-American ❏ -1   Hispanic ❏ -3   Native American ❏ -5
          Asian ❏ -2   White ❏ -4   Other _____ ❏ -6

4. Are you: Single ❏ -1 Married ❏ -2 Separated ❏ -3 Divorced ❏ -4 Widowed ❏ -5

5. How many brothers and sisters do you have?   Brothers: _____   Sisters: _____

6. If you have brothers or sisters, are you:
     The oldest ❏ -1   The youngest ❏ -2   Or somewhere in between ❏ -3

7. Which of the following best describes how you were raised?

By your natural mother and natural father	❏ -1	By your natural father and a stepmother	❏ -5
By your natural mother only	❏ -2	By another relative	❏ -6
By your natural father only	❏ -3	By an adoptive parent or parents	❏ -7
By your natural mother and a stepfather	❏ -4	In an orphanage	❏ -8
		Other	❏ -9

8. Which best describes your family? Wealthy ❏ -1   Middle Class ❏ -2   Poor ❏ -3

9. Have any members of your immediate family ever been convicted of a felony?
Yes ❏ -1 No ❏ -2

If you answered "yes," please tell us their relationship to you (father, sister, etc.) and what they were convicted of.

<u>Relationship to you</u>   <u>Convicted of</u>   <u>Any other comments</u>

10. As a child or teenager, were you ever in trouble with the law? Yes ❏ -1 No ❏ -2
    If you answered "yes," please tell us what type of trouble you were in:

11. During your childhood, what was the harshest punishment you received from your family?

12. What was the worst thing that happened to you as a child?

13. As a child, did you ever spend a night in the hospital because of an injury?
    Yes ❏ -1 No ❏ -2
    If you answered "yes," please explain:

14. What was the highest level of education you completed before your conviction?
    (Please check only one.)

1st grade	❏ -01	7th grade	❏ -07	Vocational/tech school	❏ -13
2nd grade	❏ -02	8th grade	❏ -08	Some college	❏ -14
3rd grade	❏ -03	9th grade	❏ -09	College graduate	❏ -15
4th grade	❏ -04	10th grade	❏ -10	Law/medicine/	❏ -16
5th grade	❏ -05	11th grade	❏ -11	post-graduate degree	❏ -17
6th grade	❏ -06	12th grade	❏ -12		

15. Which of the following best describes your religious preference?

Catholic	❏ -1	Protestant	❏ -4	Atheist/Agnostic	❏ -7
Jewish	❏ -2	Muslim	❏ -5	Other: _____	❏ -8

16. Do you consider yourself to be: Heterosexual ❏ -1 Homosexual ❏ -2 Bisexual ❏ -3

17. How old were you when you first had sex? _____

18. What was your last regular job? _____

20. The last regular job you held, how much money did you make a week?

$250 or less	❏ -1	$501–$750	❏ -3	$1,000 or more	❏ -5
$251–$500	❏ -2	$751–$1,000	❏ -4		

21. If you have ever used drugs, how old were you when you first tried drugs?

Under 9	❏ -1	13–15 years old	❏ -3	Never tried drugs	❏ -5
9–12 years old	❏ -2	15 or older	❏ -4		

23. If you have ever drunk alcohol, how old were you when you first tried alcohol?
Under 9 ❑ -1 13–15 years old ❑ -3 Never tried alcohol ❑ -5
9–12 years old ❑ -2 15 or older ❑ -4

24. Do you believe that you ever had a problem with alcohol? Yes ❑ -1 No ❑ -2

25. Have you ever been treated for drug or alcohol abuse? Yes ❑ -1 No ❑ -2
Treated for drug abuse ❑ -1 Treated for alcohol abuse ❑ -2 Treated for both ❑ -3

26. Did you consider the treatment successful? Yes ❑ -1 No ❑ -2

27. Have any members of your family been regular drug users? Yes ❑ -1 No ❑ -2
If "yes," please tell us which one(s):
Mother ❑ -1 A brother/sister ❑ -3 Other: _____ ❑ -5
Father ❑ -2 A child ❑ -4

28. Have any members of your family ever had a problem with alcohol? Yes ❑ -1 No ❑ -2
If "yes," please tell us which one(s):
Mother ❑ -1 A brother/sister ❑ -3 Other: _____ ❑ -5
Father ❑ -2 A child ❑ -4

29. Have you ever been treated for a psychiatric problem? Yes ❑ -1 No ❑ -2
If you answered "yes," please explain:

30. Do you have any long-lasting physical illness or disease? Yes ❑ -1 No ❑ -2
If you answered "yes," what: _____

31. Were you ever sexually assaulted or abused as a child? Yes ❑ -1 No ❑ -2
If you answered "yes," please tell us who abused you:
A parent ❑ -1 An acquaintance or friend ❑ -3
A brother or sister ❑ -2 A stranger ❑ -4
Other, please describe: _____ ❑ -5

32. Were you ever physically abused as a child? Yes ❑ -1 No ❑ -2
If you answered "yes," please tell us who abused you:
A parent ❑ -1 An acquaintance or friend ❑ -3
A brother or sister ❑ -2 A stranger ❑ -4
Other, please describe: _____ ❑ -5

33. What is the <u>one</u> thing in your life that you are proudest of?

34. Who is the <u>one</u> person, living or dead, you most admire? (Tell us what his/her relationship is to you.)

35. If there was <u>one</u> thing that you could do differently in your life, what would it be?

36. Aside from being on death row, do you think you are significantly different from most other people? Yes ❑ -1 No ❑ -2 If you answered "yes," please explain how you're different from most other people.

CRIME

1. Which of these statements is closest to your view? *(Check only one.)*
   - People are born good or born bad ❑ -1
   - People are neither born good nor bad; it's circumstances and experiences that make them what they are ❑ -2

2. Under what circumstances do you think violence is okay? *(Check all that apply.)*
   - To punish wrong-doing ❑ -1
   - To defend yourself ❑ -2
   - To get what you want ❑ -3
   - To protect your standing or reputation ❑ -4
   - Other: _____ ❑ -5
   - It's never okay to act violently ❑ -6

3. Please check what you think are the <u>three</u> most important causes of crime in America.
   - Breakdown of the family ❑ -01
   - Violence on TV or in movies ❑ -02
   - Drugs or alcohol ❑ -03
   - Lack of values or morals ❑ -04
   - Lack of religion in people's lives ❑ -05
   - Lack of parental supervision/discipline ❑ -06
   - Children or teens joining gangs ❑ -07
   - Poverty ❑ -08
   - Pornography ❑ -09
   - Failure of the justice system ❑ -10
   - Lack of education ❑ -11
   - Racial prejudice ❑ -12
   - Availability of guns ❑ -13
   - Other: _____ ❑ -14

4. Do you think that people who commit crimes enjoy doing it? Yes ❑ -1 No ❑ -2
   If "yes," please explain:

5. In your opinion, how many inmates on death row in the United States are guilty?
   - Nearly all of them ❑ -1 About half of them ❑ -3 Almost none of them ❑ -5
   - More than half of them ❑ -2 Less than half of them ❑ -4

6. Do you think executions should be shown on TV? Yes ❑ -1 No ❑ -2

7. If executions were on TV, do you think it would cut down on crime? Yes ❑ -1 No ❑ -2

8. Finish this sentence: The death penalty discourages people from commiting violent crimes . . .
   A lot ❑ -1 A little ❑ -2 Not at all ❑ -3

LIFE ON DEATH ROW

1. Since you've been on death row, how important would you say that religion is in your own life?

   Very important ❏ -1   Fairly important ❏ -2   Not very important ❏ -3

2. Is that more, less, or about the same than it was before you were sent to death row?

   More important ❏ -1   Less important ❏ -2   About the same as before ❏ -3

3. Do you think those death row inmates who turn to religion do so for any of the following reasons? *(Check all that apply.)*

   Peace of mind   ❏ -1   To save their souls   ❏ -3   Other ❏ -5
   To help their case ❏ -2   To make up for what they've done ❏ -4

4. Are you allowed to work outside of your cell? Yes ❏ -1   No ❏ -2
   If "yes," what is your job? _____

5. What is your most cherished possession on death row?

6. In an average month, how many books or magazines do you read?
   None ❏ -1   Less than 5 ❏ -2   5 to 10 ❏ -3   More than 10 ❏ -4

7. In your opinion, which manner of execution is the most humane?
   Gas chamber ❏ -1   Electric chair   ❏ -3   Firing squad   ❏ -5
   Hanging   ❏ -2   Lethal injection ❏ -4

YOUR CASE

1. Even if you are innocent, what did officials say happened in your case? *(Check all that apply.)*

   A police officer was killed   ❏ -1
   Someone was killed during a robbery   ❏ -2
   Someone was killed during a rape   ❏ -3
   Someone was killed during a kidnapping   ❏ -4
   A child was killed   ❏ -5
   Someone was hired to kill someone else   ❏ -6
   More than one person was killed   ❏ -7
   Other: _____   ❏ -8

2. Even if you are innocent, please tell us which statement describes what you were convicted of.

   Actually causing someone's death   ❏ -1
   Being a party, or accomplice, to a death
       someone else actually caused   ❏ -2

3. How long have you been on death row? Years _____ Months _____

4. Have you ever had an execution date? Yes ❑ -1 No ❑ -2
   If "yes," how many execution dates have you had? Number of dates: _____

5. Prior to your conviction, were you offered a plea bargain? Yes ❑ -1 No ❑ -2
   If "yes," what were you offered?

6. What was the race of the victim(s) in your case? *(Check all that apply.)*
   White ❑ -1   African-American ❑ -2   Hispanic ❑ -3   Other ❑ -4

7. What was the sex of the victim(s) in your case?   Male ❑ -1 Female ❑ -2

8. Which of these best describes the victim in your case?
   A family member ❑ -1 A stranger ❑ -2 Just someone you knew ❑ -3

9. During your trial, what was the race of the judge:
   White ❑ -1   African-American ❑ -2   Hispanic ❑ -3   Other ❑ -4

10. The lead defense attorney:
    White ❑ -1   African-American ❑ -2   Hispanic ❑ -3   Other ❑ -4

11. The lead prosecutor:
    White ❑ -1   African-American ❑ -2   Hispanic ❑ -3   Other ❑ -4

12. Regarding the jury in your case, how many members were:
    White _____   African-American _____   Hispanic _____   Other _____

13. How many jurors were men and how many were women? Men _____ Women _____

14. Do you believe discrimination — either against your race or against your sex — helped
    convict you?   Sex discrimination ❑ -1 Race discrimination ❑ -2 Neither ❑ -3

15. What was the name of your main trial lawyer? _____
    Was he/she: Hired ❑ -1 Appointed ❑ -2 A public defender/resource center lawyer ❑ -3

16. What was the name of your main attorney on appeal? _____
    Is he/she: Hired ❑ -1 Appointed ❑ -2 A public defender/resource center lawyer ❑ -3

17. During your trial, did your lawyer use any expert witnesses, such as jury selection
    specialists, defense psychiatrists, or private investigators? Yes ❑ -1 No ❑ -2

18. Have you ever been arrested for driving while under the influence of alcohol or drugs
    or for public intoxication? Yes ❑ -1 No ❑ -2

19. Have you ever been arrested for a sex crime? Yes ❑ -1 No ❑ -2

20. Besides your current capital crime conviction, what crimes, if any, have you been convicted of? Please tell us the offense, the sentence you received and the year. (Check this box ❑ if you've never been convicted before.)

Offense _____ Sentence _____ Year _____

Offense _____ Sentence _____ Year _____

Offense _____ Sentence _____ Year _____

Offense _____ Sentence _____ Year _____

21. What events or circumstances would have changed the direction in your life so that you would not be on death row today?

22. What do you think will happen to most of the inmates on death row today?

Their conviction will be overturned and they will be cleared of any wrong-doing ❑ -1

Their conviction will be overturned and they will get a new trial ❑ -2

Their death sentence will be changed to life in prison ❑ -3

They will eventually be executed ❑ -4

They will die on death row of other causes before they're executed ❑ -5

23. What do you think will happen to you, personally?

Your conviction will be overturned and you will be cleared of any wrong-doing ❑ -1

Your conviction will be overturned and you will get a new trial ❑ -2

Your death sentence will be changed to life in prison ❑ -3

You will eventually be executed ❑ -4

You will die on death row of other causes before you're executed ❑ -5

24. If you could be free for one day, how would you spend it?

THANK YOU

If you want to tell us anything else about yourself, your life on death row, crime in general, or your case, we'd like to hear your comments. Please use this space to tell us anything you like.

Thank you for answering our questions. Of course your answers are confidential and will be used in combination with those of other death row inmates from all over the United States — none of your individual comments will be quoted without your permission. Because it's difficult to reach you, we're asking you now for permission to use your name in stories published with survey results in *The Dallas Morning News*. You will not be quoted unless you check below and sign your name.

❏ Yes, you may use my name with my responses. Sign below.

Name _____ Date _____

❏ No, please do not use my name with survey responses.